A Climate of Success

A Climate of Success

Creating the right organizational climate for high performance

Roderic Gray

AMSTERDAM • BOSTON • HEIDELBERG • LONDON • NEW YORK • OXFORD
PARIS • SAN DIEGO • SAN FRANCISCO • SINGAPORE • SYDNEY • TOKYO
Butterworth-Heinemann is an imprint of Elsevier

Butterworth-Heinemann is an imprint of Elsevier
Linacre House, Jordan Hill, Oxford OX2 8DP, UK
30 Corporate Drive, Suite 400, Burlington, MA 01803, USA

First edition 2007

British Library Cataloguing in Publication Data
A catalogue record for this book is available from the British Library

Library of Congress Cataloguing in Publication Data
A catalogue record for this book is available from the Library of Congress

ISBN: 978-0-7506-8368-5

For information on all Butterworth-Heinemann publications
visit our web site at http://books.elsevier.com

Printed and bound in The Netherlands

07 08 09 10 11   10 9 8 7 6 5 4 3 2 1

Working together to grow
libraries in developing countries

www.elsevier.com | www.bookaid.org | www.sabre.org

ELSEVIER   BOOK AID
International   Sabre Foundation

Contents

Contents

List of Figures

Foreword

We are all learning to recognize the importance of climate change, whether society as a whole and its concern for global warming or managers and employees and the climate in which they work. This book focusing on organization climate therefore covers an increasingly important topic and brings together a body of knowledge in an organized and easy to read format illustrated with critical incidents and cases in real world organizations.

Over recent years we are seeing considerable changes in the way organizations operate; managers strive to lead and employees contribute their services. It is no longer taskmaster and servant. Power is diffused and shared. In contrast with traditional management models that generations of MBA students have been forced to learn in which structures and systems are derived from a mechanistic predefined strategy, the new workplace seeks to balance what matters for the company (its strategy) and what matters for the individuals (their life strategies).In this new paradigm in which priority for sustained personal development goes hand-in-hand with the employer's business performance and growth, a supportive and enabling corporate climate is the new source of authority. The climate provides the whole contextual environment defining much of the essence of the relationship between an organization, its employees, customers and shareholders and the environment in which it operates.

From the start, the author differentiates clearly between inherent organization culture and organization climate and emphasizes the latter is strongly influenced by the behaviours of leaders and managers which they themselves can change. Chapters 3, 4 and 5 are particularly helpful to the reader as they provide an important summary of the key underlying models and frameworks and how climate can be assessed and categorized. The origins and facets of corporate climate are not simply attributable to a single variable and the author brings together issues of behaviour, perception (what it feels like), motivation, and work satisfaction etc.

But this is more than a review of theoretical constructs. There are 16 mini-case studies that serve to illustrate these key ideas. They cover a wide spectrum of incidents in a range of different businesses. They address many of the fundamental issues that managers have to consider – such as goal setting, participative decision making, innovation, job satisfaction and motivation, as well as threats and opportunities from and in the external business environment. This case study approach has the advantage of making the issue of organization climate very real for the reader and readily transferable to their own experience and frame of reference.

Organizations often focus on systems and process changes. But the key message from this book is the importance of behaviours and actions by leaders and managers that can lead to a supportive climate that respects and reinforces employee commitment that thereby contributes to the longer term sustainability of the organization. When a climate is put in the context of realizing business objectives and solving business issues, its results are greatly enhanced.

This book will be of value to managers to help them understand how their behaviours have consequences for the working context of their employees and thereby how they can synergize the needs of the organization with the needs of the individual employee and secure the best for all. It will also be of value to students of business and management who need to learn and understand the increasing importance of these 'soft issues' of work and organizations, over and above functional disciplines and business economics.

As the author extols in Chapter 14 ('The way ahead'), the process of improvement begins with self-knowledge and the first step towards a better climate is an assessment of how things are now and can be. This book will help the reader achieve these ends.

Professor Peter Woolliams, PhD
Emeritus Professor, Ashcroft International Business School, Anglia Ruskin
University, UK
and
Senior Partner and co-owner of The Centre for International Studies, Amsterdam,
The Netherlands

Preface

A happy sailor is an efficient sailor
**Lt Cmdr Dean Woodruff RN, at the launch of HMS Daring – 'the
world's most advanced destroyer' – on 1 February 2006**

Happiness and profits have something in common: both are elusive if pursued directly. Profits usually come as a by-product, or side effect, of doing or making something that has value for other people, in the same way that glycerine is a valuable by-product from the manufacture of soap, or grapeseed oil from winemaking. The range of activities which may produce profits is almost infinitely varied but the basic mechanism is always the same: people buy your product or make use of your service and in return they pay you, if you've organized things correctly, more than the activity has cost you. The difference is profit.

Happiness, too, is a by-product of other activities. Again, the range of activities which may bring happiness is infinitely varied (a fact which is a rich source of profit for tabloid newspapers) and very often it is only when those activities are combined with other factors that we feel happy. The ingredients of this cocktail are fairly constant: freedom – to make decisions and to exercise some control over our own lives; relationships with other people who value us; security or freedom from threat; challenge – within the limits of our own individual comfort level; and usefulness, or the feeling that what we are doing has purpose and value.

This book deals only with workplace activities. It's only very recently, in evolutionary time, that the designations 'work' and 'non work' have had any meaning for human beings. It may make sense in our current social environment to distinguish between them, but psychologically it isn't very helpful to us. 'Passive' and 'active' are more meaningful for us, but our active phase is very much the same whether we are performing a task in return for pay, or engaged in a leisure activity, cutting the grass, doing DIY, shopping, playing with our children, learning a foreign language, taking part in sport or doing voluntary work.

It is because our minds, deep down, don't recognize the distinction between working for an employer and every other kind of activity, coupled with the fact that we spend a significant proportion of our lives in our workplaces, that it is necessary for those workplaces to fulfil the basic requirements of a social setting where we can function as human beings. If they don't, we won't feel comfortable and we won't perform to our full potential. That's what this book is about. It isn't (mainly) about happiness, although I hope and believe that increased happiness will be an evident side effect of putting this book's message into practice. Making people happy won't, directly, lead to their becoming efficient, but a work environment in which people can be happy is also one in which they can be effective, which is much more valuable than mere efficiency.

I began my exploration of the concept of organizational climate after observing the deeply negative impact of a threatening environment on people at work. I reasoned that removing threats should lead to better performance. As I researched this proposition in more depth I came to realize that eliminating negative influences wasn't the whole story; there were positive influences to be promoted as well. In fact, the holistic package that determined 'what it feels like to work here' needed to be kept in balance if people were to give their best. I met with opposition. People told me that employees had to know that there would be penalties if they didn't measure up, otherwise they would get lazy and complacent, and take advantage. So I checked, and I found through rigorous research – my own and other people's – that this idea didn't fit with the evidence; work outcomes tended (and we can seldom assert more than this where human activities are concerned) to be significantly more successful where threat was low and positive factors more prominent.

Over several years I have applied and developed this valuable lesson, both as an observer and as an active participant in organizational change. This book is largely the product of that experience. It's in three parts. First (in Chapters 1–5) there is an explanation of the concepts and theory, and I present evidence to show the characteristics of an organizational 'climate of success'. Then (in Chapters 6–13) there are narratives, or case studies, to illustrate each of eight climate factors in a real world setting. Finally (in Chapter 14), there are suggestions of how the ideas in the book might be put to work in a variety of workplace situations.

I believe, in fact I'm sure, that the application of the concepts explored in this book will lead to noticeable improvements in organizational effectiveness. Inextricably bound up with this increased effectiveness will be an extra helping of that elusive by-product – individual happiness.

Roderic Gray
Leigh-on-Sea

1

Metaphor and reality

Metaphor is often regarded as a device for embellishing discourse, but its significance is much greater than this. For the use of metaphor implies a way of thinking and a way of seeing that pervade how we understand our world.

Gareth Morgan, *Images of Organization*, 1986

The term 'organizational climate' is, of course, a metaphor, but rather a good one for my purpose. Actual (meteorological) climate is a highly complex phenomenon, with characteristics that can be individually measured such as high, low and mean temperatures, rainfall, prevailing winds, seasonal variations, hours of sunlight, and so on. It is also subject to local exceptions, known as microclimates, which seem to defy the regional norms and standards. And sometimes the climate seems to lose its senses and completely unexpected climatic events occur which have the potential to do enormous damage. In any case, measurement and documentation of individual characteristics only tell part of the story: the term 'climate' only conveys real meaning as a package of characteristics taken as a whole. The proper term for this is a 'system' and systems have 'emergent properties', i.e. characteristics of the whole package which don't obviously come from any of the component parts. I will explore this in a little more detail later.

There is another property of meteorological climate which isn't easy to observe and measure, and that is what it *feels* like. This arises from another package of components, those that go to make up the individual experiencing the effects of climate on his or her well-being. This is very subjective and it would be risky to make assumptions about that experience. Only the individuals themselves can tell us definitively how the climate suits them: if we want to know we have to ask them. However, because we are all genetically very similar it's possible to predict very broadly the kind of climate which will probably be acceptable to, if not ideal for, most people and this gives us at least a starting point.

What this means is that if we were to ask as many people as possible about their preferences concerning some of the main climate factors we might well find that their answers followed what statisticians call a 'normal distribution'. That is, if plotted on a graph they would produce a shape like a bell, which is close to being symmetrical, with most people's preferences lying towards the middle, as illustrated in Figure 1.1 (see over).

I'm writing this in south-east England, where I don't meet too many people who would enjoy genuinely arctic conditions. Many people do, though, enjoy a bright

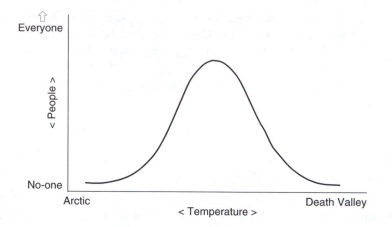

Figure 1.1 A normal distribution curve.

frosty winter morning, so their comfort zone would begin towards the left of the curve in Figure 1.1. Similarly, most people here would find sustained temperatures of 40–50°C quite unbearable, but many (like myself) have a strong preference for moderately hot weather. Our comfort zone would be towards the right of the curve. The majority would find their preference towards the centre.

This would give an indication of one of the many contributing factors in meteorological climate, but climate is much more than just temperature. If we prepared a similar graph for, say sunshine, it's likely that the curve would be a little skewed, because (probably – I haven't any research evidence to substantiate this) more people like sunny weather than cloudy. If we then combined the two graphs it would show that the appeal of cold, dull weather was quite limited, but cold bright weather fell within the main body of the bell-shaped curve, with warm sunny weather close to the centre. Do the same for rainfall, then for consistency versus variety, then for every other identifiable climate factor, and combine all the graphs. We would have a description of a climate that would at least be acceptable to most people, although, importantly, there would still be some who wouldn't be happy or comfortable in it.

Of course, we have very little control over meteorological climate. We can take palliative measures to warm ourselves up, cool ourselves down and protect ourselves from the elements, but in the end if our local climate doesn't suit us our only recourse is to move somewhere else. In practice, though, most of us are able and willing to compromise. We may have our preferences but between quite wide parameters we accept things as they are and get on with our lives. Familiarity, or perhaps just time to adapt, has a big influence on this. Human beings, or their predecessors, are believed to have originated in central Africa. As our species slowly spread out across the world we had time over many generations to adapt to a wide variety of climates, using our high intelligence to find ways to compensate for conditions that were too extreme for human bodies to cope with unaided. We wore the skins of other animals, made fire and built ourselves shelters, so that long before recorded history we were surviving and thriving in climates that would quickly have finished off our earliest ancestors.

When the climate metaphor is applied to organizations we find that some, at least, of the characteristics of organizational climate are also susceptible to observation and measurement, and I will examine some of the research activity that has been directed towards this in the following chapters. We also find 'microclimates' within organizations that seem to be markedly different from that of the wider setting. Sometimes things go wrong and the climate seems to change suddenly or unexpectedly, leading to confusion and depression among employees (theoretically, of course, the change might be for the better but somehow this is less often seen in practice). Again, the subjective element is absolutely crucial: the experience of organizational climate is essentially an individual, personal experience which is governed by the degree of synchronicity between the objective, measurable characteristics of the organizational environment and the idiosyncratic needs and preferences of the unique human being on the receiving end. Because of this, I will argue that the essence of organizational climate is to be found in the deceptively superficial-sounding question 'what does it feel like to work here?'.

Of course, each employee is likely to give a different answer to this question:

> Different individuals, working side by side in the same organization, may be working in organizations that are in effect different – one person may experience the organization as a hostile and malevolent force, bent on destruction, while a second experiences the same organization as a model of everything that is good and right and a third 'is only doing a job' and does not care one way or another for the organization.
>
> Gabriel and Schwartz, 1998

These variations in the ways that individuals perceive the organizational climate in which they work will certainly influence the ways in which they respond to it and, therefore, the effectiveness of their workplace performance. This presents a real challenge for managers, which has to be addressed on several levels.

Fortunately, unlike the weather, organizational climate can be influenced, even controlled to a certain extent, by the actions of managers. First, we need to identify those characteristics of organizational climate that are likely to be most conducive to good performance. This is actually at the core of one of the oldest, and one of the most contentious, issues in management theory and practice, although it's more recognizable with the label 'management style'.

It's important to recognize that the view expressed by Cmdr Woodruff that 'a happy sailor is an efficient sailor' is actually considered quite heretical in some management circles. How indicators of contentment among employees, such as 'satisfaction', relate to productivity is disputed. Back in the 1950s Douglas McGregor reviewed the available management literature and detected a clear underlying set of assumptions – which he labelled 'Theory X' – which led him to the conclusion that 'the principles of organization which comprise the bulk of the literature of management could only have been derived from assumptions such as those of Theory X. Other beliefs about human nature would have led inevitably to quite different organizational principles' (McGregor, 1960). The assumptions of Theory X are:

1. The average human being has an inherent dislike of work and will avoid it if he can.
2. Because of this human characteristic of dislike of work, most people must be coerced, controlled, directed, threatened with punishment to get them to put forth adequate effort toward the achievement of organizational objectives.
3. The average human being prefers to be directed, wishes to avoid responsibility, has relatively little ambition, wants security above all.

Whilst management thinking has moved on quite a lot in the half-century since McGregor, the Theory X command and control assumptions are still very common, and modern computerized monitoring systems make their implementation easier and more intrusive than McGregor could possibly have foreseen (Arkin, 1997). It's clear that the happiness of employees doesn't figure very prominently in this kind of thinking but there is a clear assumption that this is the way to maximize productivity. It would be fair to assume that people working in an organization based on these principles would be likely to find the organizational climate rather harsh, although McGregor did accept that in practice Theory X can be expressed as a more benign, paternalistic regime.

When I first began investigating organizational climate some ten years ago, I came across some venerable expressions of allegedly 'motivational' thinking which helped me to define the two ends of the spectrum. The most coercive, threatening style is captured by the Roman statesman Accius (150–c90 BCE) who said 'let them hate, so long as they fear'. Of course, twenty-first century managers can't apply the methods that were available in ancient Rome, but I have certainly come across managers who were thoroughly detested, and feared, by their staff and who showed every sign of being convinced that this was the only reliable way to get things done. I call this the 'Accius Orientation'.

The alternative view was expressed by Shakespeare in *The Taming of the Shrew*, where Tranio advises Lucentio that 'No profit grows, where is no pleasure ta'en'. In other words, people need to enjoy their work and get satisfaction and fulfilment from it if they are to perform well. Because *The Taming of the Shrew* is set in Padua (which by a happy coincidence is a rather nice, historic town with an agreeable climate), I call this perspective the 'Padua Paradigm' (Gray, 2002). Just as McGregor's Theory X reflects an updated version of the Accius Orientation so the Padua Paradigm captures in a few words the essence of McGregor's alternative vision of managerial attitudes, which he called 'Theory Y'. This view holds that 'the expenditure of physical and mental effort in work is as natural as play or rest'. Importantly, it is, potentially at least, within the control of managers as to whether people regard work as a source of satisfaction to be 'voluntarily performed', or as a source of punishment 'to be avoided if possible' (McGregor, 1960).

McGregor goes on to claim that, contrary to the assumptions of Theory X, 'The capacity to exercise a relatively high degree of imagination, ingenuity, and creativity in the solution of organizational problems is widely, not narrowly, distributed in the population' and warns that 'under the conditions of modern industrial life, the intellectual potentialities of the average human being are only partially utilized' (McGregor, 1960).

The issue for managers is to decide where they stand on three important questions: where the limits of acceptable behaviour lie, in terms of the effects of management behaviour on people's working lives; whether such ethical considerations override issues of profit and/or productivity; and whether a tendency towards one or other set of assumptions – Accius or Padua, Theory X or Theory Y – is more likely to promote the kind of organizational climate in which most people, most

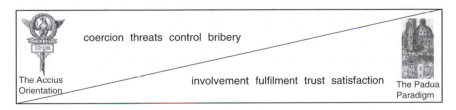

Figure 1.2   The Accius <> Padua spectrum.

of the time, will contribute most effectively towards the aims and objectives of their employing organization.

These questions don't present themselves in any particular order. For example, if managers decide that the evidence points to the Padua Paradigm (or Theory Y) as being the management style which is most likely to result in maximum productivity they don't have to worry about the other two questions; pure objective economics will determine a mode of behaviour towards employees which will pass the most stringent ethical tests without damaging or endangering profits.

On the other hand, if the Accius Orientation (or Theory X), appears to offer the best hope of maximizing profit and productivity, then managers are obliged to ask 'how far should we go?'. The boundaries may be set, albeit not very effectively, by law, but managers can't avoid forming an opinion and making choices. As Jean-Paul Sartre (1943) said, 'we cannot not choose. If I do not choose, that is still a choice. If faced with inevitable circumstances, we still choose how we are in those circumstances'. Managers are continually having to choose 'how they are' in their relations with their employees and those choices will, as I will argue, have a significant impact on the success of their organizations.

In the chapters that follow I will first try to give some academic respectability to this debate by examining the concept of organizational climate in more detail, reviewing some of the trends in research into the subject, and identifying specific performance management issues which are linked to climate issues. I will then look at how managers can assess the climate of their own organization, or perhaps that subset of the organization that most concerns them, such as their own department or team.

The major part of the book will be devoted to a collection of narratives, or case studies, each illustrating a particular aspect of organizational climate and how it might impact on performance. Each narrative is genuine, in the sense that I, or a colleague, have actually seen the incidents and situations in a real organization, or received a first-hand account from someone directly involved. However, to make them more useful to the reader I have simplified what are often fairly complex accounts and in some cases I've combined features from more than one organization. Most of the narratives are what I would call fairly low key; there are no cases of drastic re-engineering or dramatic corporate failures. Redundancies, where they occur at all, are relatively modest in scale. In short, these stories reflect everyday organizational life as experienced by many people. I've had one or two similar experiences myself.

Also, all the narratives are set in England, mostly in south-east England where I live and do the majority of my work. The principles contained in them, though, are universal. Cultures differ and this has effects on the expectations individuals have of their workplaces and the conditions that they will find most comfortable (Trompenaars and Woolliams, 2003), but this is largely a matter of 'fine-tuning'; in general the ideas expressed here can be applied with very little modification almost anywhere.

Needless to say, all the names I have used in the narratives are fictitious and none of the accounts as I present them accurately reflects any one existing organization.

THE ESSENTIALS OF THIS CHAPTER:

- Organizational climate is a metaphor.
- Like real (meteorological) climate it has measurable characteristics but the real point is what it's like for the people who live and work in it. Organizational climate means 'what it feels like to work here'.
- Individuals have different needs, but there are characteristics of organizational climate which are likely to suit most people most of the time.
- Some organizational climates are more likely than others to be associated with successful work outcomes.
- Managers can influence the climate of their organizations, or their part of the wider organization.

2

Climate, culture and perception

Central to most, if not all, models of organizational behavior are perceptions of the work environment, referred to generally as 'organizational climate'.

Patterson et al., *What is it Like to Work Here? The Climate of UK Manufacturing*, 1996

When the term 'organizational climate' first began to appear in management literature it was often used almost interchangeably with 'culture', as when Porter, Lawler and Hackman (1975) wrote about '. . . organizational climate or "culture" – a set of customs and typical patterns of ways of doing things'. Denison (1996) suggests that a kind of reversal in the terminology took place so that studies which talked about 'climate' in the 1970s would be thought of as addressing 'culture' by the late 80s. It's important to distinguish between the two concepts because, although related, they focus on quite distinct aspects of organizational life and, crucially, managers can have more influence on climate than they can on culture: 'climate is held to be a summary perception of how an organisation deals with its members and environments, and thus develops from factors primarily under managerial influence' (Wallace, Hunt and Richards, 1999).

Although it's quite reasonable to argue that 'climate can most accurately be understood as a manifestation of culture' (Reichers and Schneider, 1990) the two concepts, culture and climate, are distinct, whilst being clearly related in various ways:

> the 'feel of an organization' reflects both its *climate* and *culture*. The climate of an organization is inferred by its members . . . . The inferences organizational members make about climate are based on the policies, practices, procedures and routines that they are subject to, as well as on the kinds of behaviors that are expected and that get rewarded and supported.
>
> Schneider, Brief and Guzzo, 1996

Burke and Litwin (1992) point out that 'climate is much more in the foreground of organizational members' perceptions, whereas culture is more background and defined by beliefs and values. Climate is of course affected by culture and people's perceptions define both at different levels'. In fact, 'climate and culture are viewed as reciprocal processes, the one causing the other in an endless cycle over time' (Reichers and Schneider, 1990), which I regard as a rather wise observation.

First, organizational culture is often summed up as 'the way we do things round here' although I think Lucas (2006) adds a little to this meaning when he says that it's 'generally agreed to be a combination of values (what matters to people) and expectations of behaviour (the way things are done). It is, you could say, what an organisation does when it thinks no one is looking'.

The term 'culture' itself is borrowed from the science of anthropology and began to appear in management literature in the 1970s (Despres, 1995). Writers have used the term with different meanings even within the context of management (Baron and Walters, 1994) and anthropologists might wince at the ways some of their core concepts have been applied (Meek, 1988). One thing which most writers seem to agree about is the idea of distinctiveness; that 'the way we do things' is somehow different from the way someone else might do them. This draws attention to observable characteristics of behaviour in organizations, but it does rather invite the question *why* do we do things this way? Culture researchers have been trying to answer this question pretty much from the beginning.

The broad conclusion has been that organizational culture develops through social learning mechanisms (Schein, 1985; Kilman et al., 1985; Hofstede, 1991). These accumulated experiences build on original models put in place (consciously or not) by the organization's founders and the context in which the organization was set up, in much the same way as the personality of an individual forms and develops through the interactions of genetics and life experiences (Rose, 2003). Actions and behaviours which are associated with favourable outcomes tend to be repeated, and eventually become behavioural norms. Underlying assumptions become established in a similar way.

Because cultures become established through a process of development, it follows that they are not static, but go on developing under the same pattern of influences. This gives managers the idea that culture can be changed according to some strategy or plan. On the whole this is an illusion. Whilst writers generally agree that planned culture change is a theoretical possibility, there's fairly wide consensus that it's a long, slow, laborious task with uncertain outcomes (Trice and Beyer, 1985; Baron and Walters, 1994), leaving aside the really quite tricky question of what kind of culture would be 'better' than the one you've got. 'After countless research studies there's precious little evidence that it can be manipulated, no clear guidelines showing how to do it, and no real proof that a new culture leads to better business results' (Manning, 1990). I won't go any deeper into organizational culture here. Readers who are interested in an academic review of the literature can look at Gray (1998) or find a less formal account in Gray (2004).

The distinction between climate and culture arises from two mutually reinforcing threads. First, one of perspective. Culture – the way things are done – can, in theory at least, be observed by an objective outsider without reference to the participants. Some writers have suggested that this is the only useful level at which culture can be studied, because the underlying reasons *why* things are done are too deeply buried to be accurately identified (see, for example, Morgan, 1986, or Schein, 1985), and too complex to be disentangled. Culture, therefore, refers to impressions gained from the outside, looking in, whilst climate refers to the feelings someone on the inside has about the organizational context in which they find themselves.

Second, once the terminology had settled down it began to become apparent that researchers were often approaching their subjects from quite different disciplinary paradigms. According to Williams (1998) 'whilst the constructs of culture and climate have developed in parallel, they have been driven by researchers from different disciplines using different methodologies. There has been little cross-fertilisation of methods and ideas and considerable debate among researchers about the relatedness of the two constructs'. Climate studies have mainly been conducted from an individually-focused psychological orientation, concerned principally with personal values and attitudes and explainable in terms of personality and individual experience.

Culture studies, in contrast, have been mainly anthropological in character, if not always in formal discipline. Their 'frame of organizational reference is group understanding ... or ways of perceiving, thinking or feeling in relation to a group's problems' (Williams, 1998). In fact, one criticism that has often been levelled at organizational culture writers, including such eminent figures as Edgar Schein, is their tendency to extrapolate observations of small groups and apply their findings to much larger organizational sets (Hollway, 1991).

Another characteristic of the anthropological approach in the context of organizations and management is that the 'purpose of anthropology is to observe/describe' (Reichers and Schneider, 1990); it isn't primarily concerned with relative effectiveness of one culture compared with another. Since the main justification for researching (and teaching) organizational culture is to contribute to improved effectiveness this could be considered a potential weakness.

Still, it would be wrong to exaggerate the divergence between the two fields of study. It's true that psychological constructs, primarily those constructs that relate to group behaviour, do figure prominently in culture studies. At the same time, a number of writers on organizational climate have also tended towards a group perspective, defining their topic as 'shared perceptions' (Reichers and Schneider, 1990). This is understandable because it's difficult to talk about an *organizational* climate that is experienced as such by only one person; to be meaningful, or at any rate to be useful, what we learn about the climate has to be generalized so that it applies to a significant number of people or even to the whole organization.

However, I take the view that in this context it isn't the *sharing* which is the vital factor, because each individual's perceptions of the prevailing climate are and remain his or her own and not part of some collective phenomenon. Rather, the climate which we can perceive and, perhaps, change in positive ways is a construct of the *aggregated* individual perceptions of the people involved, 'a synthesis of perceptions' (Sparrow, 2001) or as Litwin and Stringer, who were among the earliest researchers of climate as a separate phenomenon, put it: 'the sum of the perceptions of the individuals working in [an] organization' (Litwin and Stringer, 1968).

Thus, if we were to model the climate perceptions of each person and plot them on a graph, then overlay all the graphs one on top of another, the collective description of the climate would be that central section of the bell-shaped curve which represented a broad consensus among the subjects of the enquiry. This 'high level of consensus' is very difficult to achieve (Payne, 2001), which is not surprising if we accept that climate is a construct of individual perceptions, and at best it provides a starting point, a kind of base camp from which to explore the complexities of climate and performance in any particular organization.

So, although I have emphasized the importance of individual perceptions in modelling and assessing climate, it is important to remember that when we talk about organizational climate we are usually referring to the sum or aggregate product of those perceptions, making climate 'an attribute of the *organization*' (Ekvall, 1996, my use of italic for emphasis), rather than simply of individual members of it. It's here that the climate metaphor, like all metaphors, reaches a limit of useful meaning.

Meteorological climate isn't a product of the perceptions of the inhabitants of a region; its characteristics would still be the same even if there were no people there to experience them. Organizational climate, in contrast, exists only as a psychological construct – a product of 'a conglomerate of attitudes, feelings, and behaviours which characterizes life in the organization' (Ekvall, 1996). I disagree with Ekvall when he goes on to say that climate 'exists independently of the perceptions and understandings of the members of the organization' although, as with other group norms, certain patterns of behaviour can outlast any – or indeed all – those individuals who make up the membership of the organization at any particular time (as shown by Jacobs and Campbell, 1961). This is partly why Tagiuri and

Litwin (1963), in their early investigations into organizational climate, quickly identified the fact that it was a 'relatively enduring quality of the internal environment of an organisation that (a) is experienced by its members, (b) influences their behaviour, and (c) can be described in terms of the values of a particular set of characteristics (or attributes) of the organisation'.

Some writers have suggested definitions of climate that seem to try to shape the meaning of the term to fit organizational aspirations, as when Watkin and Hubbard (2003) suggest that 'colloquially, organisational climate is … how it feels to work in a particular environment and for a particular boss. More precisely, it is a measure of employees' perception of those aspects of their environment that directly impact how well they can do their jobs'. I see this as wishful thinking. How well people can do their jobs matters as one ingredient of the overall quality of working life, but it would be naïve to imagine that this is the most, much less the only, important factor colouring people's perceptions.

Lawthom et al. (1995), after reviewing a number of definitions, came to the conclusion that 'a precise and unitary definition of climate is yet to be found but amidst numerous definitions, two qualities distinguish climate as a concept. First, it is perceptual in that individual perceptions are elicited: second, it is descriptive rather than evaluative in its orientation'. In the end it is the perceptions of individual employees which really matter to us if we are to make our organizations more effective and successful at what they do, so the working definition of climate as 'what it feels like to work here' seems to me to be highly fit for purpose.

THE ESSENTIALS OF THIS CHAPTER:

- Climate isn't the same as culture. Culture is the personality of the organization and very hard to change. Climate is strongly affected by managers' behaviour, which they can change if they want to.
- Climate is perceived by individuals – as organization's climate is the collective or aggregate product of those individual perceptions.
- We can't make other people perceive things the way we think they should. We can only acknowledge their perceptions and use that information when deciding how we should behave.
- How managers behave has a big impact on people's perceptions of organizational climate. This is both a danger and an opportunity.

3

Theoretical foundations

There's nothing so practical as a good theory.

Kurt Lewin, *Field theory in social science,* 1952

Before looking at the performance issues that are intimately connected with employees' perceptions of climate it will be helpful to define some related concepts. The first of these, which influences practically all workplace behaviour, is the 'psychological contract', defined by Rousseau (1995) as 'individual beliefs, shaped by the organization, regarding terms of an exchange agreement between individuals and their organization'.

The psychological contract is a special kind of contract for several reasons, not least because 'the essence of the psychological, as opposed to the economic, contract is that the expectations concern non-tangible, psychological issues' and because it is 'to a large extent informal, and implicitly rather than explicitly understood. It is, therefore, essentially subjective' (Makin, Cooper and Cox, 1996).

This, of course, is fraught with difficulties. In a formal, legal contract the terms are usually made clear: one party will do or deliver something, in return for which the other party will do or deliver something else, as when someone undertakes to perform some work for another person in exchange for an agreed sum of money. Both sides are supposed to know what is expected of them. Even so, lawyers get rich on resolving disputes about what the words in contracts really mean, and whether what was delivered really fulfilled the agreed terms.

How much more problematic would be a contract where each side had expectations of the other but neither had any objectively-based idea of what the other party expected from *them* in return. It would be even more difficult if these subjective interpretations were continually changing. There's great potential here for either or both parties to feel cheated because, in their perception, despite delivering their side of the bargain they had not received their due return.

The psychological contract between employees and their organizations almost inevitably suffers from this to a greater or lesser extent because the terms are very rarely made explicit. Rather, they develop or evolve as employees build a picture of what is expected of them, and of how they are treated, rewarded (or punished), praised or corrected during the course of their daily interactions with management. This picture is also heavily influenced by observations of how other people are treated, and how much and in what ways those others seem to be contributing to the organization. Over time the terms of the bargain become established in the perceptions of both managers and employees and are further reinforced as behaviour is consistent and predictable. As Rousseau (1995) puts it, 'we know a contract has been kept when neither party is surprised by the behavior of the other'. Any future departure from this established model seems like a violation of the agreement between them.

According to Makin, Cooper and Cox (1996) 'long-standing and close relationships can tolerate considerable periods when one partner is continually giving, while the other is only receiving. (In fact, one way to tell when a relationship is under stress is when the time scale over which the "balance sheet" is balanced, shortens. In such situations the participants begin to expect almost immediate repayment of favours done.)'. Incremental changes may pass almost unnoticed but over time have the power to alter perceptions of the way that the psychological contract is being fulfilled or violated.

These changes are not necessarily the same for the two sides: managers may increasingly come to expect higher performance in terms of quality or quantity, longer hours, greater responsibility, more flexibility and more modest demands for reward in its various forms. They may well believe that these gradual evolutionary changes in the contract terms are accepted by the employees, especially if there are no or only muted protests. The employees, on the other hand, may well regard these changes as an attack on their rights and privileges, which have been established over time by custom and usage, and therefore a wilful violation of the agreement which they believed governed the relationship between themselves and their employer.

Perceived violations of the psychological contract affect the organizational climate directly. Trust, which is based upon predictability coupled with a perception of goodwill (Gray, 2004), begins to break down and the organizational environment begins to feel harsher and less benign. If an employee feels that managers cannot be relied on to keep their (inferred) promises an important safety factor is removed from the relationship, which has serious implications for performance.

Employee engagement. A second concept which tends to recur in any consideration of climate and performance is that of employee engagement. Engagement is characterized, according to Robinson, Perryman and Hayday (2004) by 'a positive attitude towards, and pride in, the organisation', belief in its products and services, 'a perception that the organisation enables the employee to perform well, a willingness to behave altruistically and be a good team player' and 'an understanding of the "bigger picture" and a willingness to go beyond the requirements of the job'. Engaged employees are 'respectful of, and helpful to, colleagues' and are likely to 'keep up to date with developments in the field'.

Buckingham (2001) comments on a survey carried out by Gallup which defines engagement in similar terms to those used by Robinson et al. Gallup's engaged employees are 'loyal and productive. They not only get their work done effectively, but they are also less likely to leave and more inclined to recommend their company to friends and family', whilst disengaged employees are 'not psychologically bonded to their organisation'. They are 'less collaborative than their colleague, less innovative, less tolerant of change and more vocal about their many dissatisfactions'.

Konrad (2006) analyses the concept of employee engagement into 'three related components'. The cognitive aspect 'concerns employees' beliefs about the organization, its leaders, and working conditions. The emotional aspect concerns how employees feel about each of those three factors and whether they have positive or negative attitudes toward the organization and its leaders. The behavioral aspect . . . is the value-added component for the organization and consists of the discretionary effort engaged employees bring to their work in the form of extra time, brainpower and energy devoted to the task and the firm'.

Clearly it would make sense for managers to do what they can to foster the attitudes and behaviour of engaged employees, so it's regrettable that the Gallup survey (Buckingham, 2001) found that more than 80 per cent of UK employees are not engaged at work. 'Engagement is two-way: organisations must work to engage the employee, who in turn has a choice about the level of engagement to offer the employer' (Robinson et al., 2004). Many of the changes in managers' behaviour which Buckingham, Robinson et al. and to a lesser extent Konrad recommend to help improve matters have close parallels in models of good management practice which emerge from climate research, which suggests that engagement may be a useful 'visible' correlate for climate perceptions.

Commitment. Robinson et al. (2004) say that 'engagement has clear overlaps with the more exhaustively researched concepts of commitment and organisational citizenship behaviour'. 'Organizational commitment has been defined as an individual's dedication and loyalty to an organization' (Adela et al., 2004) or as 'a psychological state that binds the individual to the organization (i.e. makes turnover less likely)' (Allen and Meyer, 1990). Just as Konrad (2006) found that the construct *engagement* had three constituents, so Allen and Meyer suggest that *commitment* has three components, each of which is individually measurable: 'The *affective* component . . . refers to employees' emotional attachment to, identification with, and involvement in, the organization. The *continuance* component refers to commitment based on the costs that employees associate with leaving the organization. Finally, the *normative* component refers to employees' feelings of obligation to remain with the organization'. The first of these is a powerful force in the perception of climate, since an organizational climate which is inferred to be hostile, threatening or otherwise inimical to employees' well-being is, almost by definition, incompatible with 'emotional attachment to, identification with, and involvement in, the organization'.

The second component of commitment – continuance – perhaps surprisingly has the potential to exercise a negative influence of employees' perceptions of climate. The reason for this is that we allow other people – in this specific case, managers or employers – to influence our behaviour at several levels. Kelman (1958) called the most basic level 'compliance', which means no more than simply 'going along with what we think, or are told, is required, without necessarily believing it's the right or best thing to do . . . Compliance tends to last only as long as the external influence which is driving it persists' (Gray, 2004). One reason why we might comply with a request or instruction is because we desire the rewards associated with complying, or fear the consequences of not doing so.

The next level identified by Kelman (1958) is 'identification'. This is usually driven by admiration of another person or group, leading to a wish to adopt what are seen as their characteristic behaviours, such as style, manners, speech, dress code, typical actions, etc., in order to be more like them, to appear to others to be like them, or to be accepted by them. This behaviour is much more voluntary in nature than compliance and it tends to last rather longer; probably as long as we continue to admire the reference group or person, or still want to be accepted by them.

Kelman's deepest level of referent-inspired behaviour is 'internalization':

> which means changing our ideas, values and behaviours because we have come to believe that the new ways are better and more valid. Once the level of internalization is reached the behaviours or values concerned can be said to have been incorporated into personality; they become *our* behaviours and *our* values, rather than someone else's that we are merely copying.
>
> Gray, 2004

So, if the dominant aspect of commitment at a particular time is the continuance component it may be that the employee's choice to remain with the organization has little to do with any 'emotional attachment', but only with the balance of advantage, likely to be primarily economic, associated with leaving. This can easily come to be perceived as threatening; a kind of 'golden handcuffs' keeping the employee in a place he or she doesn't want to be but can't escape because the penalties of doing so are unacceptable. This is unlikely to lead to excellent performance.

The third of Allen and Meyer's (1990) components of commitment, the 'normative' component, is similarly problematic, although for different reasons. A 'feeling of obligation to remain with the company' is unlikely to be rooted in economic advantage or disadvantage. It's more likely to arise from favours done in the past, good or generous treatment, perhaps in times of personal difficulty, or the sense of an undischarged debt owed to the organization. In the end, though, an employee in this situation can begin to feel trapped. The organization comes to feel like what Gareth Morgan (1986) graphically calls a 'psychic prison' in which he or she is condemned, by those originally quite positive feelings of obligation, to remain indefinitely, or at least, until resentment and frustration overtake the sense of indebtedness and the employee comes to see the organization as oppressive.

This is potentially dangerous for the organization. An employee held against his or her will by the, mainly economic, golden handcuffs effect may, of course, also become resentful, but the strong emotional turmoil generated by a normative commitment which has gone sour can lead to highly negative behaviour ranging from the passive, such as doing only what is measured, through militancy or support for extremist viewpoints (Drummond, 2000) to denigrating the organization or senior personalities, or even direct sabotage of procedures, systems or property (Gray, 2004). As Congreve (1695) poetically puts it 'Heav'n has no rage like love to hatred turned'.

If, on the other hand, the employee has come to *identify* with the organization and/or its managers, then his or her apparently compliant behaviour is voluntary and likely to become more and more attuned to the organization's norms and attitudes over time until eventually they become *internalized*. This used to be thought of as a thoroughly good thing which would lead employees naturally to act in the organization's best interests and do things 'the company way' without continual close supervision. Unfortunately it has a serious downside because a lack of diversity can lead to 'groupthink' (Janis, 1982), which is perhaps best summed up for this context as a dysfunctional inability to think differently. Organizations need their members to have independent perspectives, ideas and approaches, otherwise they are likely to become blind to changing environments and unreceptive to new and better ways of doing things. This independence of mind can't happen if employees morph, over time, into clones of the senior managers and of each other.

It is, perhaps, natural that managers feel more comfortable if their employees think and act like them, i.e. correctly:

> management is largely populated by positivists . . . by positivism I mean the conviction that there is some matrix or framework of reality to which we can appeal in determining the nature of truth . . . or more correctly, The Truth.
>
> Despres, 1995

However, the world isn't really like that. 'The Truth' is a chimera; in reality there are multiple, continually changing, truths and survival depends on keeping up with them. This will be greatly helped by listening to people who don't think exactly as we do.

So, the goal of organizational management is to foster positive feelings in the *affective* dimension of employees' commitment so that the people who are, after all, members of the organization, at every level, feel that they want to promote its well-being and positive development, and act in its best interests. This is what careful attention to organizational climate is all about. Adela et al. (2004) found in a wide-ranging survey that there was a 'significant correlation (.66) between organizational commitment and organizational climate'. It's certainly time for management attention to be directed towards the issue of commitment, because it seems that the situation is deteriorating.

Taylor (2002) refers to the 'striking ... apparent deterioration that has taken place among workers in having any sense of personal commitment to the company that employs them'. Scase (2002) suggests that 'one reason may be that companies underestimate the intelligence of their staff, who are hardly likely to be committed to their bosses while they feel their jobs are on the line through constant restructuring of their duties and responsibilities and intensifying demands to achieve improved performance targets'. Unless they are alert, managers may not notice that there's a problem, especially if they wait for people to complain. Swan (2005) refers to research by Working Families, a charity dedicated to improving the lot of parents who work, which showed that 'unhappy parents are far more likely to look for another job that offers greater flexibility than they are to raise the issue with their employer'.

It doesn't have to be this way. Leary-Joyce (2004) identifies lessons to be learned from the results of the *Sunday Times* '100 Best Companies to Work For' awards and explains how organizations can create a working environment which attracts employees and inspires them to give of their best. She describes the benefits, in terms of recruitment, retention, high levels of creativity and innovation and improved customer service, of a company culture in which staff feel valued and respected and in which they can flourish. In the end people do have choices. Jean-Pierre Garnier, CEO of GlaxoSmithKline, calls his workforce 'volunteers' because, he says, 'they could choose to work anywhere they like, so we have to look after them' (2006).

This is not a new concept. Back in 1954 Drucker was advising that 'managers should treat their staff as though they were volunteers', and Lawler (1973) comments that 'those individual behaviors that are crucial in determining the effectiveness of organizations are, almost without exception, voluntary motivated behaviors'. The task for managers is to ensure, through a favourable organizational climate, that employees *want* to make a positive contribution to organizational success.

Job satisfaction. It would be hard to make any meaningful assessment of an organization's climate without considering the concept of job satisfaction among its employees. In the early days of climate research Litwin and Stringer (1968) found through controlled experiments that different kinds of climate could directly influence levels of job satisfaction; there seemed to be a straightforward cause–effect relationship. This led some writers to suggest that the two concepts were essentially the same thing, a view which was rather reinforced by the fact that climate measurement often used the same instruments and techniques as research into job satisfaction (Guion, 1973). Al-Shammari (1992), however, maintains that 'there is evidence to suggest that while climate and job satisfaction concepts do tend to be related, they are eventually different constructs. A large number of research studies have supported this view'.

One issue that arises is that the term 'job satisfaction' is almost always left undefined. Or rather, it seems to be assumed that it doesn't require definition in the countless studies which set out to measure it, usually with a view to correlating it with some other organizational benchmark such as productivity, staff turnover or customer satisfaction. These studies usually allow an implicit definition to emerge as they seek to discover how 'satisfied' or 'happy' employees feel with various contributing factors, such as the work environment, colleagues, supervision, work content, challenge, rewards, security or prospects. Job satisfaction is seen as the sum of the answers to questions about these contributing factors. This may, in fact, be a perfectly satisfactory way to understand it, but they do, in my opinion at least, tend to leave job satisfaction as a construct of limited usefulness. There is more value to be extracted by mining beneath the surface for performance correlates.

Of course, this is also true of the word 'job' itself. We use this with a variety of meanings ranging from someone's whole lifetime at work down to a single brief task. It only takes on rich meaning when analysed, but it's still quite a useful little word.

This is reinforced by the results of studies of links between job satisfaction amongst employees and the success of their organizations. Attempts to show direct causal relationships between the two variables have not been very successful (Beech and Crane, 1999). On the other hand, it does seem to be the case that a range of human resource management practices which are seen to *produce* satisfaction amongst employees also correlate to improved productivity (for example, Patterson et al., 1997; Rogg et al., 2001; Patterson et al., 2004).

Pass (2005) observes that 'an association between HRM practices and the competitive advantage of firms has been well established. But the precise mechanism of this causal chain is rarely specified, and frequently based on assumptions about employee outcomes of commitment, motivation and increased competence. As a result, a "black box" has been created, with organisations left wondering how it works'. Beech and Crane (1999) suggest that 'the answer to this puzzle may be the collective climate of satisfaction which impacts on performance as this would enhance peer-group support and pressure towards performance'. Pass conducted her research with production line factory workers who, she says, were quite clear that 'you don't work in a factory to get job satisfaction'. However, she was able to correlate measurable performance outcomes with good relationships between workers and managers, managers treating their staff with respect and giving recognition to good work. These can all be related to factors in organizational climate.

Reeves (2002) comments 'frankly, the jury is out on whether happy or satisfied workers are more productive. On balance, as jobs become more creative, knowledge based and service oriented, it's likely that the link between work happiness and profit will strengthen. But this is a secondary concern, in any case. The point is that because work is so central to our well-being, we should be happy at it regardless of whether or not it improves the bottom line'.

Motivation. Motivation concerns 'those psychological processes that cause the arousal, direction and persistence of behaviour' (Ilgen and Klein, 1988). In the context of management the word 'motivate' is often used as a transitive verb: motivation is something done by one person or group to another. This also tends to imply that the motivated parties need to be induced to perform some action or expend a degree of effort which they wouldn't otherwise wish to do. There have been many theories about human motivation, most of which have been, or still are, taught in business schools as though they can be used as management techniques, or at least as guides to management behaviour. Not many of them were originally intended to be used in this way. According to Kanfer (1994), most motivational theories are 'not intended to predict performance but rather to predict decision processes and volitional behavior'. All the same, some admittedly do contain nuggets of wisdom of which managers could very usefully take advantage.

Theories of motivation have been grouped or classified in many ways (Gray, 2000a). Perhaps most directly useful to managers is the consideration of whether a person's observed behaviour is caused by intrinsic or extrinsic factors. Extrinsic motivation refers to behaviour which is instrumental, i.e. that's performed in order to achieve some subsequent reward or objective, whereas 'intrinsic motivation has often been defined as behaviour performed in the absence of any apparent external reward' (Kanfer, 1990). In practice, of course, most behaviour is likely to be motivated by a mixture of these factors, in varying proportions.

Reinforcement theory. Reinforcement is a basic mechanism which influences much human and animal behaviour. This is most easily explained by Thorndike's (1911) 'law of effect', which says that 'actions which are rewarded tend to be repeated'. The reward, or reinforcement, associated with a specific behaviour can be any pleasant or satisfying effect, so the reinforcement mechanism may be triggered by intrinsic factors, as when we do something because the activity itself is enjoyable, or extrinsic factors, when we only do something because we anticipate some reward *afterwards*. The principle of reinforcement crops up, in one form or another, in many theories of motivation.

Expectancy theory. Perhaps the most influential theory to be applied regularly to the context of the workplace is known as expectancy theory. The most complete form of expectancy theory is probably that devised by Victor Vroom and his associates, working in the 1950s and 60s (Vroom, 1964). Expectancy theory is essentially a reinforcement model, because it assumes that behaviour is motivated by the rewards that it brings. It is a *cognitive* model, because it assumes that people will work out (a) how likely they are to be able to do what is required, (b) how likely it is that doing what is required will lead on to the desired outcome, and (c) how much they really want that outcome anyway. It is also, usually, an *extrinsic* model: assuming that the motivation comes from what will follow after the behaviour – which could be work – is completed, although Vroom does acknowledge, rather reluctantly, that some things may be done for the pleasure or satisfaction that comes from the activity itself. Vroom proposed a rather obtuse mathematical model, my interpretation of which is illustrated in Figure 3.1.

To give the model some kind of life, consider the following scenario: an employee is asked by her boss to translate a document, which is in Turkish, into Japanese. The employee has no knowledge of either language, so immediately

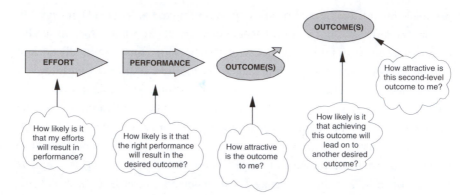

Figure 3.1 Expectancy theory.

assesses that no amount of effort on her part is likely to result in performance. It doesn't matter how attractive a reward she is offered, the task isn't worth attempting. So, her motivation is effectively nil. (Of course, it might make sense to invest part of the promised reward in the services of a translation agency, but we'll assume this wasn't an option in this case.)

If, on the other hand, the document is in French, which she learnt at school but has now largely forgotten, and has to be translated into English, her native language, she might decide that effort on her part *could* possibly result in 'performance'. So the next question becomes relevant: will it produce the desired outcome? Let's assume that this desired outcome is to impress her boss with her skills or resourcefulness. She may decide that a successful translation would indeed be likely to produce this outcome. She must then decide how attractive this outcome would be for her: is it worth the effort of struggling with French dictionaries and grammar manuals, etc.? It may help her in this decision if she considers what second-level outcomes might become possible if she manages to impress her boss in this way – perhaps a promotion, or secondment to the Paris office. According to expectancy theory the answers to all these questions will combine and interact to determine how much effort she will be motivated to put into the task.

If we extend Vroom's version of the theory to allow for intrinsic factors we could also take into account the enjoyment she might get from the activity itself: perhaps she likes intellectual challenges and would get a lot of pleasure from the task. This would make the attractiveness of the *outcomes* less significant in the calculations.

Reward. There are two main problems associated with applying expectancy theory as a management tool. The first is the fairly obvious difficulty of being able to answer the questions it poses: how could a manager know what assessment a particular subordinate would make of the difficulty of the task, or the attractiveness of the outcomes, etc. – an assessment which is, in any case, likely to be subconscious. The second problem is a more general one concerning the association between extrinsic rewards and performance. Many, though certainly not all, incentive schemes link rewards of various kinds with outcomes or results. Research has shown that this has a very real potential to divert attention and energy away from the work itself and into doing whatever is required to gain the reward instead. Of course, the intention of such schemes is that these two factors should be the same thing, but achieving this is much harder than many people imagine.

The role played by rewards, especially extrinsic rewards (i.e. those that you only receive after the work is done) is there in the background of most ideas about workplace motivation, and the association between rewards and performance has been investigated by many researchers. On the whole, the consensus seems to be that extrinsic rewards often don't do what people think they will do. For example:

> A meta-analysis of 98 studies showed by statistical analysis that financial incentives produced no significant effect overall. Financial incentives were unrelated to absenteeism or turnover. Training and goal-setting programmes did, however, have a positive impact on productivity.
>
> Guzzo, Jette and Katzell, 1985

The term 'meta-analysis' here means a study which takes the data from many earlier studies, puts it all together, and re-analyses it. This was consistent with Deci's (1972) finding that 'the more we obtain an extrinsic type of reinforcement [e.g. money] for performing a task, the more likely we are to lose our intrinsic motivation to perform that task. On the other hand, the more we receive verbal reinforcements, the more we come to develop intrinsic motivations to perform the task'. This is supported by extended research at Toronto University, which found that 'a series of studies confirmed that the larger the incentive we are offered, the more negatively we will view the activity for which the bonus was received' (Freedman et al., 1992), and by Kanfer (1990), who says that 'the undermining effects of extrinsic rewards on task interest and free-choice behavior have been shown in numerous studies'.

In my own research (Gray, 2000b) I have found that incentive payments, which are intended to motivate people to exceed 'standard' performance, often get included in what people expect to be paid. Then the possibility that they won't be received looks more like a threat of punishment for not performing well enough, and threats have been strongly linked to poor work outcomes. Purcell (2000) observes that 'research into individual performance-related pay ... in the UK over the past decade has failed to show that such systems have an effect on performance. Instead, the growing conviction is that a pay system can at best have no effect on performance, but, at worst, it will damage competitiveness'.

Although researchers have been aware of this, admittedly rather counter-intuitive, negative effect of reward for so long, the idea that performance-related pay, incentive bonuses and so on are the right way – perhaps the only way – to get people to deliver good results is still very widespread. If this view is mistaken, what other motivational approaches might be more successful?

Theory X and Theory Y. I've already mentioned McGregor's (1960) theories, which are often advanced under the heading of motivation on business and management courses. Unfortunately, Theory X and Theory Y are labels for whole sets of attitudes and assumptions which are genuinely held by the managers involved, not techniques which can be adopted at will. Their relevance to the practice of management, in my view anyway, lies in their power to inform practice and influence management development. McGregor said of Theory Y that managers who hold these assumptions will *naturally* behave very differently in their interactions with employees, creating a climate of 'integration' in which members of an organization can 'achieve their own goals best by directing their efforts toward the success of the enterprise' (McGregor, 1960, my use of italic for emphasis). He maintained that the assumptions of Theory Y 'are far more consistent with existing knowledge in the social sciences than are the assumptions of Theory X'. Both sets of assumptions are capable of being translated into behaviours which, if consistent and sustained, can influence organizational climate. In a very real sense, organizational climate research is the logical progression of the work begun by McGregor in the 1950s.

Maslow. McGregor's theories were based, at least in part, on the work of Abraham Maslow in the early 1940s. Working on earlier notions that behaviour is caused by 'needs' which have to be met or satisfied, Maslow (1943) identified initially five such needs: Physiological, Safety, Love, Esteem and Self-actualization. The last one means a need to be whatever one is capable of becoming. His idea, which has not really been supported by subsequent research (Lawler and Suttle, 1972) was that we try to meet those needs roughly in that order, so we won't be primarily concerned about safety whilst we still have unmet physiological needs, such as hunger or thirst, and love will have to wait until we've met our need for safety (not sex, though – Maslow tells us that's a physiological need).

It's suggested that this model can be transferred to the workplace, where people seek to meet their needs at all these levels. Of course, 'organisations don't ... always see themselves as places of safety and security for their employees. The workplace may provide opportunities to feel accepted, to "belong" and to form friendships, and it may well give some people scope to achieve higher levels of self-esteem and the respect of others' (Gray, 2004). They might also, conceivably, provide opportunities for self-actualization.

On the whole, Maslow's hierarchy of needs doesn't have much to tell us about motivation in a structural or deterministic sense, but it does give a useful set of considerations which anyone who has some degree of power to affect the quality of someone else's life should take into account. I am particularly struck by his remark that 'a man who is thwarted in any of his basic needs may fairly be envisaged simply as a sick man. This is a fair parallel to our designation as "sick" of the man who lacks vitamins or minerals. Who is to say that a lack of love is less important than a lack of vitamins?'. This has compelling ethical implications, in the workplace and in society as a whole:

> If we were to use the word 'sick' in this way, we should then also have to face squarely the relations of man to his society. One clear implication of our definition would be that [1] since a man is to be called sick who is basically thwarted, and [2] since such basic thwarting is made possible ultimately only by forces outside the individual, then [3] sickness in the individual must come ultimately from a sickness in the society. The 'good' or healthy society would then be defined as one that permitted man's highest purposes to emerge by satisfying all his prepotent basic needs.
>
> Maslow, 1943

If we accepted Maslow's theory, even in the limited context of the workplace, we would be accepting responsibility for the well-being of our colleagues at all levels, and many workplaces would be very different from the way they are today.

Herzberg. Based on some rather flawed research (Adair, 1990; Robertson et al., 1992) Frederick Herzberg concluded that there are some factors in an employee's experience of working life, which he called 'motivators', which can make him or her feel good and lead to increased effort, involvement, loyalty and productivity. These were principally to do with the work itself, a sense of achievement, responsibility and the recognition and respect of others. Another set of factors can cause de-motivation, resentment and high staff turnover if they are missing or unsatisfactory, but if these factors are already satisfactory, increasing them or enhancing them doesn't lead to increased motivation. These were mainly to do with working conditions, the 'system', relations with supervisors, and pay (although there are some complications attached to this). Because he believed that these factors could not produce job satisfaction, but were necessary for the avoidance of **dis**satisfaction, Herzberg called them 'hygiene factors' because:

> hygiene operates to remove health hazards from the environment of man. It is not a curative, it is, rather, a preventive. Modern garbage disposal, water purification, and air-pollution control do not cure diseases, but without them we should have many more diseases.
>
> Herzberg et al., 1959

Although the notion of two distinct categories of 'factors' hasn't held up under scrutiny (Burke, 1966; House and Wigdor, 1967; Wood and LeBold, 1970), the idea that motivation is most effectively facilitated by concentrating on the intrinsic rewards of being at work and doing the job is consistent with subsequent research, including climate research.

Equity. The last motivation theory I want to discuss here is equity theory (Adams, 1963). Essentially, equity theory suggests that 'people will be most satisfied and work most effectively when they believe that their rewards or outcomes are in balance with their inputs' (Deci, 1992). How we arrive at such a belief is by comparison with other people: 'When such comparison reveals that similar persons are better off than oneself is, a state of relative deprivation may arise' (Jung, 1978). 'The basic premise . . . is that individuals seek fairness and justice in the employee–employer social exchange relationship' (Kanfer, 1994). Fairness in this context takes two basic forms: 'distributive fairness pertains to perceptions with respect to the distribution or allocation of outcomes; procedural fairness refers to perceptions about the organizational procedures used to make outcome decisions' (Kanfer, 1994). Adams (1963) emphasizes that the employee–employer relationship is not 'usually perceived by the former purely and simply as an economic matter. There is an element of relative justice involved that supervenes economics and underlies perceptions of equity or inequity'.

Equity theories predict dissatisfaction (or rather, 'dissonance') from over- as well as under-reward. Adams (1963) says that a worker has a drive to equate production with the perceived fairness of reward. So, a worker who believes himself to be overpaid will try to produce more, in order to redress the inequity, and a worker who believes himself underpaid will produce less. Cynics will not be surprised that the evidence for the overpayment effect is rather mixed. Adams' own experiments showed that hourly paid systems did produce the predicted results, and piece-rate systems did produce better quality for overpayment but didn't produce greater quantity. He interpreted this as a means of redressing the inequity by giving better value.

Kanfer (1990) remarks that 'studies of overpayment inequity ... provide mixed support for Adams' theory (which) predicts an increase in performance under conditions of perceived overpayment' but the effects of underpayment have been 'found to be broadly consistent with Adams' model', that is, people who feel they are underpaid by comparison with certain others do typically decrease the quality/quantity of their output. Equity theory is therefore helpful as a general guide, even if it's a little unsatisfactory at the detailed level. My broad interpretation is that people need to feel that they are being dealt with fairly. If this is the case then a lot of minor issues seem to fade into the background and attention can be focused on the job itself, which is in everyone's interest.

In fact, I take the view that rewards, whatever form they take, should always aim to reflect an individual's overall contribution to the success of the organization, rather than be linked to any short-term specific target or transitory success. When something we do turns out well it tends to make us feel good anyway, and this effect is amplified considerably if other people notice. Provided that other people are treated in similar ways (i.e. we don't perceive ourselves to be dealt with less favourably than others) goal-related rewards are unlikely to improve overall contribution anyway. This isn't, of course, easy to implement; our own perception of the value of our contribution may be quite different to our bosses' opinions. All the same, it's worth striving to achieve the best balance possible, because perceived fairness is the key to this whole complex area:

> the compensation received by an individual for the contribution of his job is much more than a simple material exchange for services rendered. Because it is so tangible, compensation functions as the most immediate and direct commentary on job performance. As a reward it is also a measure of the individual's worth as an employee and, to some extent, as a human being.
>
> Gordon and Cummins, 1979

This isn't a trivial matter. Whenever we have the power to influence someone else's self-perception of his or her 'worth . . . as a human being' (Gordon and Cummins 1979) we take on an awesome responsibility for their psychological health. It's vital that we invest the highest degree of effort, diligence and sensitivity into the task of assessing and communicating what someone's contribution is actually worth to the organization.

Note also the use of 'compensation' as a euphemism for pay or reward in the above quote from Gordon and Cummins. There's a strong flavour of Theory X about it; someone needs to be 'compensated' for the unpleasantness and loss associated with going to work. If we can turn this around, so that work is full of rewards; personal, emotional, intellectual and financial, we would have made the workplace a much better place to be and, as I contend in this book, much more successful on every level.

There are, of course, many theories and perspectives on workplace motivation which I haven't mentioned here. This isn't just because of lack of space, but rather because I don't find them very helpful in making organizations more effective. All those I have mentioned have been around a long time, and have attracted criticisms both on methodological grounds and on their conclusions. More recently, attention has shifted away from trying to isolate 'motivation' from the holistic workplace experience. This is realistic because the reasons why anyone feels motivated to do anything, with what level of intensity, focus, persistence and mental and/or physical effort are so complex and so variable from person to person and from moment to moment that there is effectively no answer to the question 'how can I motivate people?' that's likely to be of much use to managers. In contrast, 'how can I facilitate excellent performance?' is a rich and useful substitute. The factors which tend to contribute to this (and 'tend to' is probably as good as it gets) are explored in the remainder of this book.

THE ESSENTIALS OF THIS CHAPTER:

- The psychological contract is the unwritten agreement which defines what each party – employee and employer – has to give the other and what they will get in exchange. Unfortunately, neither party knows what the other believes to be the terms of the contract, and in any case it changes over time. The potential for misunderstandings, disappointment and resentment is considerable. Managers have to take active steps to find out what their people think about this if they want to maintain good relationships.
- Engagement is the feeling an employee may have of belonging to an organization, being proud of it and wanting to help it do well. Engagement is in short supply and the damage this causes is considerable.

- Commitment is an employee's loyalty and dedication to an organization, often shown by a willingness to stay rather than leave. Reluctance to leave can be induced by financial considerations but the most valuable kind of commitment is 'emotional attachment to, identification with, and involvement in, the organization' (Allen and Meyer, 1990).
- People's motivation to work can have many causes, which can interact in complex ways. Rewards in the form of money or other benefits play a part but their influence is far less straightforward than many people assume. The most effective motivators are intrinsic: i.e. they arise from the work itself rather than from any reward that may be forthcoming after the work is done.

4

The good life – and good performance

There are many visions of the good society: the treadmill is not one of them.

J K Galbraith, *The Good Society: The Humane Agenda*, 1997

Gavin and Mason (2004) also address the question of what makes a good society. For them 'three things – health, happiness and productivity – are the ingredients of a good society. Improvement in productivity alone, which is almost the sole emphasis of many organizations today, is not enough'. I agree, but there are grounds for optimism because these 'ingredients' are not mutually exclusive. In fact, it's a basic premise of this book that they are mutually reinforcing; organizational climate influences performance, and the kind of climate in which most people are likely to feel that sense of well-being, which is closely related to happiness, is also the kind of climate in which work is performed most successfully. This is excellent news because 'work by itself, of course, cannot make a person happy, but a person cannot be genuinely happy if he or she is unhappy at work' (Gavin and Mason, 2004). In this chapter I will review some of the evidence for the positive effects of a benign organizational climate, and consider some performance issues that are related to organizational climate in various ways.

According to Watkin and Hubbard (2003) 'research has ... consistently shown how an organisational climate can directly account for up to 30 per cent of the variance in key business performance measures'. Wiley and Brooks (2000) cite 'a significant body of research ... that examines the relationship between how employees describe their work environments and the relative performance success of those work environments'. They say that this research 'suggests that the more present certain organizational or leadership practices are in a given work environment, the more energized and productive the workforce'. Malcolm Patterson, who with various colleagues has conducted ongoing research on human resource practices over many years, feels able to give precise figures in at least one aspect of this relationship: 'We can explain some 29 per cent of the variation between companies in change in productivity over a 3 or 4 year period in human relations terms' (Patterson et al., 1997).

The body of research which has led to such conclusions is extensive. Williams (1998) surveyed 40 UK manufacturing companies and compared climate with performance. He found that 'most of the climate variables are both positively and significantly related to each other, and to organisational performance' with 'strong positive correlations on almost all climate and performance measures'. Watkin (2001) reports that 'a few years ago my organisation carried out climate surveys at 10 identical bottling plants belonging to one of the world's largest soft drinks companies. The results showed that the plants with the most favourable working environment were also the most profitable. This confirmed what a large body of research had already demonstrated: that organisational climate – how it feels to work in a particular environment, the atmosphere of a workplace – makes a difference to organisational performance'.

Further evidence from Patterson et al. (2004) reports that 'in a study of 42 manufacturing companies, subsequent productivity was significantly correlated in controlled analyses with eight aspects of organizational climate' and Bilmes (2001) analysed 200 companies in the USA and Germany, comparing a 'people scorecard' with shareholder returns. She found that the companies with the highest 'people scorecard' scores had shareholder returns almost three times the levels of those with the lowest scores.

My own research in this area (Gray, 2000b) involved extended interviews with 44 managers from 17 organizations, all major well-known names, in a total of seven industry sectors, public and private. Informants were asked to discuss the last completed project in which they were involved, and from their comments an analysis was made of the organizational climate in which the work took place, and of how successful the project had been. The interviews were quite probing; statements were not accepted at face value, and the subsequent analysis was rigorous.

When the relevant organizational climate for each project was compared with the outcomes the correlation between the two was much higher (at +0.74) than I or my colleagues had expected. If one anomalous case of low project success is excluded: 'This was something which was good on paper but just didn't work out. So we ended up after a period of time going back to (the previous system)' (Gray 2000b), the correlation rating rises to +0.80. This striking correlation is illustrated in the graph in Figure 4.1.

The evidence shows a clear linkage between organizational climate and the success, assessed in a variety of different ways, of the work being done. This immediately raises the question of why this should be so; what are the mechanisms at work here, and, if we can answer these questions, how can managers make practical use of this understanding.

Williams (1998) raises the question of 'whether climate perceptions are a consequence rather than a cause of organisational performance'. He goes on to say that in his own research 'some evidence was found that suggests the relationship between organisational climate and performance could be interactional and in

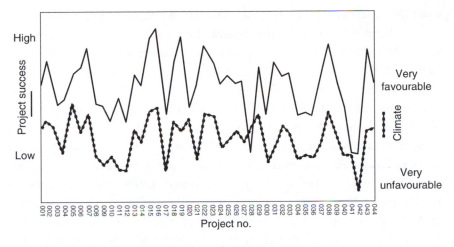

Figure 4.1 Organizational climate and project success.

either direction depending on contextual features'. This is a valid point, even if we accept (as I certainly do) that 'the case can be thoughtfully made … that causality is not a workable concept when it comes to human behavior: People are not billiard balls, but have complex intentions operating in a complex web of others' intentions and actions' (Miles and Huberman, 1994). In other words, the complexity involved in any human behaviour is such that it becomes almost impossible to say that one thing causes another in a direct linear sense. Intuitively, it seems reasonable to suppose that people would feel better if their organization was performing well, and that this would 'lift' the organizational climate, in a general sense; I have no good grounds for thinking that this doesn't happen.

However, I feel that the evidence for this being the prevailing direction of causality is rather weak. This is partly because of anecdotal evidence from the informants in the research quoted above (Gray, 2000b). In the course of this research the assessments of both climate and work outcomes were made from detailed analysis of the data, and in some cases didn't altogether agree with the assessments made by the managers themselves. For example, there was a strong tendency for informants to overstate the success of their projects, despite being aware of shortcomings that were discussed quite freely during the interviews.

The mean success rate, as assessed by the researchers, for projects where informants expressed some reservations was actually higher than for projects where the informants asserted unequivocally that they believed their project to have been successful. It's possible that the assessment criteria applied in this research were more stringent than those customarily applied by the informants themselves but, whatever the reason, it means that the objective (although qualitative) assessment of the relationship was not based uncritically on the informants' perceptions alone. The indications were that, in those cases where it was possible to make a judgement, the strongest direction of influence was from climate to outcomes, rather than the other way round.

This view is consistent with that formed in a rather different context by Litwin and Stringer (1968), who were impressed by early work done by Kurt Lewin with artificially created climates in boys' clubs; 'the climate itself proved more powerful than previously-"acquired" behavior tendencies, and it was able to change the observed behavior patterns of the group members' (Lewin et al., 1939). Watkin and Hubbard (2003) say that 'climate makes a difference because it indicates how energising the work environment is for employees' and although this expression of the principle may seem a little facile it does fit very well with the advocacy of 'positive psychology' advanced by West (2005).

West says that 'when we feel positive emotions we think in a more flexible, open-minded way, and consider a much wider range of possibilities than if we feel anxious, depressed or angry. This enables us to accomplish tasks and make the most of situations. We adapt more effectively to the demands around us and are more likely to see challenges as opportunities rather than threats'. He argues that under the influence of positive emotions we tend to adopt an open, questioning and understanding style with others, are likely to feel greater self-control, cope more effectively and be less defensive in the workplace. This leads on to 'pro-social behaviour' – co-operation and altruism – which in turn 'encourage organisational citizenship … the tendency for people at work to help each other and to put in extra effort beyond what is required'.

Caulkin (2006), commenting on differences between attitudes about employment conditions in continental Europe and Britain/USA, agrees: 'productivity is not just a matter of investment and skills. It also depends on the morale which governs discretionary effort – the willingness to "go the extra mile". This is unforthcoming if workers feel insecure'.

Ekvall (1996) suggests that 'in the context of organizational processes climate plays the part of an intervening variable which affects the results of the operations of the organization'. He believes that climate comes between the application of resources, including people, and the effects of that application. Feedback about those effects then influences climate, so again the direction of influence is not simple and linear, but two-directional. The key 'organizational processes', in this context, are those relating to the way people are managed.

Briner (2002) says 'there is growing evidence that HRM policies have an impact on organisational performance. Even though the absolute strength of these relationships might be relatively weak, researchers argue that small relationships can translate into tangible and important changes in performance', a view confirmed by Rogg et al. (2001) who also found evidence from their research on '351 small businesses ... that human resource practices influence organizational climate which in turn influences customer satisfaction indices'. They observe that the effects were indirect, but 'significant and very large'.

Many factors go to make up an employee's perception of his or her organization's HRM policies or, in the broadest sense, of how he or she is managed. Some of these factors are determined quite remotely from the individual, so although they may certainly feel personal to the individual on the receiving end, the interaction is with a corporate entity – 'them' – rather than with another individual. The influence of these factors on organizational climate is important, but the strongest, most significant factor seems to be the employee's interactions with his or her immediate supervisor(s); the 'day-by-day behavior of the immediate superior and of other significant people in the managerial organization' (McGregor, 1960). 'McGregor's view of climate was that managers create the climate in which subordinates work by what they do, how they do it, how competent they are, and their ability to make things happen through upward influence in the organization' (Reichers and Schneider, 1990).

'Just as climate is one of the major determinants of motivation, research findings indicate that the manager is one of the major determinants of climate. His actions, his personality, his leadership style all act to generate certain patterns of motivation, and this framework will allow us to trace some of the important causal relationships involved' (Litwin and Stringer, 1968). Watkin (2001) says that his organization's research 'building on the work of Litwin and Stringer at Harvard University – also indicates that 50 to 70 percent of an organisation's climate can be traced to its leadership or management style. In other words, good managers create good climates, while poor managers create poor climates. Both affect performance. This holds true in all sectors'.

Whilst I take a rather jaundiced view of the current fashion for 'leadership' studies, because it seems to me that the frequent use of the word 'leader' has more to do with massaging managers' egos than with accurately describing what they actually do, I think that in this context the terminology is unimportant. Previous generations would have referred to 'supervisors', more recently to 'managers'. Just occasionally the word 'leader' is right and appropriate. Whatever label is used it means here someone whose opinion, and whose behaviour, matters to the employee concerned.

There's considerable evidence that relationships between employees and their bosses are not as good as they might be. Worrall and Cooper maintain a regular 'Quality of Working Life' survey and report from the latest update (2006):

> perhaps one of the most striking findings is the extent to which the views and perceptions of directors differ from those of all other levels of management, including senior managers. Directors were far more likely to think that organisational change had improved morale, flexibility, employee participation, the speed of decision-making, profitability, productivity and motivation. They were much less likely (even compared to senior managers) to think that organisational change had led to a loss of knowledge and key skills in the organisation. We see this dissonance between the views of directors and other managers as significant and a cause for concern. The findings indicate the gap between the perceptions of those in the boardroom and the workforce as a whole which cannot be healthy for UK plc.

In an earlier edition of the survey there was 'a huge gap ... between what companies thought they provided and what workers believed they received. Most companies claimed to offer training, performance evaluation and employee involvement in decision-making, yet only a third of employees said they received such benefits' (Bilmes, 2001).

Why people at the most senior levels in organizations should be so unaware of the feelings of their subordinates, or even of straightforward factual information about their organizations, is difficult to understand, although I suspect that Douglas Adams (1987) might have been on to something when he observed that horses 'have always understood a great deal more than they let on. It is difficult to be sat on every day by some creature without forming an opinion of them. On the other hand, it is perfectly possible to sit all day, every day, on top of another creature and not have the slightest thought about them whatsoever'.

In the 1980s the practice of team briefing became very popular and I was frequently involved in helping to set up briefing systems. The idea of team briefing, which was 'promoted by the Industrial Society as a means of communicating systematically with managers and employees throughout an organisation' (CMI, 2006) was that managers or supervisors would hold regular face to face formal meetings with their teams to discuss current work issues, answer questions and, crucially, pass down information that senior levels wanted everyone to know. This 'cascade' of information grew as it travelled down the organizational levels and each manager added locally-relevant material.

On the whole I found that the downward flow usually worked quite well, although checks needed to be put in place to see that the information really did get passed down, uncensored and uncontaminated, and that superfluous items were discarded at the appropriate levels to avoid overload (inundation was a constant danger). The real problem was in getting anything useful passed back up the system so that top people actually found out what concerned the people at the 'coal face'. Middle managers were highly skilled in sanitizing – or just plain blocking – the messages in that direction.

Perhaps the root of the problems is in deep-seated adversarial attitudes between managers and managed. Scase (2001) remarks that despite an 'explosion in management education' and widespread knowledge of people management theories and models, 'employees and managers still do not trust each other'. Researchers bear this out. Patterson et al. (1996) surveyed 5500 employees in 54 UK manufacturing companies. They report that 'the survey results indicate that current human resource management practices are less enlightened than current rhetoric suggests … manufacturing companies are still characterised by an 'us' and 'them' attitude between management and shopfloor employees'.

Findings from their research into people management and performance led Patterson et al. (1997) to comment that 'in the majority of organisations, people are not viewed by top managers as their most important asset', and Peter Drucker (1998) observes sadly from the perspective of half a century of personal experience in organizational research and consultancy that 'all organizations now say routinely, "people are our greatest asset". Yet few practise what they preach, let alone truly believe it. Most still believe, though perhaps not consciously, what nineteenth century employers believed: people need us more than we need them'. All of which makes it difficult to answer Lewin and Regine's (1999) rhetorical question: 'how come we refuse to see the obvious – that when people are treated as replaceable parts or as objects to control, and are taught to be compliant so as to be used as fuel for an existing system – then inevitably you are going to have an organisation that is fraught with frustration, anger and isolation, which ultimately is detrimental to business?'.

It isn't just the business, or the organization, which suffers when the approach to working life is unhealthy in this way. Worrall and Cooper (2006) say 'what has emerged is a picture of managers coming under increasing pressure from the imposition of targets, performance management systems and league tables'. This puts a great strain on individuals and their families, which has serious implications both for employees and for their organizations: 'in recent years economic productivity has been wrung out of the average worker, in large measure, at the cost of his or her health and happiness. This trend towards pathological and dysfunctional effects needs to be reversed' (Gavin and Mason, 2004).

One glaring symptom of this increasing pressure is a comparison of working hours. Quoting the latest figures available to them, Gavin and Mason report that average working hours for 2002 in the UK were 1707, compared to Germany's 1444. Among the leading industrial nations, only the USA had longer average hours, at 1815. Contrary to 'flexible market' mythology, the 'anglo-saxon' long hours culture doesn't make us more efficient: 'there is some intellectual confusion here, not least because, on the measure of GDP per hour worked, France, Germany and some of the smaller member states in the EU 15 already have productivity levels equivalent to or better than the USA' (Coats, 2006).

On the other hand 'World Health Organisation … research proves that rates of mental illness are three times higher in Anglo-Saxon, compared with European, nations' (James, 2005). The underlying reason for this is almost certainly increased stress levels arising from a variety of work-related factors. In a recent 'poll of over 3000 people' (Skillsoft, 2006) 'a staggering 97 per cent of people working in IT claim to find their life at work stressful on a daily basis' and several other professions were not far behind. Workload was the most frequently cited stressor. This didn't include 'having to take on other people's work', which was listed as a separate category. 'Feeling undervalued' was the second most common stressor.

Stress is 'a reality like love or electricity – unmistakable in experience but hard to define' (Teasdale and McKeown, 1994). McLean (1985) remarks that 'the word is sometimes used to denote stressful events, sometimes to denote the effect of these events on work performance, and sometimes to denote an individual's reaction in terms of disordered health'. This confusion about the terminology detracts from what is a very real issue.

It's undoubtedly true that something of a 'stress industry' has developed over recent years, with counselling, physical exercise and other palliative steps becoming available to try to tackle the effects of stress. Alongside this a cynical anti-stress movement has emerged to argue that complaints of stress are either the whingeing of people who aren't up to the job or, quite often, deliberate fraud. This can sound credible if it can be said, without any intent to mislead, that 'some stress is necessary' as a spur to performance. It wouldn't be possible to say this if the terminology was more precise. For example, the sharpening of mental and physical processes to deal with a demand of some kind is properly called 'arousal'. Actually, unless we're fighting or fleeing from some acute danger we don't want too much of this because at the same time as providing increased resources to tackle the emergency it also tends to reduce our ability to handle complexity (Yerkes and Dodson, 1908; Hockey and Hamilton, 1983). Also, the cocktail of chemical messengers that flood our bodies under these conditions are meant to deal with acute, rather than chronic demands (chronic meaning continuing over an extended period of time). If they don't get used up by physical activity they can contribute to a range of damaging symptoms.

'Stress itself is not an illness, rather it is a state. However it is a very powerful cause of illness. Long-term excessive stress is known to lead to serious health problems' (Teasdale and McKeown, 1994). Cox (1993) reviews a number of studies in the field of psychoimmunology that strongly indicate a connection between the experience of stress and changes in the operation of the immune system, which has been identified as a probable mechanism by which stress may lead to ill-health.

In a review of the research on the associations between occupational stress and coronary heart disease, Landsbergis et al. (1993) found that 12 out of 14 studies reviewed showed a clear link. Cooper (1994) points out that 'it must be remembered that heart disease is only one of the physical manifestations of an unhealthy organisation, research shows that there are many more possible diseases and negative health outcomes (e.g. gastro-intestinal disorders, immune system failures, neurological problems, etc.)'. People suffering from stress are also more accident-prone (Cartwright et al., 1993).

And they don't perform very well: 'Although their illnesses may not lead to an economically measurable health care cost, exhausted or depressed employees are not energetic, accurate, or innovative at work. The losses that result loom larger than health care as preventable costs' (Karasek and Theorell, 1990). These losses mount up: 'Stress costs British business over £400 million a year, and the Health and Safety Executive predict that the bill will continue to rise. The World Health Organisation estimates that stress will account for half of the ten most common medical problems in the world by 2020' (Bunting, 2004). Bunting refers to 'The longest-running research on stress', known as the Whitehall Study (Stansfeld et al., 2000). This extensive study, sponsored by the Health and Safety Executive, involved over 10 000 civil servants. It

> found that stress was related to three variables: the amount of control the employee had in the job, the demands of the job, and the degree of support from colleagues and managers. How the three interacted was where the stress resulted; for example, if the support was excellent, an employee was more likely to be able to manage high job demands, but if the support was

weak, even a low-demand job could be stressful. The study identified one other source of stress – the "effort–reward imbalance": workers are more likely to be stressed if they feel they are putting a lot of effort into the job for few rewards such as income, promotion and recognition.

Bunting, 2004

This is entirely consistent with stress research over many years (Lazarus and Folkman, 1984; McLean, 1985; or Williams, 1994), and it seems to have links with equity theory (Adams, 1963).

From both perspectives – the economic and the personal – stress is a genuine issue and one that demands attention from managers. It has to be actively monitored, because 'the indicators of workplace stress are often silent. No one can see the rising blood pressure or impending nervous breakdown until it is too late' (Bland, 2000). Organizational climate, or more simply, the attitudes and behaviour of managers, can make an immediate and significant difference to the risk of stress-related damage to employees' health and to productivity.

By far the most significant factor in stress is the amount of control that people feel they have over what happens to them (Karasek and Theorell, 1990; Sauter et al., 1992). Echoing Maslow, Kanter (1983) warns that people can experience the workplace as 'a world marked by turbulence, uncertainty and instability, because their comfort, let alone their success is dependent on many decisions of many players they can barely, if at all, influence'. This is potentially highly damaging. Of course, how much control people feel they have is subjective, and personality factors come into it (Bandura, 1977), but managers can make a positive difference by actively promoting greater participation in goal setting and autonomy over the way that work is performed. Failure to do so is both culpable and very counterproductive.

THE ESSENTIALS OF THIS CHAPTER:

- Organizational climate influences performance. A climate in which most people feel a sense of well-being – closely related to happiness – is also the kind of climate in which work is performed most successfully.
- Evidence suggests that climate influences performance more than performance influences climate, so improving climate is likely to lead to better performance.

- The strongest (but not the only) influence on employees' perceptions of climate is probably their interactions with their immediate supervisor(s).
- Relationships between employees and their bosses are often less than satisfactory. Employers often don't know how employees feel and don't pay enough attention to their needs.
- Work-related stress is a serious problem, causing physical and mental illness, accidents, poor performance and financial loss. A benign organizational climate may help to reduce the experience of stress.

5

Assessing organizational climate

Some people, especially at work, like to measure everything, because this makes them feel as though they are in control. In reality, for everything that's accurately measured, there's some big and blobby unknown quantity lurking just around the corner.

Guy Browning, *How to … Measure*, 2006

I wholeheartedly agree with Guy Browning's views on measurement and I try to seize any opportunity to convince managers that measurement isn't an end in itself; its value is as a tool to be used in the process of *assessment*. Measurement, in one form or another, features to some extent in most efforts to assess the climate in organizations, and a variety of tools and techniques has been developed to help in this.

First, I need to say something about the way, or ways, in which research can be conducted in organizations in order to tell us something useful about climate, which is a subjective construct, existing in the perceptions of the people who experience it. It may seem as though *performance*, in contrast, is an objective concept in organizational life, and therefore easily measurable. In some respects this is clearly true. We can count how many units of product have been produced over a given time. We can check the share price, or note progress against a production or project schedule. But performance becomes much less easily assessable when we want to know how well people are performing some of the less well-defined elements of their jobs. For example, if someone's job involves handling complaints what measures do we use? How many complaints they deal with in a day? What if a rushed, impatient manner leads to even greater customer dissatisfaction? How about the number of customers who consider their complaint to have been dealt with properly? Did this involve making inappropriate concessions which cost a fortune? It gets more problematic as the complexity of a job increases.

When we need to assess the performance of managers the number of factors we might look at gets quite daunting. Organizations often try to deal with this by measuring outcomes rather than looking at what the individual actually does. 'Unfortunately, this isn't really the answer … The main problem here is that outcomes are the *effects* of what is being done; looking at results tells you what happened but it doesn't tell you why. Managers really need to be able to work on causes: by the time we are able to measure the results it's too late' (Gray, 2004).

In social research – and organizational research belongs in this broad category of enquiry – it's widely recognized that positivist or quantitative approaches, which are 'based on testing a theory composed of variables, measured with numbers, and analyzed with statistical procedures, in order to determine whether the predictive generalizations of the theory hold true' (Creswell, 1994), have limitations in terms of learning what we need to know. This is because 'many subjects of interest to social scientists cannot be meaningfully formulated in ways that permit statistical testing of hypotheses with quantitative data' (Trafford, 1997). When dealing with people's feelings, perceptions and responses, the 'objectivity (which) is a goal of traditional research . . . is largely an illusion' (Erlandson et al., 1993).

The alternative approach is known as qualitative, or sometimes phenomenological, research. This aims to develop 'understanding (of) a social or human problem' through a process which is 'based on building a complex, holistic picture, formed with words, reporting detailed views of informants' (Creswell, 1994). It's suggested that this kind of approach is more 'useful for hearing data and understanding meaning in context' than positivism which 'denies the significance of context and standardizes questions and responses, so that there is little room for individual voices' (Rubin and Rubin, 1995).

For most of us, these rather esoteric debates belong in academia rather than in the workplace. After all, 'in some senses, all data are qualitative; they refer to essences of people, objects, and situations. . . . We have a 'raw' experience, which is then converted into words ('His face is flushed.' . . . 'He is angry.') or into numbers ('Six voted yes, four no.' . . . 'The thermometer reads 74 degrees')' (Miles and Huberman, 1994). Miles and Huberman believe that the 'quantitative–qualitative argument is essentially unproductive. . . . In a deeper sense . . . the issue is not quantitative–qualitative at all, but whether we are taking an 'analytic' approach to understanding a few controlled variables, or a 'systemic approach to understanding the interaction of variables in a complex environment'.

For our purposes the need is very definitely for a systemic approach, and this has been broadly the line that many, although not all, climate researchers have taken. It involves examining, usually by interviews or surveys, a variety of factors that are believed to contribute to the experience of climate, and then putting them together to see what holistic picture emerges. There's still a risk, though, of losing the richness of an individual's experience in this process: 'The cold summary that researchers ask for should be seen as having as much relationship to a living process as snapshots have to the experience of a holiday' (Boulton and Coldron, 1991). We have to try to guard against this as best we can.

One approach that facilitates the understanding of interactions between many factors has become known as systems thinking. 'Systems thinking has, over the past three decades, emerged as one of the most important intellectual disciplines, and it has provided a powerful mental frame of reference in understanding problem situations and in guiding day-to-day decision making' (Yeo, 1993).

When we start to examine any complex topic the most obvious approach is to *analyse* it, or decompose it into its constituent parts. This is exactly what researchers, including myself, have done in the study of organizational climate. Unfortunately, this carries a great risk of missing those properties of the whole topic which only emerge and are only observable when the elements are conjoined. The word 'system' refers to 'a set of elements mutually related such that the set constitutes a whole having properties as an entity' (Checkland and Scholes, 1990). Systems thinking challenges the assumption 'that a component part is the same when separated out as it is when part of a whole. . . . Systems thinking is different because it is about the framework itself' (Checkland, 1984). 'The defining characteristic of a system is that it *cannot* be understood as a function of its isolated components' (Kofman and Senge, 1993).

Systems come in various forms, but the kinds of systems which interest us here are *open* systems which 'exchange ... materials, energy and information' with their environments and which have 'a set of processes in which there is *communication* of information for purposes of regulation or *control*' (Checkland, 1981). They are also *natural* systems, and *human activity* systems in the sense that they are the products of the relationships between people within certain environments.

> Natural systems are the evolution-made, irreducible wholes which an observer can observe and describe as such, being made up of other entities having mutual relationships. They are 'irreducible' in the sense that meaningful statements can be made about them as wholes, and this remains true even if we can describe their components and the relationships between the components with some precision. Carbon dioxide is not reducible in this sense to carbon and oxygen, in that however much we know about inter-atomic distances and bond angles, carbon dioxide remains a higher level whole having properties of its own.
>
> Checkland, 1981

These properties of a system that are not properties of any of its constituent parts are called 'emergent properties'.

A human activity system 'can be described as an interacting set of subsystems or an interacting set of activities. A subsystem is no different to a system except in terms of level of detail and hence a subsystem can be redefined as a system and modelled as a set of activities. Thus the term "system" and "activity" can be used interchangeably' (Wilson, 1984). In other words, 'a system is, at the same time, a subsystem of some wider system and is itself a wider system to its subsystems. What we define to be "a system" is a choice of resolution level or the choice of level of detail at which we wish to describe the activities. It is a choice: there is no absolute definition of what is a system or what is a subsystem' (Wilson, 1984).

The precise definition of what constitutes a specific system depends, according to the Checkland view, upon the perspective of the observer: 'Even if there are no closely associated systems to emphasize the grouping of the activities, as in the example . . . of "the eating habits of the octogenarians of Basingstoke", it is difficult to deny the right of an observer to choose to view a set of activities as a system if he wishes to do so' (Checkland, 1981). The notion of a system is as key to the understanding of the experience of organizational climate, as it is to understanding the much wider field of organizational behaviour in general.

I have, I think, made it very clear that organizational climate is a systemic concept, made up of constituent parts which are individually distinguishable but which together form a new, greater construct with an identity of its own; a system, in fact. Over more than four decades of climate research various writers have defined climate in terms of its constituent parts and there has been a reasonable level of consensus about what those constituents are. It is also noticeable that there has been very little development of the ideas over time; the list offered by Litwin and Stringer in the 1960s is not substantively different from the one that Watkin produced in 2001. There are differences of emphasis between the writers, as might be expected, and there are differences of opinion about what qualifies as a separate dimension. I will briefly review some of the more prominent ideas here.

Litwin and Stringer (1968), at the beginning of the era, defined nine factors (or variables, or dimensions) of organizational climate:

- 'Structure: the feeling that employees have about the constraints in the group, how many rules, regulations, procedures there are; is there an emphasis on 'red tape' and going through channels, or is there a loose and informal atmosphere.'
- 'Responsibility: the feeling of being your own boss; not having to double-check all your decisions; when you have a job to do, knowing that it is your job.'
- 'Reward: the feeling of being rewarded for a job well done; emphasizing positive rewards rather than punishments; the perceived fairness of the pay and promotion policies.'

- 'Risk: the sense of riskiness and challenge in the job and in the organization; is there an emphasis on taking calculated risks, or is playing it safe the best way to operate.'
- 'Warmth: the feeling of general good fellowship that prevails in the work group atmosphere; the emphasis on being well-liked; the prevalence of friendly and informal social groups.'
- 'Support: the perceived helpfulness of the managers and other employees in the group; emphasis on mutual support from above and below.'
- 'Standards: the perceived importance of implicit and explicit goals and performance standards; the emphasis on doing a good job; the challenge represented in personal and group goals.'
- 'Conflict: the feeling that managers and other workers want to hear different opinions; the emphasis placed on getting problems out in the open, rather than smoothing them over or ignoring them.'
- 'Identity: the feeling that you belong to a company and you are a valuable member of a working team; the importance placed on this kind of spirit.'

This seems quite a comprehensive list, until Gordon and Cummins (1979) present eight dimensions, at least some of which appear to cover different ground:

- 'Clarity with which organizational goals and plans are perceived';
- 'Rationality, implementation and evaluation of decision-making';
- 'Organizational integration (co-operation and communication)';
- 'Management style (encouragement of initiative, support, tolerance of questioning/challenge)';
- 'Performance orientation (accountability for results)';
- 'Organizational vitality (perception of the organization as dynamic)';
- 'Compensation (fair, equitable, competitive, related to performance)';
- 'HRD (people see opportunities to develop their potential)'.

Some of these are clearly overlapping; it's hard, for example, to match 'management style' to a single dimension from Litwin and Stringer's list, but aspects of it would apply to several of them.

Jones and James' (1979) dimensions are a little easier to line up. They are:

- 'Leadership facilitation and support';
- 'Workgroup co-operation, friendliness and warmth';
- 'Conflict and ambiguity';

- 'Professional and organisational *esprit*';
- 'Job challenge, importance and variety';
- 'Mutual trust'.

Gordon (1985) refers to the climate dimensions used in a questionnaire designed by the Hay consulting group. They are:

- 'Clarity of direction';
- 'Organizational reach';
- 'Integration';
- 'Top management contact';
- 'Encouragement of individual initiative';
- 'Conflict resolution';
- 'Performance clarity';
- 'Performance emphasis';
- 'Action orientation';
- 'Compensation';
- 'Human resource development'.

Anderson and West (1994) use a psychometric test, the 'Team Climate Inventory', to assess the climate of a group within an organization. 'Team climate refers to the norms, atmosphere, practices, interpersonal relationships, enacted rituals and ways of working developed by a team, so climate has a big impact on performance'. The TCI assumes that climate has four main dimensions: 'Participation and safety'; 'Vision'; 'Task orientation'; 'Support for innovation'. Again, it's arguable that some of these dimensions line up with one or more of those in the earlier lists.

Ekvall (1996) reverts to a longer list and defines ten dimensions:

- 'Challenge';
- 'Freedom';
- 'Idea support';
- 'Trust/openness';
- 'Dynamism/liveliness';
- 'Playfulness/humour';
- 'Debates';
- 'Conflicts';
- 'Risk taking';
- 'Idea time';

all of which seem to line up with dimensions from earlier lists but are, perhaps, a little more specific in some cases, which adds to the length of Ekvall's list.

Patterson et al. (1996) take this process almost to its logical conclusion by defining no less than 20 dimensions:

- 'Communication: the openness and effectiveness of communications systems within and between levels';
- 'Participation: the extent to which people are involved in making decisions that affect them';
- 'Performance Monitoring: the extent to which job performance is monitored and fed back to employees';
- 'Welfare: the extent to which employees feel valued and trusted';
- 'Supervisory Support: the extent to which employees experience support and understanding from their immediate supervisor or manager';
- 'Formalisation: the degree to which rules and formal procedures govern the way things are done';
- 'Autonomy: the degree of autonomy employees are given to do their jobs';
- 'Quality: the level of importance placed in producing quality products and services';
- 'Effort: the degree of effort and enthusiasm employees put into their work';
- 'Pressure: the extent to which there is pressure on employees to produce';
- 'Vision: the extent to which employees understand the company vision and long-term aims';
- 'Efficiency: the degree of importance placed on efficiency and productivity at work';
- 'Tradition: the extent to which traditional established ways of doing things are valued';
- 'Innovation: the level of interest in new ideas and innovative approaches';
- 'Flexibility: the extent to which the company can adapt to change';
- 'Skill Development: the extent to which employees are encouraged and supported in learning new job relevant skills';
- 'Risk: the extent to which decision makers are encouraged to take risks to capitalise on an opportunity';
- 'Interdepartmental Relations: the level of conflict or co-operation existing between different groups in the organisation';
- 'Outward Focus: the degree to which management looks outside for market opportunities and the degree of importance placed on providing a high level of service for the customer';

- 'Reviewing Objectives: the extent to which organisational members take action in changing objectives, strategies or team processes in order to achieve successful outcomes'.

Oddly enough, when Patterson's list is lined up with the earlier sets of dimensions the length of the combined list doesn't really increase. In some cases there is a slight difference of emphasis and, again, Patterson et al. seem to have separated out elements which some earlier writers have combined to form a single dimension.

Williams (1998), who conducted research into the relationship between climate and performance, defined six climate variables:

- Supervisory style;
- Co-workers;
- Work motivation (not explicitly mentioned or, I think, implied by any of the others);
- Employee competence;
- Decision-making;
- Performance rewards.

Finally, Watkin (2001) says that although the various assessment instruments 'may use different labels to describe the qualities that they aim to evaluate, most measure the following key aspects or dimensions of organisational climate' and goes on to provide seven of his own:

- Flexibility;
- Responsibility;
- Standards;
- Rewards;
- Clarity;
- Team commitment;
- 'Climate and leadership style' (sic).

In all, I can detect what I believe are 15 arguably distinct dimensions in the views of these writers, which are shown in the form of a system map in Figure 5.1.

It's a characteristic of systems that the elements are interlinked. Each element may exert an influence on, and/or be influenced by, other (potentially all the other) elements, hence the lines of connectivity between the elements.

I have omitted from the above review, and from the system map, the elements which I used in my own research. Although, as might be expected, there's a fair

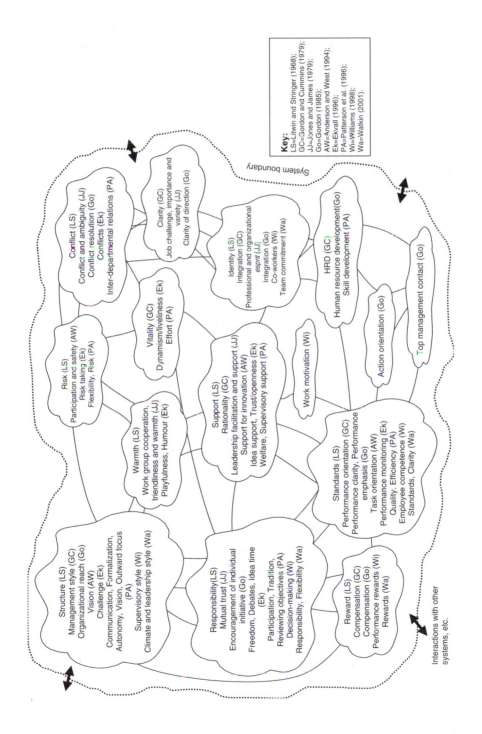

Key:
LS=Litwin and Stringer (1968);
GC=Gordon and Cummins (1979);
JJ=Jones and James (1979);
Go=Gordon (1985);
AW=Anderson and West (1994);
Ek=Ekvall (1996);
PA=Patterson et al. (1996);
Wi=Williams (1998);
Wa=Watkin (2001).

System boundary

Conflict (LS)
Conflict and ambiguity (JJ)
Conflict resolution (Go)
Conflicts (Ek)
Inter-departmental relations (PA)

Clarity (GC)
Job challenge, importance and variety (JJ)
Clarity of direction (Go)

Identity (LS)
Integration (GC)
Professional and organizational esprit (JJ)
Integration (Go)
Co-workers (Wi)
Team commitment (Wa)

HRD (GC)
Human resource development(Go)
Skill development (PA)

Action orientation (Go)

Top management contact (Go)

Risk (LS)
Participation and safety (AW)
Risk taking (Ek)
Flexibility, Risk (PA)

Vitality (GC)
Dynamism/liveliness (Ek)
Effort (PA)

Work motivation (Wi)

Warmth (LS)
Work group cooperation, friendliness and warmth (JJ)
Playfulness, Humour (Ek)

Support (LS)
Rationality (GC)
Leadership facilitation and support (JJ)
Support for innovation (AW)
Idea support, Trust/openness (Ek)
Welfare, Supervisory support (PA)

Standards (LS)
Performance orientation (GC)
Performance clarity, Performance emphasis (Go)
Task orientation (AW)
Performance monitoring (Ek)
Quality, Efficiency (PA)
Employee competence (Wi)
Standards, Clarity (Wa)

Structure (LS)
Management style (GC)
Organizational reach (Go)
Vision (AW)
Challenge (Ek)
Communication, Formalization, Autonomy, Vision, Outward focus (PA)
Supervisory style (Wi)
Climate and leadership style (Wa)

Responsibility(LS)
Mutual trust (JJ)
Encouragement of individual initiative (Go)
Freedom, Debates, Idea time (Ek)
Participation, Tradition, Reviewing objectives (PA)
Decision-making (Wi)
Responsibility, Flexibility (Wa)

Reward (LS)
Compensation (GC)
Compensation (Go)
Performance rewards (Wi)
Rewards (Wa)

Interactions with other systems, etc.

Figure 5.1 A system map of climate dimensions.

degree of commonality between my own analysis and the collective analyses of the nine other writers I have cited here, I took a slightly different view of what would be likely to be associated with performance and, therefore, what would repay management attention. For example, it is perfectly reasonable to try to assess, as Williams does, the level of motivation of individuals or groups.

However, when we look more closely at the psychological, social and economic bases of workplace motivation it becomes apparent that the concept of 'motivation' is too high a level to be very useful. There's not much a manager can actually do directly with the knowledge that someone is highly motivated, moderately motivated, or hardly motivated at all. The useful information in this case would be found at a deeper level; what is the background to the observed motivation level and what can be done to facilitate a more positive attitude towards the work that needs to be done?

Similarly, I would not dispute for a moment that clarity about what is required of an employee is likely to be a big factor in his or her feelings about the job and the employer. In fact, this is one of the most basic functions of any manager. However, there is considerable evidence that participation in defining what has to be done, and how it is to be done, is by far the best way to achieve excellent results, and it's less stress-inducing for the people concerned:

> considerable research has shown that when regulation is through choice (i.e. is self-determined) people are . . . more creative, display greater cognitive flexibility and conceptual understanding, have a more positive emotional tone, are healthier, and are more likely to support the autonomy of others.
>
> Deci, 1992

Alternatively, 'for many people, a goal set and delegated by others serves as a disincentive' (Robertson et al., 1992). Of course, it's sometimes necessary just to give instructions, but the reasons for those instructions should always be explained, on practical grounds as well as out of concern for the recipients (and out of common courtesy, which should never be neglected in workplace interactions). Therefore, in considering the holistic system of an organizational climate I think we should be looking for patterns of interaction about goal and task definition rather than asking simplistically how clearly goals are understood.

For these kinds of reasons I looked for ideas and direction in a wide range of studies on subjects which seemed to have potential to inform a practical, usable overview of an organization's climate. These topics included: individual and group processes of perception; social learning theory; attitude formation; leadership theory; the psychological and physiological effects of fear, anger and stress; hostile and extreme work regimes, such as slavery; threat and coercion; motivation; organizational culture; the psychological contract; authority, power and influence; conflict; and attribution theory. From these sources I derived a series of qualitatively testable propositions which led to the identification of eight dimensions of organizational climate (and, incidentally, to discarding some others). The final list is:

- **Free expression** of ideas;
- **Free expression** of concerns;
- **Freedom to question** (especially decisions and policies determined by more senior people);
- **Participation**: genuine participation in defining goals and objectives;
- **Intrinsic satisfactions** derived from the work itself;
- **Innovation** (freedom to try new concepts and approaches);
- **Purposive threat**;
- **Environmental threat**.

These eight dimensions fall into two groups. The first six are positive factors and are largely associated with individual autonomy, responsibility and control. I refer to them collectively as voluntarism. (I'm aware that this term has a rather precise meaning in philosophy, which is related to, but not quite the same as, the meaning I'm ascribing to it here).

In general terms the more voluntarism there is the better the climate will feel to most (never all) people in a workplace. However, this is always likely to be a moving target. To illustrate this, Figure 5.2 is based on a principle of customer satisfaction with products or services, which was developed by Professor Noriaki Kano of Tokyo University of Science, modified for this specific application (examples of the Kano method and variations of the Kano diagram are reproduced in many books and articles on product design. For a selection of helpful articles see CQMJ, 1993).

In this model, three levels of satisfaction can be distinguished. First, people's basic expectations must be met, otherwise they will inevitably be dissatisfied to some degree. If their dissatisfaction doesn't already arise from some specific cause, they will be likely to focus it on some aspect of workplace life which they might otherwise have taken in their stride. Even if basic expectations are fulfilled, there will still be needs that people have from their working life which are unmet. One real difficulty with meeting basic expectations is that they are often unspoken or even unrecognized by the people themselves; it just doesn't feel right if they are going unmet.

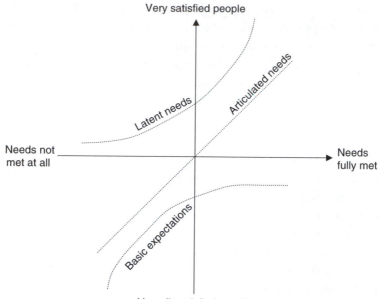

Figure 5.2   Three levels of satisfaction (with acknowledgement to N. Kano).

Second, people have articulated needs; things they know about and can express. These are often on a kind of sliding scale of 'the more the better' (like the distance a car will go on a litre of fuel, or how much talk time a mobile phone will allow for a given battery size/weight) but without a pre-set value which determines the point at which dissatisfaction changes to satisfaction.

Lastly, there are latent needs. These are things people aren't really aware that they need so their absence isn't really noticed, but whose presence is noticed and evokes a delighted reaction. In the commercial world of products and services features that address latent needs are sometimes called 'delighters'.

Organizational climates which manage to provide adequately for articulated needs, and sometimes surprise employees with unexpected 'delighters', are likely to be perceived as benign. Of course, delighters quickly become articulated needs, and then basic expectations. This is one powerful way in which the psychological contract changes and develops over time. The clear underlying theme here is the necessity for understanding employees' needs and this requires continual communication and goodwill on both sides.

The six factors collectively called 'voluntarism' are positive, and likely to improve the perception of climate. The last two, however, are negative and are likely to depress the perception of climate as benign. Threat, in a general sense, means 'the anticipation of impending change to a state less favourable than the status quo' (Gray, 2002) or 'harms/losses which have not yet taken place but are anticipated' (Lazarus and Folkman, 1984).

Threats come in two kinds. Environmental threat refers to natural events, forces or changes in society which are not being controlled by anyone, or from macro-political causes or policies that are decided so remotely from the people they affect that for all practical purposes we can regard them as being undirected. When we perceive ourselves as being subject to this kind of threat we are likely to feel insecure and worried about the future. In the workplace this can also lead to doubts about the 'continuance of context': our enthusiasm for and commitment to a current task or project is 'undermined if there seems a real possibility that it will be stopped before completion by management decision or external forces' (Gray, 2004).

Purposive threats are those which are directed quite consciously at individuals or groups with the intention of making them do (or possibly stop doing) something specific, or in some cases from malice. It's actually quite common in organizational life, even in Western liberal democracies, for purposive threats to form part of the standard repertoire of management techniques, either in the form of specific penalties or sanctions for infringements of rules or failure to meet targets, or as inverse sanctions, as when performance-related pay is withheld because targets have not been met, or when anticipated pay increases or promotions aren't forthcoming. It should be said here that many people regard this as perfectly legitimate, including some of those who are themselves on the receiving end of the penalties. Leaving aside the ethical discussion to which this might give rise, I can say from my own research (Gray, 2000b) that it doesn't seem to be a very effective management tool; when levels of purposive threat were compared with successful work outcomes the correlation was clearly negative.

There were also reports of adverse health effects which the sufferers linked to the experience of perceiving themselves to have been threatened in the ways I've described above. This isn't really too hard to explain. Edmund Burke (1756) says that 'No passion so effectually robs the mind of all its powers of acting and reasoning as fear'. This is hardly a situation to be promoted in today's workplaces. Charles Handy (1990) warns that 'a culture of excitement, of question and experiment, of exploration and adventure cannot survive under a reign of fear'. In the end, 'someone who threatens us is, by definition, an enemy; and people don't work willingly and enthusiastically to further an enemy's objectives. Furthermore, many people would positively relish the prospect of getting back at an enemy if the opportunity arises. I really don't recommend this as a basis for working relationships' (Gray, 2004).

Information about the current state of an organization's, or organizational subgroup's, climate is a vital prerequisite for making decisions and for going on to change things for the better; as Wiley and Brooks (2000) observe: 'properly designed employee-based measures of the work environment and organizational climate are key tools for the diagnosis of bottom-line organizational success'. However, because climate is a construct which exists in the perceptions of the individuals concerned, finding out about it can be problematic.

Watkin (2001) says that 'On an organisational level, there are three strategies for measuring climate'. These are (a) observation of 'work in progress'; (b) interviewing 'key members of the workforce'; and (c) conducting surveys of 'staff members using questionnaires'. Watkin recommends the last option, mainly on grounds of cost, and I have to agree that the time commitment both of the researchers and the staff involved, and the inevitable disruption caused, usually rule out interviewing on anything more than a very limited scale. This is regrettable, because I believe that the open or semi-structured interview, carried out and subsequently analysed by neutral third-party researchers, is the most reliable and productive approach to finding out about organizational climate. However, there's no getting away from the fact that it's very expensive.

Third party observation, which restricts its objectives to overall impressions, can be quite useful, because a stranger may see, or be aware of, symptoms of problems that are blurred by familiarity to the members of the organization or group. However, the usefulness of this approach for more in-depth analysis is limited. In practice, it's almost impossible to observe work as it's being done in any meaningful way because hardly anyone behaves naturally or expresses their true feelings whilst being watched.

Thus, however imperfect the method may be, we are left with the survey as the most practical and cost-effective way to learn about a particular organizational climate. This then presents the problem of what questions to ask. The objective is to build up a picture of the perceptions of each individual, and then to aggregate those individual perceptions in order to be able to make broad statements about the organization's climate. This means designing questions which focus the respondent's attention on one factor at a time and elicit answers which fit into categories so that one person's answer can be compared with other people's. This would suggest tightly-defined, closed questions. However, what we are trying to find out about are psychological states, attitudes and perceptions, which really requires open questions which people can answer in their own way, prioritizing the issues and concerns which matter most to them.

These essentially incompatible requirements make it unsurprising that 'most climate instruments have not been validated. With the exception of some domain-specific climates such as Schneider's service climate ... there are few measures with demonstrated reliability and validity' (Patterson et al., 2005). The test of *reliability* is that 'if you or anyone else were to repeat the research, you or they should be able to obtain the same results. ... *Validity* is the extent to which research findings accurately represent what is really happening in the situation' (Hussey and Hussey, 1997).

Both these qualities are hard to demonstrate in the context of what is, primarily, phenomenological research. Reliability is very difficult to establish because you can't repeat the test in any meaningful way. If you ask the same people the same questions again, three things (at least) have changed:

1. they've already been through the exercise so they know the questions already and will remember at least some of their previous answers;
2. time has passed, so their feelings may have changed; and
3. they are aware that management wants to find out what they think.

This last point is crucial. If the fact of management's interest in their feelings is taken at face value it may have the effect of evoking a warm feeling and a wish to respond positively to the organization's benign interest. Or it may provoke a cynical belief that management is going through the motions of pretending a bogus concern about employees' views. It may even be perceived as threatening if employees think that management may be trying to test their loyalty and identify those with a 'bad attitude'.

If the questionnaire is given to a different set of people, then one of the most significant criteria – the 'research population' – has changed, so it tells the researcher little or nothing about the instrument's reliability. The exception to this is that if the exercise is repeated in a wide variety of situations with large numbers of subjects and the results can be independently confirmed by a different method (which is called 'triangulation'), then the assumption may reasonably be made that the instrument is reliable. In practice this is quite a tall order.

Validity is equally hard to demonstrate. At its most basic level the questionnaire should demonstrate *face* validity: the questions and the complete instrument should at least seem to be checking the things the researcher has set out to test.

Then triangulation can be used to check on *convergent* validity; if different methods point to similar findings then confidence in the questionnaire's validity will be boosted. Easterby-Smith et al. (1991) question how important these concepts are in the kind of enquiry we are discussing here 'because they might imply acceptance of one absolute (positivist) reality'.

The way out of this maze of concepts and technical difficulties is usually to fall back on some form of Likert scale (originally Likert, 1932). These present respondents with a series of statements and ask them to '*place themselves* on an attitude continuum for each statement – running from "strongly agree" to "agree", "uncertain", "disagree", and "strongly disagree". These five positions were given simple weights of 5, 4, 3, 2 and 1 for scoring purposes (or sometimes 4–0), after more complex scoring methods had been shown to possess no advantage' (Oppenheim, 1992).

If we give respondents a set of statements, each of which is carefully crafted to reflect a specific dimension of organizational climate, and ask them to say how much they agree that 'this is the case in my organization' we will build up a picture of the holistic experience of that climate. We can make the instrument more robust by providing more than one statement for each dimension, and there are features that can be built in to minimize technical problems such as the tendency for respondents to detect, rightly or wrongly, patterns in the answers to survey questions which suggest what answers would be socially desirable or just seem to be what the researcher is looking for, and answer accordingly. This can also happen if a series of questions or statements quite legitimately produce the same answer; the pattern of consistent answers may carry on to the next item, which really should get a different response.

This form of questionnaire is the kind of instrument which I and my colleagues have developed to help in our consulting work on organizational climate (Gray, 2002, 2004). In Patterson et al.'s (2005) terms it isn't 'validated', but we would contend that this isn't the point, since it isn't used to provide academically replicable data. Rather, its use is in building a systemic picture of the current state of feelings and perceptions in an organization, or part of an organization, which managers can then use as a basis for considered action in changing their own behaviour and fixing structural problems in their own spheres of responsibility.

The narratives which follow illustrate specific organizational climate issues, some of which were brought to light by the use of survey instruments, others by observation and some by the realization among the players themselves that things could be improved, even if they weren't initially very clear just what that meant.

THE ESSENTIALS OF THIS CHAPTER:

- The only value of measurement is as a tool to be used in the process of *assessment*.
- It's difficult to assess the performance of someone doing a complex job, such as a manager, because outcomes may be determined by many factors.
- Assessing organizational climate is also difficult because it is made up of many interacting factors.
- Systems approaches have been found to be the most productive ways of assessing complex and/or subjective constructs.
- Researchers have different opinions about what factors should be taken into account when assessing organizational climate, but closer analysis shows that the differences are often more in definition than in substance.
- The best way to find out how people feel about the climate of their organization is to ask them. The cheapest (but not necessarily the best) way to do this is by means of questionnaires.

6

On the freedom to express ideas

One of the greatest pains to human nature is the pain of a new idea.
Walter Bagehot, *Physics and Politics*, 1869

Narrative No 1: EAEP

Background

In 1944 two young RAF officers, David Faber and Michael Ward, were seriously injured when their plane was hit by anti-aircraft fire over Germany. The aircraft managed to limp back to England and the two men received the best available medical treatment but after many weeks it became clear that neither of them would be fit to fly again: Faber had lost part of his right leg and Ward's right hand was severely burned and retained only minimal function. They were both subsequently discharged from the air force.

Before joining up, Faber had studied engineering at university. Ward had a degree in Classics but was an enthusiastic aficionado of all things mechanical and technical. Both were independently well off but, once recovered from their injuries, they both felt strongly that they needed a purpose in life. After looking at the job opportunities open to them, which were in fact reasonably wide at that time, notwithstanding their disabilities, they decided to set up their own company making precision-engineered machine parts, initially for aircraft.

Some fairly rudimentary market research showed them that the major companies, with government support, had the supply of aircraft parts more or less sewn up, but this also meant that other less war-effort focused demands were not being adequately addressed, so when they launched their company their attention was directed towards the manufacture of one-off or short production run parts for industrial and domestic machinery.

Neither man had any experience of business or manufacturing. In fact, neither of them had ever actually made anything even remotely comparable to their intended products. They did, however, have some theoretical knowledge and, perhaps crucially for the success of their business, they understood only too clearly the importance of top quality robust components in working machinery. They both attributed their survival to the quality of design and manufacture of their aircraft, which had managed to stay in the air despite being severely damaged. This made them very effective salesmen which, combined with their education, military training and social connections, enabled them to make valuable contacts as they went about setting up their company.

Business acumen was provided by Faber's uncle, a partner in a City investment bank, who joined them on the board of the new company. Finance was never going to be a problem and they were able to secure investment from various members of their two families without ever needing to approach commercial lenders. When Eastern Aero Engineering Parts Ltd launched it was probably one of the best capitalized small businesses in England and its factory in Essex was equipped to the highest standards.

If finding the money to set up the business was easy, finding the people they needed was anything but. The Directors of EAEP quickly realized that they needed to recruit staff with skills which were in very heavy demand at that time. Whilst Faber and Ward understood a fair amount about making precision machines they lacked the design skills to translate their concepts into executable technical drawings, and they needed skilled craftsmen to turn the abstract ideas into deliverable products. If the war had continued for a few more months EAEP would probably have folded before it really got going but fortunately the winter of 1945–6 brought many skilled men onto the labour market and EAEP was able to recruit a talented designer and several craftsmen. The stage was now set for EAEP to develop into a successful and well-respected business that survived several periods of economic gloom and, overall, has managed to be consistently profitable right up to the present day.

In 1975 Faber's uncle, who had guided the younger men through the vicissitudes of business life, died unexpectedly and after some indecision an accountant, John Ferguson, who was not a member of either founder's family, was appointed as Finance Director.

Michael Ward retired in 1985, whilst David Faber continued to run the business for a further six years, when declining health forced him to bow out as well, leaving Michael's son Peter Ward and John Ferguson in charge. Two new Directors, Alan Pitcher and Ian Jones, were appointed over the next few months, both of whom settled quickly into what was by all accounts a friendly and collegiate board-room. In 40 years of trading, all decisions of any importance had been taken at board level; staff had been hired to meet operational needs and the firm had always paid well, rewarded good work and never knowingly treated any employee unfairly in any way. The 'new' regime was, in all obvious respects, exactly like the old one, and things were expected to continue much as they had before.

The situation

In February 2002 I was contacted by Alan Pitcher. He told me that EAEP had recently been invited by a long-established customer to bid for a new contract.

Although he didn't say so explicitly, reading between the lines I got the strong impression that the contract was considered virtually a done deal, and EAEP had jumped the gun a little by doing a significant amount of development work in anticipation of getting the job. So it came as a nasty surprise to be told that the contract had gone to a competitor. Worse, this was the third time something of the kind had happened in a six-month period. Pitcher felt that something was going wrong and wanted help to pinpoint the problem and, of course, do something about it before things got really serious.

The first step was to find out why, specifically, EAEP hadn't got this order. Fortunately the long and previously very positive relationship between them made it possible to approach the customer informally and put the question fairly directly. EAEP already knew that their prices tended to be in the upper mid range in the industry but they thought it unlikely that price had been the definitive reason for losing the business. Their reputation for quality and after-sales support usually cancelled out any minor price differential.

Discussion with the customer tended to confirm this. The competitor had won the bid by being clearly ahead on two key grounds: product design and delivery dates. I suggested that Pitcher should look into the other lost orders to see if there was a common pattern. This was a little more difficult because the relationships were more formal, but after some subtle probing he was able to confirm that in one case the order had gone to a firm which offered a novel design which EAEP considered dangerously new and untested. In the other case a revolutionary manufacturing method had enabled the competitor to cut delivery times by several weeks.

I asked Pitcher what EAEP's design and production teams thought about the new methods being put into use by the competition. He seemed a little taken aback by the question. It seemed that the process by which products were developed from conception through manufacture and on to delivery was the tried and tested method of the firm's founders: the Director responsible for the customer's account would find out, through discussion, exactly what the customer needed the product to do. Then, a design specification which would meet those needs was agreed with the customer. Quite often the customer would know exactly what he wanted, so all EAEP had to do was to develop the design to the level of detail needed by the factory.

This was exactly what had been done with the latest lost order, so EAEP felt more than a little aggrieved; after all, their bid had been for a product that was exactly what the customer had asked for! Pitcher felt strongly that this was a good, professional approach; senior people kept their finger on the pulse continually and took the greatest care to give good, clear instructions to the designers and production people so that everyone knew what they had to do every step of the way. It had always served them well in the past.

Further discussions, over a fairly alcoholic meal with the customer, revealed that the winning bid had in fact offered something radically different from EAEP's product design; something quite different, in fact, from what the customer had requested. Pitcher and the other EAEP Directors were nonplussed, and seriously worried. If customers didn't want what they asked for, how could a supplier be expected to meet their requirements?

I asked to be allowed to speak to staff at EAEP and after discussion with his fellow Directors Pitcher reluctantly agreed, with the warning that I should be careful not to 'worry people' or 'cause confusion'. Over the next two days I spoke informally to nine employees. I was glad that no Director was present during these conversations because I was soon very sure that I would have learned much less if they had been. This wasn't because the staff feared the consequences of speaking out of turn. On the contrary, I soon felt reassured that the bosses were generally respected and even liked. Rather, there was a culture of carrying out instructions according to established procedures and checking with one of the Directors if anything wasn't clear, so people were more conditioned to listen, rather than give their own opinions when the boss was present.

I learned that the designers were aware of the 'new' solutions which had featured in the competitors' product offerings; they had read about them in trade journals and heard about them from fellow professionals but 'we couldn't do that here – EAEP does things the traditional way until new methods have been thoroughly tested elsewhere. That way we don't have any disasters'. This was fair enough, unless losing orders counts as a disaster. I found out that two talented young designers had left recently; 'they couldn't get on here' I was told, 'they were full of ideas but not very practical. The bosses have been in the business since the year dot and they've seen it all before. They know what works and what doesn't and they haven't let us down in the past'. The partings had been amicable, even regretful. No one I spoke to could remember anyone ever having been sacked from EAEP.

I talked to the production people, and heard a similar story. Several of the team were young, well qualified but willing to learn tricks of the trade from the old hands. Their theoretical knowledge played a part in implementing the designers' specifications efficiently and often with a certain elegance. Quality was high on the agenda and the staff were proud of their department. Whilst I was there two separate customer visits took place and I could see that the visitors were impressed with what they saw. Once again, I was told that someone had left the department a few weeks previously, but recruitment had never been a problem because of the firm's excellent reputation, so a replacement was already in post.

I learned something else from my private discussions with the staff in these two key departments; people were naturally disappointed at the loss of the orders, although there was still plenty of work on hand so real concern had not yet set in, but underneath that there was a feeling that things could be better. Some of the younger team members had tried to make suggestions, which had been received politely but not acted on. I found that even some long-serving people were willing to admit that in the past they had had ideas of their own but had been gently turned back to get on with their 'proper jobs' of implementing decisions made by others.

The management style was benign and often the rejection of employees' input went almost unnoticed, but it was consistent enough for them to give up after a while. It was rare for ideas to be accepted that didn't originate in or close to the boardroom. The people who had left were 'full of ideas', some of them original, others current in the industry but not in practice at EAEP. They had been unable to go along with the paternalistic EAEP culture and had voted with their feet. I decided to follow this up.

At my request EAEP's personnel manager (not, of course, part of the senior management structure at EAEP) contacted the leavers and asked if they would be willing to give me 'exit interviews'. Two out of the three agreed and I duly met them on neutral territory (the pub) to find out why they had left EAEP. Their responses were not earth-shattering. They had achieved advanced qualifications and en route had heard or read about many new concepts and approaches. They had also been required to come up with ideas of their own for evaluation by their peers and tutors. They had expected these talents to be valued at EAEP, and indeed, this had been strongly implied in the recruitment process, but once established in the job they had found that ideas were not what was required. They were only expected to apply themselves to making other people's ideas work. This in itself sometimes required a certain amount of ingenuity, so the jobs weren't entirely without intellectual challenge, but it wasn't what they wanted, so they left.

Rather more revealing was the fact that both had gone to work for EAEP's competitors and both had been involved in the winning bids which had beaten EAEP's tenders. In each case they had made suggestions to their new bosses which had been eagerly accepted, implemented and placed before the customers as examples of how radical, cutting-edge thinking from a young, brilliant, dynamic team could produce fast, practical and cost-effective solutions to the customers' needs. In one case the solution was quite different from the one the customer had identified, but it met the requirement in a new and effective way.

Both the ex-EAEP employees were enthusiastic about their new employers. They felt valued and saw bright futures for themselves. Equally, they were both already aware that among their new colleagues were people who were, perhaps not exactly patronized, but certainly treated in a slightly offhand manner by apparently much more junior staff. These were people who had been rising stars in their time, but who hadn't come up with any startling ideas for a while.

The young ex-EAEP men had quickly absorbed the unspoken condition of their new jobs; that people's ideas were highly prized, recognized and rewarded, but when the ideas dried up your status dropped accordingly. Even so, neither regretted making the move; they were still full of ideas, some practical, others less so, but people were listening to them and that felt good. They were confident of their ability to play an active role in their new organizations. EAEP hadn't treated them badly – I didn't detect any bitterness in their attitudes – but they both felt they had things to offer which EAEP simply didn't want from them.

Analysis

Organizational cultures are like individual personalities – a product of the interaction between genetic 'hard wiring' and learning from experience. EAEP's 'genetic' origins were in the deference to authority and incontestability of orders, which the two key players had learned in their war-time military experience. They had no other management models to work from.

It would be unfair to say that this culture served the company well 'to begin with' because in fact EAEP has been successful for over 60 years, is still profitable and has an excellent reputation. It has loyal and capable staff who show strong commitment to the organization, and the bosses are personally well liked and respected (it is quite possible to be both).

The transition from the founders to the current management team had been more or less seamless and the old values still prevail in the company. The learning that has taken place over the years has, if anything, served to reinforce those values because behaviour which is perceived to be successful (in whatever sense is meaningful for the context) tends to be repeated. EAEP has done well and on the principle of 'if it ain't broke, don't fix it' there has been little inducement to change.

Most people still find EAEP a good place to work and on the whole I would say that little is wrong. However, the departure of at least two potentially valuable members of staff for almost identical reasons (we can't be sure about the third because he declined to be interviewed) starts alarm bells ringing. I asked the

Directors of EAEP to let me carry out a climate survey. They took some persuading. They believed that they knew how people felt about working there because they talked to their people all the time (which was true). However, eventually they conceded and I was able to send a climate survey questionnaire to all staff. Return was, as I always try to insist, anonymous and direct to my practice address, so no individual's response was seen by any Director.

There was a high response rate. In fact, only a handful of questionnaires were not returned, which is a very positive sign. The results confirmed my suspicions. Six of the eight climate factors scored towards the top of the range, indicating that EAEP felt like a good place to work. One – Participation – was hard to pin down because the responses covered such a wide range, indicating mixed feelings among the workforce. On the dimension 'Freedom to express ideas' the response was consistently low; hardly anyone marked the questions relating to this dimension above the mid-point.

I reported these results back to the Directors, making it clear that on the whole things were pretty good in EAEP. The climate was generally positive and they had a lot to be pleased about. However, climate is systemic. When one or more dimensions get out of step with the others it's a sign that things are beginning to go wrong. Sometimes this is because something has changed; perhaps a new manager has been appointed whose style is different, or a new commercial situation has developed. In EAEP's case the real issue was that internally nothing much had changed, but the world outside had moved on. Whereas people had once been glad of the security and benign paternalism of the EAEP culture, now even old hands were beginning to find it stifling. Newer appointees noticed it even more and some found it so unacceptable that they felt they had to get out.

The solution was simple to define, but hard for the EAEP Directors to implement. They needed to listen more and make use of the ideas of people at all levels. I advised them that a sudden change of behaviour by senior people can itself be very alarming and often isn't very credible.

We agreed that they would first of all make the results of the climate survey public, and explain that the Directors were concerned that a wealth of talent was going untapped. We would then implement a fairly basic suggestion scheme, where any employee could put forward an idea and be guaranteed a comment from a senior manager within a specified time. If the idea could be used immediately the initiator's name would be publicized and there would be a modest reward. If it seemed to have potential for the future the initiator would be advised and the idea would be reviewed at a specified time. I warned that if this got overlooked it could destroy the scheme's credibility. If an idea really didn't seem to have any merit the initiator would be told, respectfully, that the company couldn't see how to apply it at the moment, but that future suggestions would be welcome.

It was important that some ideas arising from the scheme should be implemented quickly, so we waited anxiously for suggestions to come forward. We weren't disappointed. The positive relations between management and staff made communication fairly easy, and there was some friendly competition to come up with the most practical ideas.

Among the early suggestions were several relating to working practices; people already had ideas about how their own jobs could be made easier and more productive, and they welcomed the chance to put those ideas across to managers. Several virtually cost-free suggestions were implemented in the first few weeks, and other more radical ideas followed. The EAEP Directors were genuinely amazed at both the quantity and the quality of the ideas that were put forward, and at the enthusiasm there was for implementing change.

EAEP is a success story. A developing problem was identified and addressed before serious damage could be done, and genuine changes in attitude occurred on all sides. There were two critical events in this process: the first was when Alan Pitcher was astute enough to recognize that lost orders could be due to something wrong in the company, and this led him to call in an organizational consultant rather than a marketing firm or a production expert. The second critical event was when the Directors of EAEP decided that it was possible for them to put their own firmly established attitudes to one side and give something new a try. Without this we couldn't have done the analysis that allowed them to move on to make changes 'on the ground'.

Narrative No 2: Gonville Data Services

Background

Gonville Data Services was founded in 1997 as a management buy-out from a multinational computer services corporation. As such, its history can be traced back to the early years of computing via successive corporate identities. Most of the staff are young, although some of the original 1997 Directors are still very much in charge. They were, after all, quite young themselves when they took what the industry considered to be a very big risk in taking on an ailing data division, second mortgaging their homes and working often 18 hours a day to get the shaky business back on its feet. Marriages had failed and health had suffered – one of the 'team of '97' died from a heart attack two weeks short of his 40th birthday – but they had succeeded in bringing the company round and, after many nail-biting moments, in establishing it as a middle-ranking player in a highly competitive business.

Risk is still applauded in Gonville, which may come as something of a surprise considering that their core business involves the provision of secure back-up facilities for clients' data. However, people are encouraged to try out new ideas, praised lavishly, and given more tangible rewards as well, when things work out, and when things go wrong there's a culture of 'better to have tried and failed than never to have tried at all'.

The company would say that they don't encourage recklessness; ideas have to be thought through and risk-assessed, but an outsider like myself might think that recklessness was tacitly rather admired behind a veneer of official disapproval. People soon learn, when they join Gonville, that the way to survive and thrive is to have lots of ideas and express them vocally so that everyone knows about them, and be ready to try them out in practice as soon as management gives the slightest hint of approval.

The situation

Although Gonville had often had a presence at trade shows and fairs in the past, they planned to make the 2004 Madrid Compuferia their biggest showcase ever. As well as their well-established disaster recovery, data back-up and data warehousing businesses they would be exhibiting a range of new data handling products aimed at the small to medium business market. The sales people were champing at the bit for the opportunity to put the Gonville product range in front of old and new customers, and the marketing team were equally full of enthusiasm and ideas to maximize Gonville's impact at the fair.

The Marketing Director, who had overall responsibility for both marketing and sales, was very much in the Gonville risk-taking mould, but he saw very clearly that some firm project management would be required if he was to avoid all that exuberant enthusiasm getting out of hand and things going horribly wrong. One of the senior marketing people, Sue Davies, was appointed as Project Manager and asked to get a properly-defined project team set up to coordinate the effort.

Sue is a clever, bright and experienced marketeer and had been a member of project teams several times in the past so she had a general idea of what the role of Project Manager entailed, but she had never actually been in charge of a significant project herself. One thing she did know, however, was the importance of getting off to a good start so she asked a colleague of mine, Tom Evans, to work with her on a project launch event, which we call an 'Onboarding event'. The real meat of this kind of event is that all the potential project team members are identified and invited to attend. (Actually, a three-line whip needs to be issued because if even one key player is missing the value is severely diminished and if two or three don't come there's little point in continuing.)

At the event the project's purpose is clarified, the specific objectives and 'deliverables' are outlined and the areas of responsibility of each person or group are defined. A senior manager who is the project's sponsor comes along to give the project organizational authority and explain its significance in the wider context, and also to make a couple of absolutely vital points: one, that project team members report to the Project Manager, and not to their usual line manager, for all matters relating to the project; and two, that the success of the project depends on everyone contributing from their own areas of expertise towards the common objective (and that these contributions will be visible wherever it matters). Usually this heavy stuff is balanced by some semi-playful exercises on teamwork and cooperation, and the whole thing usually ends with a good meal off site.

Tom was pleased with the way the Onboarding went and so, he thought, was Sue. The team seemed to bond well, there weren't any serious disputes about who does what (there's always some horse-trading) and no one felt that they would have too many problems back on the 'day job', which is often the first serious obstacle to successful projects. It was a lively team and even though various issues were identified there was a willingness to tackle them together, which gave plenty of grounds for optimism. At that early stage in the project life-cycle it was all looking very positive.

In the following weeks Tom contacted Sue several times to check how things were going. At first she seemed very positive and buoyant, but after a while her demeanour gradually changed. She complained about various members of the team who, she said, weren't pulling their weight. She had to come up with all the ideas herself and then she found the others didn't give her the support she thought she deserved, and certainly needed.

Although Gonville hadn't allocated any budget for further consultancy support after the Onboarding event, Tom offered to call on Sue to talk things over. He found her defensive and despondent. She complained of a lack of cooperation from the team and a lack of support from the line managers of several of the team members. She thought her own work was suffering whilst she had to devote more and more time to the project. Tom made some sympathetic remarks but without appearing to be touting for business it was difficult for him to offer any more practical support, which would have to be charged for.

Fortunately, the Marketing Director, in his project sponsor role, was also aware that things weren't going too well, and with an immutable deadline looming and some serious investment riding on a successful Compuferia he was anxious to deal with any problems without delay. Hearing that Tom was in the building he gate-crashed the meeting in Sue's office and asked Tom if he would talk to the team members and try to lift the mood. He was very supportive of Sue, who he said had come up with some excellent ideas and seemed to be very clear-sighted about the project. He couldn't understand why the others weren't contributing, especially as he knew that in their own departments they were all well thought of and known for coming up with imaginative solutions.

As soon as Tom met the other team members he began to get a feel for the problem. During the first couple of weeks the project team had been extremely lively, with problems being knocked down as soon as they were identified and excellent progress had been made. Sue seemed to have the full confidence of the project sponsor and the rest of the top management group, and the project team felt that this added kudos to their own efforts. Gradually, though, they began to feel that Sue's manner was becoming unwarrantedly autocratic. She could be charming and friendly, which was how many of the team had found her in the past, but if her instructions weren't followed to the letter (and sometimes even if they were) she could change in a moment and say some quite wounding things.

Team members also began to realize that the senior managers were bypassing them. Instead of friendly enquiries about the project, which had been common-place to begin with, they now seemed quite formal and tended to channel every-thing through Sue. One sales rep who had single-handedly worked out a way to bring a group of French and German buyers to the fair at virtually no expense through a deal with a travel company was surprised to be asked by his manager, almost as an aside, when he was going to make his mark on the project. Further probing revealed that the travel scheme was regarded by top management as hav-ing been Sue's idea.

Without asking anything too directly, Tom heard similar, if slightly less well-defined, stories from many of the project team. They had all put ideas and sugges-tions forward to begin with, and many had been incorporated into the project plan but few, if any, had received any personal credit for the innovations. Tom went back to the project sponsor and asked for a briefing on the project plan. Every time an item was mentioned that he had heard about from team members he asked where the idea had come from. Monotonously, the answer usually turned out to be 'from Sue'. Sue was clearly regarded as a very clever person; without her input the project would be getting nowhere.

Tom now had something of an ethical dilemma. Although Gonville was paying his bills, like many consultants he tended to regard the individual manager who had commissioned him as 'the client'. In this case he had started off working with Sue and still felt a sense of personal commitment to her. On the other hand, Gonville would be the loser if the problem wasn't sorted out quickly, and the only way he could see to put things right would be for Sue to come clean about the sources of 'her' ideas. This was certainly not going to be easy for her to do and would inevitably mean a loss of face. If she refused Tom would have to make a hard decision.

Tom is pretty thick-skinned and has a tendency towards blunt speaking, but his interview with Sue was one of the toughest he's had with a client. He laid on the line just what he had found out and put it to her that by taking credit for other people's ideas she was jeopardizing the whole project, as well as making herself extremely unpopular. At first she seemed to be stunned by what he said. This quickly gave way to anger and she furiously rejected the charge of poaching ideas. As Project Manager she didn't expect to be popular, her job was to get things done. Whatever ideas came up in the project team were, she implied, hers by right. After all, she took responsibility so she should take the credit. Tom explained that things didn't work like that. Her actions, besides being unfair to some talented people, had had the effect of stifling any new ideas from the team; they saw no point in putting in the intellectual effort if someone else was going to be credited with their contribution. Worse, the perception outside the team was that they were being ineffective, which was damaging their career prospects.

Eventually, Sue began to come round to Tom's point of view. She very reluctantly agreed to go to the project sponsor and explain that there had been 'misunderstandings' which had resulted in various members of the project team not receiving the appropriate credit for their contributions. Tom offered to go with her for support, but his offer was declined. Not by any means convinced that Sue would give a full and frank account, but unable for the time being to influence matters, Tom waited to hear the outcome of the meeting. He never heard from Sue or the sponsor, and they were never available to take his calls.

Later, though, he read in the press that Gonville had been a hit at Compuferia, so with some trepidation he used that as an excuse to ring Sue one more time to congratulate her on a successful project outcome. Sue, however, was no longer with the company. Hoping that he hadn't played a part in her losing her job, Tom asked to speak to the Marketing Director and this time he was put through. He learned that soon after his difficult conversation with her, Sue had approached the Director and asked to be relieved of her responsibilities as Project Manager. In the circumstances, and despite the operational difficulties this inevitably caused, he had agreed and another member of the team had stepped up to take over.

Sue returned full-time to her day job but found that her relationships with colleagues had cooled, and she no longer felt comfortable or confident at work. Within a few weeks she had found another job and had left Gonville. The move had been her choice, but everyone agreed that it was probably for the best. In the project team, creativity had quickly built up again and, as Tom already knew, the project had been highly successful. It had been a learning experience for everyone, including, Tom hoped, for Sue.

Analysis

Unlike EAEP, which had a culture that stifled ideas from employees albeit in a comfortably paternalistic manner, Gonville's culture actively encouraged ideas and suggestions, even when cooler heads might have advised caution. All the same, Sue Davies managed to create a sub-culture – or microclimate – within her project team where ideas were actively discouraged.

By effectively stealing other people's intellectual property she took away all the personal value the ideas might have had for their originators and so ensured that no one had anything to gain from putting forward their own suggestions. In some ways this was a more powerful barrier to innovation than simply ignoring people's ideas. Being ignored can damage our self-esteem and make us feel depressed, rejected and frustrated. Having something valuable and deeply personal stolen from us is more likely to make us angry, which can be very damaging in an organization. In Gonville, as in EAEP, the suppression of ideas was an indicator, or symptom, of the early stages in a process of decline.

Project teams often act as organizational hot houses where processes which take much longer in 'business as usual' work groups tend to speed up, and the decline in morale and contribution in Gonville's Compuferia project team was a prime example of this; the overall climate within the team was in freefall. Luckily, it was caught (just) in time; it could so easily have been a disaster.

THE ESSENTIALS OF THIS CHAPTER:

- The freedom to express ideas about work, and to have those ideas treated with respect, is an important contributing factor towards a satisfactory, or satisfying, organizational climate. If people aren't happy or comfortable with this aspect of their working lives, other aspects will be adversely affected.
- People need to be listened to. Almost everyone has ideas at or about their work and some of these will be valuable. An organization that fails to utilize the creativity of its people is wasting a precious resource.
- Ideas are a very personal form of property. If someone's ideas aren't respected it's as though they themselves aren't respected. This will have consequences.

7

On the freedom to express concerns

... to censor one's own thoughts – To sit by and see the blind man
On the sightless horse, riding into the bottomless abyss.

Arthur Waley, *Censorship,* **c1943**

Narrative No 3: Mackenzie's House

Background

Samuel Mackenzie was an eighteenth century writer, philosopher and radical political thinker. Born in Dundee in 1720, he was brought as a small child to Oxford where his father apparently had some kind of academic appointment. Little of Mackenzie's original work has survived but he is known to have been something of a polymath. Many of the scientists and creative intelligentsia of the era make references to having discussed ideas with him or been encouraged by him to pursue their theories and research.

He was also quite a colourful character, who spent at least two periods in prison. In 1760 he was imprisoned for debt, but was released after two months through the intervention of a benefactor. More seriously, following publication of a controversial pamphlet in June 1768 he was arrested on a charge of sedition and held until the following April when the charges were dropped, for reasons which have never been fully explained. After his release he spent several months in America where he is known to have met several of the architects of American independence. He is thought to have maintained correspondence with at least some of them until the outbreak of the war of independence.

Among the prominent people of the time who counted Mackenzie as a friend, and perhaps as a mentor, was the revolutionary Tom Paine, who corresponded with him over many years. The older and perhaps more politically astute Mackenzie is credited with exercising considerable influence on Paine's radical thought, especially about the necessity and justification for revolution in France and in the American colonies. Mackenzie remains quite obscure in Britain but his connections with the founding fathers are remembered in the USA by a small but devoted group of Mackenzie followers who meet annually on 3 November (the date of his death in 1802) to celebrate his role in the founding of their nation.

Mackenzie was well travelled but he kept the house which his father had bought in Oxford and lived in part of it for most his life (in later years the lower floors were occupied by a succession of tenants, with whom Mackenzie was often in dispute over rents). He married and outlived two wives, but had no children, and on his death the house was sold to pay his numerous debts.

In 1998 the house came onto the market and the Mackenzie Foundation was able to purchase it for conversion into a museum of his life and times. They formed a trust to take formal ownership of the property and appointed Mary-Anne Wysbeck as General Manager. Despite having a demanding job in an Oxford PR agency, Wysbeck took to the role with enthusiasm. Under her direction, a major restoration project was initiated and two staff were appointed to coordinate the construction and refurbishment work on site, and to show visitors round when required. John Scott was one of those employees.

The situation

John was twenty-two, with a first-class degree and a variety of work experience. He was ready for a permanent job which could form the first step in a career and saw the job with the Mackenzie Foundation advertised on the internet. It sounded ideal. The salary was attractive, the location was quite convenient, the historical context seemed really interesting, and working on a development project with clear objectives gave the whole thing purpose and a sense of challenge. He applied for the job and was invited to come for an interview.

John had been to plenty of interviews before and he found this one rather odd. Mary-Anne Wysbeck had said she could only see him in the evening because of her full-time job with the agency, so they agreed to meet at Mackenzie's House at eight o'clock. He arrived on time but Wysbeck was busy showing visitors around the shell of the old house and it was almost ten o'clock before she was at last ready to see him.

The interview took the form of a fairly rambling discussion in which Wysbeck gave John some background information about Samuel Mackenzie himself and about the history of the house, and explained the Foundation's plans for the building once it was fully restored. John thought she was rather vague about exactly what his duties would be but got the general impression that he would be the on-site project coordinator with a secondary role as tour guide and information centre. He learned that there was already another, part-time, employee at the house called David Pike who had gone home by the time John arrived for the interview. The job still seemed attractive and at the end of the interview he thought that Wysbeck had implied that he had been successful, although what she actually said to him was rather ambiguous.

John waited several days without hearing anything and eventually tried ringing Wysbeck to ask for a decision. His call was referred to Mackenzie's House and answered by David Pike, who told him that he had been successful and was expected to start work straight away. With nothing in writing John was reluctant but David told him that this wasn't unusual and he shouldn't worry about it. So John started work for the Mackenzie Foundation.

John found David Pike to be a friendly and helpful colleague. Mary-Anne Wysbeck, on the other hand, had neither of those qualities. She was dictatorial, critical of everything and unreasonable in the extreme. David was clearly afraid of her and made it his sole objective to get through the day without upsetting her in any way. In his conversations with David, John found out that he had been the only applicant for the job, and that he was the fourth person to hold the job in six months. One of his predecessors had walked out in tears. Meanwhile, John managed to get by but was increasingly concerned about his situation.

In particular, five months after starting work he still had nothing in writing to say that he was actually employed by the Foundation or what the terms and conditions were. Wysbeck, despite having worked in the UK for several years, had apparently no idea about employment legislation and irritably dismissed John's attempts to raise the matter. Both John and David had to write their own monthly salary cheques, which then had to be signed by two members of the Foundation. This could involve lengthy delays whilst members were located or cheques were sent and returned by post. The same system was used for petty cash. At least they were both getting paid (eventually).

Other than the salary everything about the job was very vague. John had enquired about holiday entitlement. Wysbeck had asked him how much was normal and when he told her he thought twenty days was the minimum in the UK she had laughed. Many aspects of life in Britain, especially concerning work, seemed either to amuse or irritate her.

Wysbeck expected John to arrange his schedule to fit in with hers. She was frequently late for meetings and when this happened she took it for granted that he would wait for her. On one occasion she arranged to meet him at Mackenzie's House at three o'clock but didn't turn up until seven. John didn't feel that he could make any plans of his own and didn't feel confident enough either to say that he would only wait until a certain time or to ask for time off to compensate for the extra hours he was working. David Pike never made any kind of protest and often advised John not to do or say anything to annoy Wysbeck.

As well as the adverse effects this kind of work relationship had on him personally, John also worried about some of the business decisions he was expected to implement. On one occasion, a computer printer had been ordered, with the approval of the Foundation, which both John and David found perfectly satisfactory, but when she had seen it Wysbeck had told John that it was unsuitable and instructed him to return it. This involved some negotiations with the supplier which proved rather difficult. Later, at a drinks reception Wysbeck and John were making conversation with guests when Wysbeck mentioned the printer problem. John inadvisably asked 'couldn't we just keep it?', which earned him a frosty look from Wysbeck. The next day he was called in to her office at the PR agency and given a dressing-down. He was told bluntly that it was 'not acceptable to question' her decisions.

In fact, everything he did had to be approved and even then he found that his actions were often criticized. Because of her demanding 'day job' Wysbeck was often not readily available and feedback from her could be slow in coming. Attempts to 'chase' her for answers were angrily rebuffed but when work was delayed she had no hesitation in blaming John and David. Wysbeck insisted that any e-mail sent on behalf of the Foundation should initially be dictated by her over the telephone, typed out by John and sent to her for approval and correction. She would then return it to John to send from the Foundation's e-mail account. This, naturally, took a great deal of time, especially when several iterations were required, as they frequently were. Working late was often the only way to keep on top of things.

John was also worried about health and safety issues. Mackenzie's House was virtually a building site and conditions there were dirty and dusty, and potentially dangerous. John mentioned this a couple of times, making a particular point of the problem of dust, but Wysbeck became annoyed and he backed off. Even when she acknowledged that his concern was 'understood' nothing was done.

Eventually John and David arrived for work one day to find the entry barred by scaffolding and builders' equipment. The only way in was to climb under the scaffolding and through a window. They went home and worked as best they could from there. In a subsequent telephone conversation John was told that working from home was unacceptable. He pointed out that there were contractors' signs on the building saying that hard hats and masks must be worn, but the Foundation's employees were expected to work there without any protection at all. Eventually Wysbeck agreed that they would have to work off site for a while and made arrangements for them to use the empty flat of a Foundation member who was abroad at the time. This had no internet access, which they needed on a regular basis, and was far from satisfactory but at least it was clean and safe.

John tolerated this increasingly stressful and thankless job for almost a year. He was still interested in the project itself and for a while he had every intention of staying long enough to see it through to the public opening of Mackenzie's House but he became increasingly worn down by the relentless criticism and dismissal of any concerns he expressed.

He also witnessed his colleague, David Pike, becoming what John described to me as 'a broken man'. The time came when John realized he couldn't cope with the situation any longer and needed to take a break. He planned to go on holiday and requested permission to take a particular week off. Wysbeck's response was that he would be needed that week and would have to take his holiday a fortnight later. He knew that it would actually make no difference which week he was absent from Mackenzie's House and regarded this refusal as no more than Wysbeck's way of demonstrating her control over him. He decided on the spot that he had reached the end of the road with the Mackenzie Foundation and handed in his notice.

When I interviewed John Scott a year had passed since he had left the Mackenzie Foundation. He had done some temporary work in the interim and had just started a new permanent job. He seemed cheerful and balanced but still felt angry and let down when he looked back on his time in Mackenzie's House. He had been sufficiently interested to check up from time to time on the progress of the refurbishment project and was able to tell me that it had over-run by several months (the Foundation had wanted to have a grand opening on the fourth of July, but this had been cancelled).

He had never had any idea of the project budget, so he couldn't say if this had been exceeded but it seemed highly probable. The Mackenzie's House website, which he had started to develop shortly before he left, had gone live as an amateurish affair which did little justice to the project and this seemed to upset him as much as any factor in his experience. The House is now open to the public, by appointment, and visitors are shown round by guides in period costume. John Scott won't be joining them.

Analysis

Mary-Anne Wysbeck is a fairly classic example of a workplace bully. With a demanding full-time job she was out of her depth after taking on, in addition, the part-time role of General Manager for the Mackenzie Foundation, but this was no excuse for treating her two staff the way she did. The consequences of her attitude were exacerbated by her lack of understanding of, or sympathy for, the slightly more employee-friendly conditions obtaining in the UK compared with her native USA.

However, at the core of the problem seems to have been her insecurity, which was both chronic and acute. She was unable to believe that her staff could take responsibility for anything without her detailed direction, and she had to check everything to ensure that it was done the way she wanted and wouldn't rebound on her in any way. Bullying tends to increase where there is insecurity and pressure and Wysbeck's 'micromanaging' is a fairly typical symptom of it. She was unable to see that this was crushing all spirit and initiative and building up resentment in her staff.

Both John Scott and David Pike were, in their different ways, capable of making a very positive contribution to the project. The Foundation was lucky to get them. In our discussions, it was very clear to me that even after all he had gone through, John still retained an interest in the history, and the future, of Mackenzie's House. If only this had been harnessed the whole project would, I am certain, have been immeasurably more successful. But Wysbeck's behaviour made it impossible for either employee to do anything beyond obeying her instructions, wilfully squandering what should have been a valuable asset.

When John expressed, or tried to express, his reasonable concerns about his own situation as an employee he was rebuffed and it was implied that he was making a fuss about nothing. When his concerns were about the way the work was being handled, Wysbeck took it as personal criticism and became angry. Both his own experience and what he learned from his colleague inhibited him from raising legitimate concerns which Wysbeck really needed to hear.

The members of the Mackenzie Foundation, who were Wysbeck's employers, should have been aware of all this. Appointing someone as General Manager doesn't absolve trustees or Directors of their own responsibilities and they should have been alerted by the rapid turnover in staff that something wasn't right. Instead they chose to turn a blind eye and leave Wysbeck to get on with it. This put both the project and the Foundation at risk. Not only was the project likely to come in late, over budget and with an inferior end product, there were health and safety risks to the employees (and incidentally to the office equipment too) from working in an unsafe environment. Had there been an accident or health problems attributable to the conditions it's entirely possible that Wysbeck and some or all of the Foundation members could have been held personally liable at law.

John Scott went on to work on a temporary contract for a charitable organization where the climate was benign and his talents were much better appreciated. When this contract expired he moved to another charity where he still works. His experience at the Mackenzie Foundation left him bruised but taught him something about management (principally, how not to do it) and about the value of a good quality of working life.

Narrative No 4: Toreston Housing

Background

Toreston Borough Council is a Unitary Local Authority responsible for the administration of a socially and economically mixed area in the south of England. About 95 000 people live in Toreston itself, but natural expansion has meant that three other adjacent smaller towns have merged with it to form a conurbation with a total population of nearly double that figure.

Originally separated from Toreston by farmland, or in one case by the river Torrey, these districts each have their own distinct character and one in particular, Northam, has seen a rising immigrant population over the last 15 to 20 years. The majority population there is still white British, and among the ethnic minorities no one group dominates. Community relations are good, crime is below the national average and unemployment appears to be just marginally above the norm, although jobs in the area are not well paid and average earnings are well below national levels.

The Borough Council is itself a major local employer, with a total staff of about 3000 people. Among the Council's many responsibilities is that of providing publicly funded or subsidised social housing, and to do this it owns and manages approximately 4000 properties. It also works cooperatively with the voluntary sector and with private landlords to extend this provision.

As with many other English local authorities, Toreston's housing services are mainly provided by an 'arm's length management organization', or ALMO, which is wholly owned by the Council but which operates as a quasi-independent business called Toreston Housing. TH has its own office premises in a rather run-down part of central Toreston, a few minutes' walk from the Town Hall, which further emphasizes its autonomy.

TH is committed to helping local people who need housing to find a home which, as far as possible, meets their current and future needs, and above all to provide a fair and impartial service. As a first step in this process it maintains a 'Home Seekers' Register' on which applicants' names and details are entered as soon as they make contact. Demand for social housing exceeds supply and TH operates a points system, approved by the Council, by which applicants are prioritized. Realistically, only those applicants who are in genuine need are likely to be allocated a home from TH's limited stocks, although its network of contacts does often enable less pressing cases to be helped through the private sector.

I came into contact with Toreston Housing through working with managers in the Council itself on another assignment. Whilst I was working on that something of a cause célèbre arose concerning TH which intrigued me enough to follow it up.

TH has a fairly flat management structure in which 30 full- and part-time housing officers report through five team leaders to a Chief Executive, who is answerable to a Management Board made up of Councillors, local residents and independent members. At the time of my involvement the staff of TH represented an ethnic and cultural mix which was very similar to that of the Toreston area, in that most were white British but there were a number of people of Asian origin, several of whom were Muslim, one was Sikh, one Catholic and a few others whose religion, if they practised one at all, was not obvious to their colleagues. Most of the staff, of all ethnic origins, were local people who knew Toreston well.

Michael Byrne joined TH as a housing officer in the spring of 2001. After university he had worked for about 18 months with a charitable organization helping homeless people but funding constraints had prevented them from renewing his fixed-term contract and he had been out of work for several weeks until he applied for and got the job with TH. He was new to the area but now lived in the Northam district of Toreston in a studio flat. He was bright, his experience, though limited, was useful, and he proved to be energetic, enthusiastic and idealistic.

The situation

Byrne hadn't been with TH for more than a couple of months when he began to feel that all was not as it should be. He was aware that prioritizing applicants' housing claims was a fairly complex procedure involving allocating points for various aspects of need such as family size, income, mobility or medical factors, domestic violence, community problems, and so on. The lengthy application form asked about all these factors and judgements were made about the appropriate points allocation against each factor by the responsible housing officer, based on a set of criteria approved and regularly reviewed by the Management Board. When all the factors had been scored individually the total was calculated and used to prioritize the case. Applicants sometimes needed help to fill in the forms which were complicated and intimidating, especially if the applicant had language or literacy difficulties. Giving assistance in such cases was part of the housing officers' responsibilities.

As he settled in to the job Byrne began to suspect that some of his colleagues were not applying the prioritization criteria on an absolutely impartial basis. He thought that people from ethnic minorities were sometimes being given lower need ratings than white British people. He discretely asked a colleague whose impartiality he thought he could rely on whether he had noticed anything of the kind, but was told very firmly that it wasn't done to second-guess another HO's judgements; team leaders sample-checked applications and that was sufficient to ensure fairness and consistency.

He was far from satisfied with this, partly because he had formed a rather poor opinion of his own team leader and at least one other. He noticed that the two men were often at each other's desks, chatting, and frequently visited a nearby pub at lunch times. He called in at the pub himself once or twice and felt rather uncomfortable there. Without exception the customers were all white, and he thought he overheard one or two racist remarks among the general chatter. He also noticed that his team leader always bought a national tabloid newspaper which regularly featured what he regarded as anti-immigrant headlines.

None of this gave him confidence that he could mention his suspicions to his own boss, and he didn't feel he could go to one of the other team leaders, even if there was one he felt he could trust, without running the risk of provoking a confrontation. He considered going directly to the Chief Executive, but he strongly suspected that this would not be considered acceptable. This was confirmed when a colleague was reprimanded for forwarding some information to the Chief Executive, which he had requested, without sending it via her team leader. She was told, within the hearing of Byrne and several others, that everything had to go 'up the line'.

When he approached one of the Asian staff he got a more thoughtful hearing but after he had finished explaining his concerns his colleague told him that he didn't think anyone at TH would abuse their position in this way. Byrne's suspicions were not allayed but he resolved to keep a careful eye on things whilst avoiding any premature moves.

Over the next few months Byrne took every opportunity he could to check up on applications from ethnic minority claimants which had been handled by the colleagues he suspected. He would secretly remove the completed forms from the files and make his own assessments based on the official guidelines. In some cases he was sure that the factors had been scored too low, and there were others where he thought the applicant's answers to the questions on the forms seemed odd. He made careful notes but still didn't report his concerns to anyone in authority.

His next tactic was to listen-in when colleagues were advising claimants about how to complete their applications. He wanted to know if ethnic minority applicants were being misled about how to make the best claim. Once again, it seemed to him that the verbal guidance some ethnic minority claimants were receiving might tend to disadvantage them. He would have helped them to put in a much more convincing application. This view was reinforced when he discovered that applicants who had received advice from community help organizations rather than from TH officers often did rather better in moving up the priority listings.

By now Byrne had a substantial dossier of 'evidence' of racially motivated discrimination in the prioritization procedures and he felt that he couldn't stand by and do nothing about it any longer.

Toreston Borough Council has a published policy on 'whistleblowing', which broadly sets out to incorporate into Council policy the protections provided by English law. Since July 1999 people must not be sacked or victimized for reporting criminal behaviour or other specified forms of wrongdoing in their workplace. This applies not only to employees but also covers contractors, agency workers, home workers and people on vocational and work experience schemes.

On checking the details, Byrne felt confident that the kind of discrimination he had discovered would fall into one of the categories of behaviour covered by the policy, either because it was a criminal offence or because it represented a failure to comply with a legal obligation. He therefore thought that he would be protected if he revealed the 'malpractice', provided he did so in the correct way.

The first problem was who to tell. The Council policy said that employees should inform their line manager immediately if they became aware of any malpractice. For Byrne, this wasn't an option because he suspected that his team leader would side with the perpetrators; a view based on very little more than the team leader's choices of newspaper and pub. Where the allegation related to the actions of their line manager the policy gave employees the option of raising the issue with a more senior manager, bypassing lower management levels. It also promised that employees would not be penalized for informing management about any sincere concerns, and to respect any requests by whistleblowers for their concerns to be treated in confidence.

Byrne decided to ask for a meeting with the Chief Executive at which he would produce his dossier. Access to the Chief Executive was guarded assiduously by his PA. When Byrne dialled the Chief Executive's extension it was answered by the PA who insisted that Byrne speak up because she couldn't understand his whispered request. As discretely as he could, Byrne repeated that he wanted to speak to the Chief Executive on a confidential matter. The PA told him firmly that any such matter should be discussed with his team leader, who would then decide if it needed to be referred to the Chief Executive. Byrne told her that that wasn't possible in this case and it was essential that he speak directly to the Chief Executive. When he declined to explain what he wanted to discuss and why he couldn't talk to his team leader, his request was refused. This was a serious blow. Not only was the Council's own policy being blatantly ignored, Byrne was now worried that the

PA might complain about his actions to his team leader, which would leave him with some explaining to do.

He decided that the only course open to him was to take his concerns to one of the members of the Management Board. Not knowing any of them personally, or how to contact them, he picked one who had an Asian-sounding name, found his home address in the telephone directory, and sent him a brief letter saying that he had evidence of racial discrimination being practised by housing officers and hoped that the Board member would take the matter up. He signed the letter and gave his own address, but he didn't make it clear that he was a housing officer himself and that he was effectively now acting as a whistleblower.

A few days later he was astonished to see a front page spread in the local paper headlined 'Council accused of racism in housing'. The story, which was extremely short on facts, included interviews with Asian applicants who had been unsuccessful in finding accommodation and a photograph of an angry-looking family on the pavement outside the TH offices.

By the end of the afternoon Byrne had been called into the Chief Executive's office and asked whether he was the source of the story. He denied it and tried to explain what he had actually done, but his protests were not accepted. He was summarily dismissed for gross misconduct.

Byrne lost no time in lodging a complaint of unfair dismissal with his local Employment Tribunal. He hadn't joined a union (if he had he might have received advice earlier on and none of this might have happened) so he went to a solicitor at his own, considerable, expense. Eventually, after several months, the case was heard and the Tribunal accepted Byrne's contention that he had acted in good faith and was therefore entitled to the protection of the relevant legislation. This automatically made his dismissal unfair.

There is no limit on the amount of compensation Employment Tribunals can award to employees who have been sacked or victimized for whistleblowing and Byrne's Tribunal was severely critical of the Chief Executive for not allowing Byrne a proper opportunity to explain his actions before dismissing him. Whilst Byrne himself was also criticized for going about things in such a clumsy way, the Tribunal awarded him a substantial sum which was sufficient to reimburse him for his lost salary since his dismissal and his legal costs, and to provide for his needs until he could find another job. Toreston Housing and Toreston Borough Council were slated for failing to operate their own whistleblowing policy.

What was not criticized was TH's application of its prioritization rules. Once matters had blown up, to the considerable detriment of community relations and public confidence, the Council had insisted that the Management Board call in the auditors who had rigorously re-examined every case that had been processed during the relevant period, including all those which Byrne had documented. They found no evidence at all of any malpractice. Some errors and questionable judgements were found, as might be expected, but these were as often as not in the applicant's favour. No reason was found to criticize any housing officer or team leader on the grounds of racial or any other form of discrimination.

TH took a severe knock from these events. Morale plummeted and relations between management and staff, and between peers, cooled and became more formal. Complaints from the public reached three times their 'pre-Byrne' levels, not only about alleged discrimination but also about staff being rude or unhelpful. When I heard about the case matters were slowly getting back to normal but still had a long way to go.

Analysis

To some extent it must be admitted that Michael Byrne brought this trouble on himself. He was young, clever and idealistic and when he saw something that he thought was wrong he wanted to put it right, but the way he went about it contained all the seeds of disaster. However, the whole situation was made exponentially worse by the failure of Toreston Borough Council's putative whistleblowing policy.

The legislation in Britain (and there is similar or equivalent legislation throughout the European Union and elsewhere) protects a whistleblower who gives information to his or her employer, provided that this is done in good faith and the whistleblower has a reasonable suspicion that the alleged malpractice has occurred, is occurring, or is likely to occur. This isn't very helpful if in practice access to a suitable person is blocked.

Informants are also protected if they give information to statutory bodies, such as regulators, or other bodies, subject to some additional conditions, so Byrne basically acted correctly in going to a member of the Management Board but should have made his status clear. Even so, the Management Board member should never have leaked Byrne's complaint to the press. This was a serious breach of his responsibilities and raises serious questions about his suitability for such a role.

However, the real issue here is that Byrne saw no way in which he could bring his early misgivings to the attention of someone who could do something about it. His lack of confidence in his team leader may well have been quite unjustified, but he genuinely felt that way and if there had been a culture of openness in TH there would almost certainly have been alternative routes for him to express his concerns. In that case he could probably have been reassured at an early stage. In fact, if there had been such a culture he would have been less likely to suspect anything underhand in the first place. Instead, the channels of communication which should have been open to permit worries to be aired – and quickly dealt with if they proved to be without foundation – seemed to him to be blocked wherever he turned.

What started as a suspicion turned almost into an obsession which he felt he had to investigate and expose all on his own. He could see no route by which he could bring his worries to the attention of someone who would have taken the responsibility of checking them off his shoulders. That was the real tragedy of Toreston Housing and the damage to its organizational climate will take a long time to repair.

THE ESSENTIALS OF THIS CHAPTER:

- In any workplace there will be things which worry people. A good manager will always take employees' concerns seriously.
- Management can't take account of people's concerns if suitable channels of communication don't exist.
- Bullying causes enormous distress and should be totally unacceptable in any organization. Responsibility for ensuring that bullying is identified and stopped lies at the very top of the organization and requires active enquiry; bullied people are often too intimidated to complain, especially if they don't think they will be listened to.
- If people feel unable to express their concerns, or that their concerns won't be taken seriously, the effects will be felt through all aspects of their life at work. If it's just one person who feels this way their effectiveness will be reduced. If it's several people then the whole organization will be adversely affected.

8

On the freedom to question

Theirs not to make reply. Theirs not to reason why.
Alfred, Lord Tennyson, *The Charge of the Light Brigade*, 1854

Narrative No 5: Mark Wodman

Background

Mark Wodman was a middle-ranking HR manager in a UK blue chip corporation. I met him at a social event and we got talking about work in general and, when he found out my interest in organizational climate, about this in particular. Mark had a boss, the Divisional HR Director, who ran what he clearly thought of, but managed to avoid actually calling, a 'tight ship'. The HR function was a blend of administrative and professional or specialist roles. They ensured everyone got paid the appropriate amounts at the right time, processed expenses claims, having vetted them for errors and compliance with rules, chased up annual appraisals, ran the annual staff satisfaction survey, and provided expert support to line managers in recruitment and promotion interviews, disciplinary procedures, grievances and industrial relations.

Mark didn't like his boss much. When he had transferred into the department on promotion from a similar but more junior role in another division, the Director had conducted the interview himself and had seemed amiable enough. Mark came well recommended and the appointment process had been fairly painless. As he settled in, however, Mark had found his boss increasingly trying. It wasn't that he was a bully, exactly, but he had what I have to capitalize as FIRM VIEWS about practically everything.

On his first day in the job Mark had received a piece of advice from a colleague: 'don't challenge him', which he found disturbing but for a long while he had managed to avoid anything that would really count as 'challenge' or confrontation. In fact, most of the time Mark was allowed to get on with his job without very much interference, and he'd found the Director usually willing to listen to suggestions, although he would be curtly dismissive of anything that didn't tally with his own rather restricted world view. So, on balance, working life could certainly have been easier and more enjoyable but was far from being intolerable.

The situation

One topic on which the Director's views were particularly firm was what he called 'cohesion', by which he seems to have meant departmental loyalty. The first real problem arose when the company's main board announced a phased programme of voluntary redundancies. Over the next year the total staff complement was to be reduced by 5 per cent – about 600 full-time equivalent posts altogether.

Although it was promised that there would be no compulsion, anyone who happened to be occupying one of the jobs which was to be cut would inevitably be in an anomalous situation. The policy was that fairly generous redundancy terms would be offered and it was expected that the take up would be quite high. This would leave vacancies which could then be filled by people whose own jobs had disappeared.

It was the kind of plan which looks quite reasonable on paper, provided you assume that people have no attachment to their current roles and can drop what they've been working on and switch to something different with unabated enthusiasm and a minimal learning curve; much like British cabinet ministers.

Mark didn't, in fact, really object too strongly to this. He could see that there would be operational difficulties and a great deal of work for HR, but dealing with the practical consequences of top management's decisions was a well established part of his job, so he began to work out what was involved and how his team would handle the task. One issue that he identified early on, and which he found replicated in equivalent HR departments all over the company, was what to do with people whose jobs had been abolished, but didn't want to leave and couldn't find a suitable new posting.

Over the next few weeks Mark heard rumours of people being put under pressure to apply for the redundancy package. In many cases these were staff whose performance had been questionable, which raised both ethical and operational issues. If someone's performance wasn't up to scratch there was an established procedure which Mark knew from experience was robust enough, if followed correctly, to protect the company from unfair dismissal claims. Usually it didn't have to come to that because following the procedure also enabled (actually, obliged) line managers to take every reasonable step to encourage improvements in performance and this could often be very effective.

Now there was a strong suspicion that the redundancy scheme was being seen in some quarters as a way of managing individuals out of the company. It was relatively easy to declare someone's job surplus to requirements, which left them with the responsibility of applying for one of the vacancies. If their skill set or experience didn't fit them for one of the new roles they were left in limbo. This was especially likely to happen to people who didn't have glowing appraisals from their former jobs and were therefore less attractive as candidates for new ones.

There were cases of people being advised that there was unlikely to be a place for them in the company and that the next round of redundancies would be on much less generous terms, so the wisest course would be to take up the offer while it lasted. And it wasn't only genuinely poor performers who were being singled out; Mark heard credible reports of this tactic being used against people whose 'faces didn't fit' or who had fallen out with their bosses or other influential people. In his role as HR manager he kept a sharp eye out for things of this kind in his own division and informally cautioned a few line managers against unfairness in the implementation of the scheme.

Matters came to a head when Mark was called in to the Director's office and told that his own team of 18 was to be cut by one post. Mark had really been expecting this because the 5 per cent cut was being applied almost everywhere in the company, but it presented real difficulties.

First, and regardless of personalities, implementing the scheme put a heavy additional workload on HR, so his 18 staff were actually overstretched already. Cutting one post might not sound too drastic but it was hard to see how he would be able to get the job done with a reduced team. Second, the work was shared out among an experienced and efficient team; there was no single identifiable job which could be cut. Mark modestly took no credit for the effectiveness of his department, saying that all but one of the team had already been there when he took over, but as he told me his account I could tell that he had worked hard to build good relationships with his people.

Mark tried to explain the difficulties to his Director, especially the operational one of reducing staff at the very time the workload was increasing. He got little sympathy. He was told that cutting one post was mandatory and needed to be done within the next two weeks. Worse, he was told that the way to do it was to advise three members of staff, who the Director named, that they must all, effectively, apply for their own jobs and only two of them would be successful.

Mark's immediate reaction was one of anger, which he managed to suppress at least until he had left the meeting. He felt that the instruction was an unreasonable intrusion on his own area of responsibility and that the three people who had been identified were all excellent team members whom he wanted to keep. He would have preferred to give the whole team the option of applying for the redundancy package in the hope that one of them would actually want to go. That wouldn't get over the workload issues but at least no one would be forced out.

After he had given the three staff the bad news Mark set about planning the fairest way of selecting the two people who would be retained in his department. All had fully satisfactory appraisals and each had particular individual skills. He felt that if he had been recruiting he would have been impressed by all three. He decided that he would hold formal job interviews with an HR manager from another division to ensure impartiality.

When arrangements had been made he informed his boss, more or less as a courtesy. The reaction was unexpected. He was asked why he had done such a thing when it was obvious that the person who should go was X, a junior HR officer who had, in Mark's opinion always done an excellent job and been quietly helpful and efficient. The 'two from three' mechanism had only been intended to soften the blow; having received the three applications the Director had intended to announce his decision and that would have been that.

Mark couldn't see why the individual concerned was being picked on as the prime candidate for redundancy. When he said this the atmosphere changed markedly. The Director told him bluntly that he expected his managers to give him their complete support and he was 'disappointed' that Mark was trying to undermine his decision. Mark protested that he had had no idea the Director had already made a decision, but in any case it was essential for the process to be seen to be fair, so picking someone for redeployment to an unidentified new role elsewhere in the company without letting them at least try to justify being retained in the department had seemed wrong. This hadn't helped. The Director told him that by telling the three staff that there was to be a formal interview process and, even worse, involving a manager from another division, he had committed the department to an unnecessary administrative burden and run the risk of the 'wrong' outcome. Mark was to ensure that this didn't happen. In other words, Mark felt, the interviews were to be a sham.

Mark held the interviews without telling the colleague from another division who was supporting him anything about the instruction he'd received from the Director. He tried to be as objective as he possibly could be with all three applicants and made assessments on a range of factors in strict compliance with the company interview procedures. He wasn't sure whether to be relieved or frustrated when the individual pre-selected to be the loser turned out to have marginally the lowest scores in his assessments, but he felt the burden lifted somewhat when the other HR manager told him that she had reached the same conclusion.

Mark didn't know whether he had misjudged his Director; perhaps he really had been able to identify the 'weakest link' and had simply put sentiment aside to make what some managers like to call 'a tough decision'. Anyway, Mark was off the hook and spent the next few days contacting people to boost his subordinate's chances of finding another job. In this he was successful, which, he felt, brought an unhappy experience to a fairly acceptable conclusion.

Mark's relations with his boss were cooler now, but life went on without any more unpleasantness for a while. A couple of months later one of Mark's people came to him with an expenses claim which, he felt, was unjustifiable. Normally, line managers decided whether to accept such claims; HR's role was only to check them for accuracy and for compliance with company policy and regulations. In his case the HR officer had seen that a claim for hotel accommodation explicitly mentioned both bar bills and paid-for films, neither of which was allowed. He authorized the officer to return the account for the disallowed items to be deleted. Two days later the same claim came back with what was clearly a new account from the hotel stapled to it. This time there was no mention of bar bills or films, but the overall sum for 'accommodation' was the same as before. The HR officer, and Mark, suspected fraud but, without proof, decided that the claim had to be passed.

Mark mentioned the episode to colleagues in HR across the company and found that they had had similar examples. The general view was that some hotels were colluding with company staff by issuing 'top-level' bills that didn't detail the illicit items. On the 'don't ask don't tell' principle line managers, some of whom were undoubtedly doing the same thing, were authorizing the claims and HR were processing them.

At their next weekly 'one-to-one' meeting Mark informed his boss of his concern that expenses claims were being abused, but was told not to worry about it. When he persisted, adding that the practice seemed to be quite widespread, he was angrily told that his job was to process the paperwork, not to make waves. He took the none too subtle hint and dropped the matter, but told his staff to return any claims about which they were suspicious with a request that the line manager personally certify that the claim complied with regulations.

A few days later he was called in to the Director's office and accused of 'disloyalty' in once again going against his wishes. Puzzled, worried and a little angry, Mark asked what it was that he had done. He found that another senior manager had complained to the HR Director that HR were blocking expenses claims. This was causing annoyance and involving managers in extra work. Since Mark had been told not to worry about the issue, the HR Director held him responsible for the complaint and seriously wondered about his reliability.

Mark knew that his appraisal was due in a few weeks and he didn't want any black marks. He apologized and explained that he was doing no more than implementing company procedures. This didn't seem to mollify his boss very much. 'Stop looking for trouble' he was told. He reluctantly gave instructions to his staff to put through any authorized expenses claims unless they clearly contained errors.

Over the next month Mark and his team were very busy with the redundancy and redeployment exercise and he had little contact with his boss other than routine meetings. Relations were cool but polite and Mark accepted any instructions he was given without demur, even when he felt misgivings. He had learned his lesson and wasn't going to stick his neck out again.

Then, one Friday morning, Mark arrived for work to find his office occupied by people from the company's Security department. Two of his staff were hanging around outside, having arrived earlier and also been denied access. He was told that a special audit was in progress and no one would be allowed into the office until it was completed. He waited for an hour and was then told by a senior Security manager that he would not be able to do any work for the rest of the day and he should go home until he was contacted.

Seriously worried, Mark did as he was told and spent a very stressful weekend wondering what was going on. On the following Monday he was telephoned and asked to attend a meeting with a Director from another division of the company. He was told that the meeting was to be 'exploratory', but that he should consider it to be potentially part of a disciplinary procedure. As an HR manager, Mark knew these procedures very well and asked to be told what he was suspected of doing wrong. He was told that there were irregularities in expenses claims processed by his department and he would be required to explain how they had got through.

Mark attended the meeting, accompanied by another HR manager. All his department's records of expenses claims had been removed and examined in detail, and a dozen or more were being followed-up. The 'revised' hotel account, which had been the subject of his earlier suspicions, was one of them and the investigating Director wanted to know why he had given instructions for it to be passed. He was also asked to explain why he had told his staff not to follow-up suspect claims. Mark asked explicitly if he was suspected of colluding with the claimants to process invalid claims and was told 'it hasn't come to that, yet'.

However reluctant Mark might have felt to shift the blame to his boss, he could see that there was a prima facie case against him, if not of dishonesty then at least of incompetence. It was, after all, his responsibility to see that claims were properly checked. He decided on the spot that he wasn't going to be the fall guy and explained in great detail the chain of events that had led to his giving the instruction to pass any claim that wasn't glaringly invalid. The investigator's response was non-committal, and he was formally suspended on full pay while further enquiries were made.

Two days later, to Mark's enormous relief, he received a call telling him that no action was to be taken against him and he could return to work. Disciplinary action was to be taken against a couple of claimants and a line manager had received 'advice'. Mark wasn't looking forward to meeting his boss but found him to be rather subdued. It wasn't possible for the recent events to be ignored, but a short, businesslike meeting was sufficient to establish that all claims must be thoroughly checked in future and anything out of order would be formally recorded and returned to the claimant's line manager for correction, which was, of course, the policy that Mark had tried to operate before.

Shortly afterwards, his boss was seconded to a senior position in the team overseeing the redundancy programme, ostensibly only a temporary 'sideways' move but when another HR Director was quickly appointed to take his place it became clear that the move would not be reversed. At the time of our conversation Mark had yet to meet his new boss, but he knew her by reputation and was feeling optimistic. He didn't know how his own career prospects had been affected, if at all.

Analysis

There are two very basic tenets of human interaction that Mark's boss had either forgotten or had never properly understood. One is that every single person we meet knows things that we don't know. The other is that everyone sometimes gets things wrong. Everyone at work needs to have the freedom to ask their boss (in their own words, of course) what Oliver Cromwell expressed in 1650 as 'I beseech you … to think it possible that you may be mistaken'.

Denial of the freedom to question is a hangover from the command and control management styles of the past and can be highly counter-productive, as well as having a negative influence on organizational climate. If we make it difficult or unpleasant for people to question our decisions, to point out when they think we may be making a mistake or acting on wrong information, or simply to ask 'why?', so that they can better understand what we are hoping to achieve, then we put ourselves and our organization's objectives at risk. At the same time we make them feel diminished and unvalued, and we lower ourselves in their estimation. It's hard to go on respecting someone whom we firmly believe to be wrong, but seems too arrogant to be told so.

Mark began by thinking that as a professional his opinion would be useful to his boss and also that he had his own personal responsibilities, which meant that he couldn't just accept instructions which appeared to prevent him from doing his job properly. His boss saw any questioning or even lack of enthusiasm as a sign of disloyalty. For him, the duty of subordinates was to do as they were told and carry out his policies to the best of their ability. He was happy for them to use their initiative, indeed he expected it, but not if this caused them to question his decisions.

It seems likely that on this occasion the consequences of this management style may have raised doubts in the minds of his own superiors about his judgement; a sideways move to a special project may be a mark of high confidence but on this occasion it looks more like problem-solving, especially as a permanent replacement was appointed so quickly. There also seems to be a possibility that Mark's record may have been blemished by the events, although it's to be hoped that his involvement will be seen to have been governed by a *force majeur*, and the company will continue to value his contribution.

Narrative No 6: 'A Quality Organization'

Background

Franklyn Tapes is, or rather was, a small independent manufacturer of magnetic media for the IT industry. As its name implies, it started off in 1976 making recording tapes for data storage. Franklyn more than kept pace with advancing technology and by the mid 1980s it apparently had an excellent reputation as a specialist or niche supplier of high quality tapes and discs. A few years later, though, it was in trouble and after some disastrous losses it was taken over in 1994 by one of the major names in the industry.

Unlike many such takeovers, this one turned out to be very good news for the 200 or so people who worked at Franklyn. The new owners wanted to exploit their acquisition's good name and had given the firm a thorough examination from which it was concluded that Franklyn was still viable as a wholly-owned trading entity, but needed a radical shake-up of its management structures and processes. It was decided that all Franklyn's problems would succumb to a vigorous application of TQM: Total Quality Management. It must have worked, because Franklyn was still operating in 1998 when the world was beginning to panic about the 'millennium bug'.

I need at this point to say a little about TQM. Total Quality Management began life as a way to improve production-line manufacturing. The idea was to develop and then stick to a set of processes and/or techniques which would reduce product variations and faults so that firms would 'build quality in' instead of 'inspecting faults out'. In other words, they could cut down on rejected products or components by putting the effort into getting them right in the first place. The rigorous post-production inspection regimes, which were the norm before TQM, would become unnecessary and the inspectors could be redeployed to more productive work. This would cut manufacturing costs and improve customer satisfaction.

The prime evangelist of the TQM gospel, W Edwards Deming, found his ideas slow to catch on in his native USA so he took them to Japan, where they proved to be spectacularly successful. The Japanese Emperor even awarded Deming an honour for his services to Japanese industry. A documentary called 'If Japan Can … Why Can't We' broadcast in the USA in the early 1980s introduced these ideas to a wider American audience and TQM began to take off there and in Europe in a big way.

It soon became clear that TQM wasn't limited to the production line, but could be applied to the supply of almost any kind of product or service, and in other contexts too. In fact, by the mid 1980s TQM was being applied practically everywhere including administrative work and management. With the spread of the TQM approach came a desire to prove to the outside world that yours was a 'quality organization' and for this many UK companies turned to the British Standards Institution, which already had standards for quality assurance, evolved from similar ideas which had originally been developed for the military to prevent accidents in munitions factories.

The relevant standard at the time was BS5750, which was later proposed to the International Organization for Standardization as the basis for an international standard that became ISO9000. Registration for the BS or ISO standard involved inspection, usually by third parties on behalf of the registration body, and it quickly became virtually essential to have the appropriate certificate to do business with government or large commercial organizations. Non-registration could exclude a bidder from even being considered.

Although full of good intentions, the most visible implication of these standards tended to be the careful documentation of processes, each of which should, of course, be the 'best' way of carrying out the particular task. 'Quality' then consists in following the process to the letter, and this was what, in practice, inspectors usually checked when deciding whether the organization merited initial or continued registration. It wasn't supposed to be like that; the idea was that there would be continual improvement, with processes constantly revised and the documentation amended, all according to strict document control which was itself subject to the same kind of regime. Sometimes this really was what happened. Often it wasn't. Now back to Franklyn Tapes.

Like other organizations of all shapes and sizes, Franklyn had a major project running to examine every aspect of its operation that might or could possibly be affected by the supposed millennium, or Y2K, bug, which was considered a serious threat to all kinds of computer systems from home PCs to national defence systems.

In the early days of computing, storage and processing power were both massively expensive, so programmers economized wherever they could by using abbreviations. One example of this was to use only two digits to represent the year in date fields, e.g. 62 for 1962. No one thought this would matter; programs would be replaced long before the year 2000. What they hadn't considered was the extent to which new programs were developed from old ones, so that by the late 1990s nobody really knew for sure that none of the highly complex and very extensive computer code that ran their systems might contain elements of code dating back several generations.

The fear was that when the date clicked over from 1999 to 2000 the routines would find themselves thinking the year was now 1900 or, even worse, trying to perform calculations on '00' and crash. There were scare stories in the press about aeroplanes falling out of the sky as their onboard computers failed to cope, of defence systems shutting down and banks losing all their clients' records. Prime Minister Tony Blair helpfully clarified the situation in a speech by reminding the nation about:

> an aluminium smelting plant in New Zealand, where a programmer had failed to allow for the leap year in 1996. The plant worked perfectly well until the end of 1996, but then, at midnight on 31 December, this small computer fault caused the plant to shut down completely. Shortly after, as Tasmanian time reached midnight, a sister plant failed in exactly the same way. It took one million New Zealand dollars to get them started again.
>
> Blair, 1998

I have no idea whether this story is actually true; many such accounts turn out to be no more than modern urban myths, but it certainly is true that many organizations were seriously worried about the possible consequences of Y2K and were prepared to invest significant sums in making sure their own systems were 'Y2K compliant'. Franklyn was one of these organizations.

As part of their preparations Franklyn replaced their main production control computer and the supplier offered them a choice of training packages as part of the deal. Most clients would choose training on the software that was being provided but in Franklyn's case this was unnecessary because all their staff were already quite expert in using the production software they would be running on the new machine. Instead, Franklyn's management thought that a better understanding of project management would be especially valuable for the people working on the Y2K compliance project, so they opted to send a dozen of their people on an introductory project management course. The computer suppliers commissioned a small training organization run by two colleagues of mine, Tim Simmonds and Julie Parks, to deliver this training in the autumn of 1998.

The situation

The people from Franklyn Tapes who attended Tim and Julie's course were from a variety of backgrounds and levels of seniority. They had been selected to attend the training, but no one had been coerced, and they all seemed bright and interested as the event got under way. The event was organized according to the fairly standard model of explanation followed by breakout for group work then back together again to analyse what's been done.

Tim and Julie had delivered this course many times before, so they knew pretty well what to expect, with variations, and were ready to deal with queries and objections as they came up. The approach to project management that they teach isn't really controversial; they describe the project life-cycle and deal at the overview level with everything that needs to be taken care of during the various phases. At the end of two days the delegates have usually had quite an enjoyable time and learned the basic principles of the subject, which they can then apply back at their own workplaces. This was exactly what Tim and Julie began to do for Franklyn Tapes.

It very quickly became clear that the material wasn't being received in the way they were used to. As Tim explained about project definition – how to specify the various tasks and contract with people in the organization who will carry them out – he sensed something between unease and bafflement among the delegates. When they broke into small groups to work on a definition exercise he dropped in on each group in turn to see if there was anything that they hadn't understood or that was causing them a problem.

He returned to the main training room utterly perplexed. The strategies which seemed to be emerging in the work groups didn't seem to have anything in common with his own understanding of project working, acquired over many years in the business. He shared his concerns with Julie, who was due to lead the next session.

When the groups reassembled to give their feedback Tim's misgivings were fully borne out. Each group seemed to have ignored his explanatory talk and followed a complex path of their own to get the project work defined and secure agreement for its implementation. Tim expressed his surprise and got the response: 'we can't just make it up – we have to follow the FPs'. The FPs, it was explained, were the 'Franklyn Procedures' – a set of ring binders occupying an open-fronted bookcase in the general office at Franklyn Tapes, which contained detailed instructions on how to carry out virtually every aspect of every task any employee would need to perform. They had been built up over years and were regarded as law by Franklyn's management. Any infringement was regarded as putting Franklyn's ISO9000 registration in jeopardy, so no one was allowed to do anything that wasn't specified in the FPs.

In vain Tim explained that projects were, by definition, outside the procedures adopted for 'business as usual'. It was no use – the delegates knew that even if they planned their project work along the lines he was suggesting, no one else in the company would be persuaded to carry it out. Julie, who knew something about TQM and ISO9000, tried to explain that these standards were supposed to be continually revised and improved, but this didn't get very far either. The delegates knew all about continuous improvement, but every suggestion for changes to the FPs had to be considered by a management committee, which could take weeks. Then the proposed new wording had to be circulated for consultation before finally being signed-off by a Director. This formal action didn't quite have the tone of the Royal Assent, but it came close.

The result of this was that any work which needed to be done in Franklyn Tapes was quite literally done by the book. The FPs were not to be questioned and if what you wanted to do wasn't covered by them then you probably weren't meant to do it. The delegates weren't stupid; they agreed with Tim and Julie that project management approaches could be extremely useful and cost-effective. 'You don't have to sell this to us' they told the trainers, ' we can see how valuable it could be to us, but we can't use it. We can't plan this way, or get commitments from people because even if people want to go along with it, they just can't. The only way to implement our project is to do everything by the FPs'.

Tim and Julie were stumped. There seemed little point in teaching project management to people who wouldn't be able to put even its basic principles to work. On the other hand, they were still only part-way through the first day of a two-day course and they didn't want to abandon it. In the end they got the delegates to agree that they would forget all about Franklyn Tapes for the rest of the event and pretend that the 12 of them were running their own project management consultancy. This proved to be an inspired move and the rest of the event progressed more or less like any other.

In the closing session, though, Tim and Julie asked if they could send a report back to the Franklyn Tapes management explaining that project management approaches could run alongside documented processes, in fact, many organizations had project procedures which formed part of their ISO9000 documentation, but so long as the FPs didn't allow for it the delegates wouldn't be able to put the training to use. The delegates were happy to agree to this, and promised to carry the message back to Franklyn Tapes. They hoped that the suggested changes could be put in place, eventually, but didn't think it would be in time to help them with their current project.

Tim and Julie heard nothing more from Franklyn Tapes. Six months later, in a routine marketing call, Julie spoke to her contact there, who said that their report had been welcomed and he thought there might be changes, but everyone was now totally dedicated to ensuring Y2K compliance so it was unlikely that anything would happen before January 2000. Julie noted this and early in February 2000 she rang again to see how things had gone.

She discovered that Franklyn Tapes had successfully passed midnight on New Year's Eve 1999 without disaster. In fact, without anything happening at all. Since by then Julie was aware that the millennium bug had turned out to be mostly harmless that came as no surprise. However, it didn't take much adding two and two for her to feel pretty sure that Franklyn's Y2K compliance project had not been completed on time. If there had been anything dangerous lurking deep in the code of Franklyn's computer systems it might well have escaped detection until it was too late. The special situation had required special ways of working but their procedures had prevented this.

Being right doesn't always make one popular, but for Tim and Julie – and, I think for Franklyn Tapes – there was a happy outcome to this episode. Tim and Julie prepared a proposal for designing a set of generic project management procedures which they submitted to Franklyn. This was accepted and in due course the new procedures were adopted and incorporated as part of the FPs, enabling anyone in the company to plan projects and, just as important, allowing people to work in this way alongside business as usual. Y2K is long gone, but next time Franklyn Tapes has a major complex one-off piece of work to handle there's good reason to hope that it will be much more successful.

Analysis

Contrary to the impression I may have given here I am rather a fan of TQM, having been involved in several TQM-based initiatives in the 1980s, all of which brought some degree of improvement and one or two of which led to really major advances. Applied properly TQM can focus attention on quality, by which I mean making everything you do at work fit for its purpose and cost-effective. The philosophy of continuous improvement, which is at the heart of genuine TQM, is one which has enormous benefits and few serious drawbacks.

The trouble with TQM lies in the way it's often misused. Commenting on a survey by The Economist Intelligence Unit (1992), Roger Trapp (1992) writes: 'the key problem is that the establishment of standards that are comparatively easy to meet makes companies feel they have progressed further than they actually have'. I would go further. The way that many organizations implemented TQM was to document in great detail what they already did. A few anomalies and discrepancies got ironed out but the bulk of what went into the documentation was simply descriptive. This is mainly what happened at Franklyn Tapes.

Inspection regimes have compounded this dysfunctional approach by marking organizations down for deviations from the documented processes (which is ironic when you consider that Deming's original concept was that 'quality' would do away with the need for inspection). Thus, a great deal of effort is expended in compiling the documentation in the first place, and then a great deal more goes on trying to comply day by day.

What frequently happens is what I call 'the speed camera effect'. Just as some motorists exceed the speed limits but brake sharply as they approach the known site of a speed camera, then accelerate away once they're clear of the danger zone, so organizations will have a major 'drains up' exercise when an inspection is due, retrospectively correcting paperwork and double-checking that everyone is doing everything 'right'. Once the inspection is over everyone relaxes and, I have observed, work frequently progresses rather more effectively.

In Franklyn's case the procedures – the FPs – were stifling the very real need for a special approach to the Y2K compliance project. The effect of the FPs was to prevent questioning of the way things were done because the procedures had almost acquired the status of holy writ. The answer to any question was to be found in them. Fundamentalism is always the enemy of progress, and this maxim is as true of 'quality' as of anything else. Franklyn Tapes could have faced disaster if the millennium bug had proved to be as dangerous as predicted.

THE ESSENTIALS OF THIS CHAPTER:

- No one gets it right all the time. A competent and confident manager will not feel threatened if a subordinate questions an instruction or a policy.
- Everyone we meet knows something we don't know. Maybe they know something that will prevent us making a catastrophic mistake.
- In the old days of union power 'working to rule' could almost be guaranteed to bring an organization to a standstill. Doing things by the book can sometimes be disastrous. The 'rules' and the 'book' should be questioned regularly; it's the only way to make progress.

9

On participation in defining goals and objectives

Happiness mostly results from an individual's ability to make choices. Happy people are those who can think independently and are free to choose.

Joanne Gavin and Richard Mason, *The Virtuous Organization,* **2004**

Narrative No 7: Harborough Response

Background

Ever since the telephone was invented there have been people whose job it was to deal with customers' telephone enquiries. Initially, telephone callers were treated in much the same way as personal visitors would have been in the past, but developments in telecommunications technology during the 1980s took call handling to new levels.

A shift occurred in the balance of skills required by staff. Before, the expertise and knowledge that were most valued were concerned with the subject matter of the calls, the products or services being dealt with, or the advice being sought. It was taken for granted that the medium of communication could change seamlessly from a face to face conversation to a telephone call without significant impact on outcomes, despite an awareness that some people had a better 'telephone manner' than others. Slowly, the realization dawned that telephone call handling was a skill in its own right and, later, that it was actually the prime skill required; product knowledge could be supplied more reliably and often faster by a computer screen than from the memory and experience of an employee.

The recognition that call handling was a specialist skill and that the management of teams of call handlers, and the technology that supported them, was also a specialized branch of management came more or less concurrently with the fashion for outsourcing. Following the spirit of Peters and Waterman's (1982) advice to 'stick to the knitting' companies sought to offload many of their non-core or support operations to specialist providers. Thus, cleaning was farmed out to low cost cleaning firms, caterers were brought in to run the staff canteen, payroll was handled by a specialist firm or, often, by one of the very big employers who found that they could accommodate other companies' requirements alongside their own at marginal extra costs. Even the accounts function might be assigned to firms of accountants.

It was in this atmosphere of change and increasing specialization that Harborough Response came into being. Originally the customer-handling department of a major insurance company, Harborough had been 'detached' from its parent and established as a wholly-owned subsidiary. Once its management had found their feet they looked around for other business, both as a means of natural growth and to protect them from the hazards of dependence on a single client.

They offered good service, had invested heavily in technology and training, were located in an area of high unemployment, and were keen to win business. They began to pick up contracts from a variety of sectors and opened new call handling centres in several locations as well as taking over the management (and the staff) of some existing in-house operations. Harborough was floated as an independent company in 1992 with the original parent company as a minority (though still the biggest individual) shareholder.

The situation

In 1997 I was teaching a distance-learning module (on organizational behaviour) which was part of a purpose-designed masters programme for call centre managers, and in connection with that programme I attended a presentation function in London where I found myself sitting next to the young manager of a mail order call centre in the north of England.

He told me that his operation had recently been outsourced to Harborough Response and his job had transferred with it. He had known this was coming for several months and wasn't too concerned. Harborough and his old employer had kept staff informed throughout the transfer process, his terms and conditions were protected and, in any case, he had seen Harborough's own staff contracts and found them to be virtually the same as his old one but with better holidays. As Harborough was by then a major player in the industry he thought the change would be beneficial to his career. I said I would be interested to hear how things worked out and we exchanged cards. I didn't really expect to hear from him again.

Almost six months later I received an e-mail from someone whose name – Rob Collings – at first meant nothing to me. He reminded me of our conversation in London and asked whether I was still interested in his work at the call centre. I replied that I was and we began a correspondence that became interesting to me and, I hope, useful and perhaps therapeutic for him.

When he wrote to me Rob was on sick leave. He had been forced to go home from work, suffering from severe gastric pain which was later found to be caused by an ulcer. People get ulcers for several reasons; they aren't necessarily caused by stress at work, but on the other hand, stress is known to be a frequent causal factor in gastro-intestinal problems. In Rob's case he, at least, had no doubt that it was his work that was making him ill. Whilst on sick leave he had time on his hands and he followed up his first e-mail with a detailed account of his experiences since his department had been taken over by Harborough.

Harborough had taken a good hard look at the operation Rob and his bosses had been running, and had clearly not liked what they saw. They called the managers together and gave them what they described as a briefing but which had seemed to the recipients more like a catalogue of the perceived errors they had been committing before Harborough came on the scene.

Discipline was said to be unacceptably slack, productivity was abysmal, the centre was overstaffed and sales targets, which had largely been met in the past, had apparently been ludicrously easy. Rob had been shocked. It was true that the atmosphere had been free and easy, but he knew all his staff and thought that on the whole they did a good job. The tone of the meeting was such that he knew that would be quite the wrong thing to say. He didn't want to get off on the wrong foot and be thought complacent.

Harborough appointed one of their people as General Manager of the centre and therefore boss to Rob and two colleagues who retained their former positions as managers. Over the next few weeks a new regime was introduced. The automated call distribution, or ACD, equipment was reprogrammed so that the freedom the 'agents', as the staff were now called, had previously had to signal their readiness for the next call was removed. Calls were now directed to them a fixed, and very short, period after completion of the previous one.

Staff had previously been encouraged to form a friendly relationship with customers. In fact, one of the main characteristics recruiters had looked for had always been 'people skills' and empathy. Harborough now introduced scripts, which the agents were expected to stick to, with an 'appropriate' response for every anticipated customer question or comment. Staff who had enjoyed being helpful and found interacting with customers one of the more rewarding aspects of the job now found their work constrained and restricted, and became increasingly frustrated and depressed.

People who had transferred to Harborough with Collings when the department was outsourced began to leave and were replaced, if at all, with casual workers. The job had always attracted part-time workers but now for the first time there were more people working part-time than full time, making rostering more difficult. Absenteeism rose steadily, exceeding 12 per cent for three months that summer. The highest Rob had previously known had been 7 per cent during an outbreak of flu. There were times when Rob rather wished more people would stay away. He at least was guaranteed sick pay if he was ill, but many of the casual workers had no such benefits and some of them would come in when they were clearly unwell, coughing and spluttering at the customers and spreading cold germs around the centre.

Strict monitoring of agents' performance became an increasingly important part of Rob's responsibilities. Automated systems now checked virtually every aspect of an agent's performance which was susceptible to such surveillance and reports were generated if agents spent too long on individual calls or made mistakes in keying-in information, but Rob was also expected to listen-in to a percentage of calls each day to check that scripts were being followed, sales opportunities seized and complaints deflected. He had been called in to the General Manager's office several times to explain failures to meet Harborough's exacting targets. His staff were struggling to meet a new line occupancy target rate of 95 per cent, which Rob thought was far too high.

In less than a year the whole climate of the centre had changed beyond recognition. Whereas staff had previously had a fair level of control over how they did their work and even, within reason, over the pace of it, now almost every move was dictated and monitored. Even the words they were allowed to speak were scripted. Permission had to be sought to leave their workstations and time spent away from the job was documented. Disciplinary action had to be taken if anyone was away from their desk for more than the tightly-defined allowance. It was no longer a good place to work and many people didn't stay very long. Staff turnover reached 35 per cent but Rob was told that this was considered acceptable.

Sickness rates increased but Rob couldn't be sure how much of it was genuine. One agent reported sick with 'acoustic shock', which Rob had never come across before. He looked it up and found that it was a condition caused by sudden noises, often associated with headphones, which led to tinnitus, or prolonged ringing in the ears, and heightened sensitivity to noise. He thought that, if true, this could make Harborough vulnerable to an injury claim and he wondered if he could be held personally liable in any way.

I felt very sorry for Rob Collings, but I wasn't involved professionally and from the opposite end of the country I could do little more than offer my sympathy and understanding. My work on the Call Centre Management masters programme had, though, brought me into vicarious contact with his world (my only vaguely comparable 'hands on' experience had been in a telephone exchange at the beginning of the 1980s, which had little relevance to the brave new world of call centres). I hesitated to tell him that, apart from making life very unpleasant for him and the other employees, Harborough seemed to me to be out of step with the zeitgeist of call centre management. I wasn't sure it would help him much. In the end, though, I gave him my analysis much as it's printed below.

I didn't hear from Rob for some time and I hoped that he had recovered from his health problems. When I next got an e-mail he thanked me for my input, such as it was, and told me that he had joined the exodus from Harborough. He had found that by then there were four other call centres within reasonable commuting distance of his home and had enquired at all of them for management-level jobs. He had been successful at the third attempt and had already started with his new employer. One factor which had been in his favour at the interview, in an inverted kind of way, had apparently been his experience at Harborough; he had been quizzed about his own attitudes and noticed the mood lightening as he expressed misgivings about the Harborough management style. It was early days, but he felt confident that the quality of his working life would be very much better in his new job.

Analysis

Call centres have been a byword for a certain kind of work environment ever since they first entered public consciousness. 'With rows of operators crammed together in front of computer screens using highly standardised procedures, call centres have been likened to production lines, or even to battery farms' (Arkin, 1997).

In the public perception they are often characterized by 'Intolerable working conditions, bullying managers, unachievable targets, stress, insufficient staffing, rigid attendance standards' (Caulkin, 1999). The words 'sweatshop' and 'call centre' are often linked together. Harborough clearly based their approach to running call centres on this kind of regime, and at the time they were not unusual, although new attitudes were already beginning to have an impact.

The root of most of the problems at Harborough lay in their total lack of confidence in their employees. The only way they saw to achieve high levels of 'efficiency' was to impose rigid control over their staff, enforced by electronic monitoring and surveillance backed up by regular eavesdropping by managers. But efficiency isn't really what organizations need to achieve; *effectiveness* is the real goal. As a scientific term, 'efficiency' is simply a ratio of inputs to outputs, or work produced for energy used. It's a value-free term. In management it acquires

> value-judgement overtones to mean maximum outputs for minimum
> inputs. All things being equal, this amounts to the minimisation of waste,
> which is certainly something to aim for. However, striving for maximum
> efficiency can be counter-productive if a short-term or small-scale view is
> taken. Sometimes effectiveness – which at one level means successfully

achieving objectives – can be better served if there is a certain amount of 'slack in the system'.

Gray, 2004

High occupancy rates (i.e. only very short intervals between calls) can be counter-productive, according to American call centre service expert Brad Cleveland (Menday, 1996) who says that 'occupancy becomes too high when it reaches ninety-two percent for an extended period of time … Also, the impact of taking one call after another, without any pause for breath, becomes very distressing for the agents. If such a situation becomes the norm, you will find absenteeism rises sharply'; which is just what happened at Harborough.

The effect of Harborough's regime is that control over what a worker does passes from the individual to the management, or even worse, to a computer. The almost inevitable result of this is an increase in stress levels and a drop in job satisfaction and commitment. Arkin (1997) quotes Kevin Hook, principal consultant at the Decisions Group and an industry expert who has observed this widely in UK call centres:

> What we have found is that there is a hugely significant relationship between levels of perceived control over the pace of work and people's job satisfaction and stress. As you would expect, if people have low control over their jobs, they experience high levels of stress and low levels of job satisfaction, so there is a very big problem in call centres generally.

The high turnover and absenteeism at Harborough were not significantly worse than national averages at the time. McLuhan (1998) quotes turnover rates as 30 to 40 per cent and absenteeism as 8 to 12 per cent, but things were beginning to change. McLuhan identifies call centres with staff turnover figures down to 15 per cent and absenteeism rates of 6 per cent. This would still not be considered very good in some sectors, but it illustrated an improving trend.

There are good economic arguments for making call centres more human. Hatchett (2000) says 'If workers are disgruntled and staff turnover is high, productivity will suffer. Customers don't return if the response is poor. There is a fine balance between productivity and quality – if the drive for productivity overrides service quality then the exercise will be self-defeating'.

And according to Roncoroni (1997) 'there's quite a lot of evidence that the more you control the less you get in terms of quality'. John Seddon, of Vanguard Consulting (Caulkin, 1999) thinks that call centre managers are working on a false premise by treating all calls alike. He suggests that at least 90 per cent of perform-ance variation is caused by the system and less than 10 per cent by people, but 'In traditional call centres, the emphasis of managers' attention is exactly the reverse'. Caulkin comments that

> Such is the sway of American call centre 'experts' and the expensive hardware 'solutions' that perpetuate the mass-production mould, that only a handful of call centres are operating along Seddon lines. But those that do report astonishing increases in productivity, fourfold in one case, for little or no extra cost and a wholesale improvement in atmosphere.

Many of the issues illustrated by call centres like Harborough Response can also be found, in less obvious forms, in other kinds of organizations too. People who find themselves in a work situation where they feel that they have little or no con-trol over what they do

> are likely to take whatever steps are available to them to give themselves some feeling of control over their working lives. This may take the forms of 'resistance' ... and doing only what is measured, and even that without enthusiasm. It may lead to militancy or support for extremist viewpoints. Or it may go further, including denigrating the organisation or senior person-alities, or even direct sabotage of procedures, systems, or property.
>
> Gray, 2004

If managers want to avoid this kind of situation arising they need to ensure that people don't feel that they have been robbed of the control they need.

Harborough Response is still in business, operating call centres for many differ-ent clients and, as far as I know, their approach hasn't changed very much. At least Rob Collings has escaped; it would be nice to think that other downtrodden employees will do so as well, and that Harborough will eventually be forced to rethink their 'sweatshop' management style.

Narrative No 8: Olsen Electrical

Background

At the beginning of the jazz age and with the horrors of the First World War still a recent memory, Henryk Olsen opened a small shop in Warren Street, in London's

West End. Despite his Norwegian name and ancestors, Olsen was a Londoner with a winning combination of attributes: a shrewd eye for business, a knack for making and fixing things, and a genuine passion for the new music.

To begin with his business just sold gramophone records, but he quickly saw the potential for selling the machines on which to play them too, so he began buying-in gramophones from a manufacturer in Middlesex. His shop was ideally situated to serve the wealthy residents of Mayfair and the adjacent areas and Olsen was astute enough to address this lucrative market by modelling the décor and ambience of his premises on the jewellers, art dealers and expensive couturiers who were, almost, his neighbours.

For a while Olsen prospered beyond anything he could have hoped for. Record sales were buoyant and he established contacts with producers and distributors in America and many other countries. His stock was renowned and if he didn't have a title on the premises he could almost always locate it for a customer within a short time.

The gramophone sales business worried him, though. The main problem was that the machines could be unreliable and were often brought back to the shop for repair. When this happened they had to be transported to the supplier's factory where the faults were attended to, and then returned to the shop for collection by the customer or, in many cases, delivered to the customer's home. This was time-consuming and unprofitable, which bothered Olsen more than a little.

He got into the habit of inspecting faulty machines himself before sending them on to the factory and he found that very often all that was needed was a minor adjustment, or the replacement of a part that had failed. Increasingly he was able to do the repair himself or, in due course, pass it on to his teenage son Harald, who quickly became very skilled at diagnosing problems and assembling and disassembling the machines. The back room of the shop slowly evolved into a well-equipped workshop.

The other problem was that Olsen didn't think the gramophones did the music justice. He knew what live music sounded like, and the sounds that came out of the gramophones he sold simple didn't measure up. He understood that part of this problem lay in the recording process and there was little, practically, that he could do to improve that. Music came from many different recording companies and customers would always want to play the records they had, wherever they were produced. What could, possibly, be addressed was the quality of the equipment used to play them.

By now father and son knew almost all there was to know about the construction of gramophones. They still bought-in from the original supplier but demand had grown so much that they were using others as well. They had also begun selling wireless sets. Every time they came across a new model they would critically evaluate its performance and examine its construction in great detail in order to learn all they could about it. As the best the market could offer passed through their shop – and over their workbench – the idea grew, tacitly at first and then more and more explicitly, that Olsen and Son could do better.

In 1929 the first Olsen gramophone appeared in the shop. Contained in an elegant rosewood box, with machine-turned control knobs and discretely concealed speakers, it was as much a piece of furniture as a traditional gramophone. And the sound that it produced was exceptional. Records which sounded tinny and harsh on even the best of the previous gramophones sounded rich and mellow on the Olsen. Subtleties in the instrumentation could be heard clearly for the first time.

In the first week orders were taken for 20. The price, of course, was beyond the reach of any but the wealthiest customers, but this only added to the Olsen's desirability. Olsen and Son's business changed almost overnight from a specialist retailer to a manufacturer. Staff were hired to look after the shop whilst father and son concentrated on production. Premises were found in a less expensive area of west London, craftsmen were taken on and within a matter of months Olsen gramophones had become the must-have accessories of the rich and discerning of London and far beyond.

Olsen and Son weathered the Depression of the 1930s and came through the Second World War a reduced but still healthy small business. Growth was slow and a little erratic, but the trend was positive and Olsen's reputation for quality ensured its survival.

Henryk Olsen had been fascinated by the first television broadcasts in London before the war, and when TV broadcasting was resumed in 1946 he lost no time in adding television sets to the company's product range. The coronation of Queen Elizabeth II in 1953, coupled with increasing national prosperity, put TV sets into many thousands of homes and Olsen sets were the natural choice of the seriously well-off. From that point on the future of Olsen and Son seemed assured and the company continued to grow. Henryk lived to be over ninety and was still interested in the company and its products right up to the end. Harald had gradually taken over the day to day running of what had by then become Olsen Electrical Ltd during the 1950s.

In 2002 the business still operated from its west London factory and was still run by the Olsen family; Henryk Olsen's great grandson was the Chairman and Managing Director and there were four other Olsens on the Board. The original shop in Warren Street had long been vacated and all retail sales now went through carefully vetted franchisees.

It had a multi-million pound turnover and world wide sales. Its product range would have seemed quite familiar to Henryk; televisions had ceased to be profitable when mass production in the Far East reached the standards of reliability and quality that Olsen had pioneered, but there was still a big market for the superb but very expensive sound systems which Olsen produced, so the portfolio now consisted of CD systems and, still, turntables for vinyl and tape players, as well as radios and a range of accessories.

But two dark clouds had begun to form on Olsen's horizon, in the form of increasing price pressures and, more shocking to the management than practically any other issue, there were the first inklings that all might not be quite perfect in the quality of their products.

The situation

In the summer of 2002 Olsen lost an order for in-car radio and CD players from a prestige car maker. This customer had offered Olsen products as premium optional extras for more than ten years and it came as a surprise to Olsen when they were informed that the order had gone to a German competitor. They assumed they had lost the order on price but enquiries revealed that in fact the German product was priced virtually identically to Olsen's. The order had been lost because the German product was considered to be of superior quality.

This news was met with disbelief; the Olsen management simply *knew* that their products were the best in the world, but it was equally important that everyone else knew it too. If word got round that an important customer thought otherwise the impact on Olsen's reputation could be serious.

The response was to tighten-up their meticulous production and assembly processes and increase the rigour of their already stringent product inspection regime. This, of course, added to their production costs and pushed out delivery times. Complaints began to come in from customers about late deliveries and from component suppliers about unreasonably high rejection rates. Meanwhile a major franchisee gave notice that they had negotiated a deal with another supplier and would not be renewing their contract with Olsen.

Olsen's management still believed their products were the best, but they were all too aware that several other manufacturers were close on their heels. Only an elite few of the world's finest musicians could actually distinguish the sound quality of an Olsen product from that of its nearest rivals; at the very top of the market most choices were made on aesthetics and, still much less important but gradually becoming more so, on price.

The Olsen people knew from their market research that they still had the edge on design; competitors' products often looked a lot like Olsen's and they had threatened legal action more than once to defend their unique style. They also knew that there was no more leeway for increased prices. Unable to think of anything else they could do about quality, and watching the profit curve gently turning downwards, they decided that it was time to call in expert advice. They turned to production expert Paul Morris to advise them on how to improve quality and cut costs.

Paul is a highly qualified engineer with decades of experience in assembly line operations of all kinds. His expertise is in process, rather than in any specific kind of product; in fact he has advised companies making just about everything from earth-moving machines the size of a small hotel down to micro-miniaturized components for the aerospace industry. He was heavily involved in many quality initiatives in the 1980s and 90s and we worked together on two projects; him dealing with technical aspects and me looking at people factors. Back then, Paul was very interested in the difference that people's attitudes could make to the operation of machines; an effect which he couldn't really explain but which he observed too often to be able to dismiss.

On arrival at Olsen's factory he asked to be shown the production processes, which were fairly simple and straightforward in concept. By far the greater part of the work consisted of assembling components bought in from suppliers. A few specialized components were actually made by Olsen on the premises and then supplied to the assembly lines in exactly the same way. Carefully judged stocks of required components were held close to the points of use. Olsen operated a modified version of the 'kanban', or 'just in time', supply system, relying on their suppliers to deliver components as they were needed, but keeping a small safety stock in case of hold-ups.

Paul Morris found the processes to be logical and efficient. As an engineer he recognized the characteristics of a well-designed and well-maintained machine with every part fulfilling its designated function at the correct rate and within the predetermined tolerances. It was, in its way, quite elegant, just like one of Olsen's products.

The flaw in this approach, which struck Paul almost as soon as he began to assess the operation, was that the majority of the 'parts' in this machine were people. People don't really work like the moving parts of a machine; they are less predictable, sometimes more resilient and sometimes less so, sometimes keen and sometimes lethargic, sometimes interested and sometimes bored. Paul talked to as many of the workforce as he could and was depressed by what he found. First, it wasn't easy to get the people to say anything significant. Consultants usually anticipate this, because a stranger asking questions about your work and how you do it can start alarm bells ringing and give rise to worries about where this might be leading. Paul has a good 'bedside manner', though, and he managed to overcome this initial reluctance to talk.

He discovered that Olsen were considered to be quite a good employer. No union was recognized but many of the staff belonged to one of three unions and management talked informally to all of them. Industrial relations were good. Various ethnic groups worked together without friction and management treated everyone alike. Pay was a bit above the average for the area and conditions were at least as good as at other local firms. Supervisors were strict but respected.

On the down side, Paul found little pride in the prestigious products that the factory turned out. In fact, only a minority of those he spoke to really knew much about how their efforts contributed to anything tangible. When he asked just what someone did he was more likely to be told something like 'I fix these circuit boards into this casing' than 'I'm helping to build CD players for luxury cars'.

Paul began to see an emerging picture which was not unfamiliar to him. Management viewed each production line as a steady incremental progress from the first die-stamped frame to a completed, tested and packaged product ready for sale. To those who worked on them the lines seemed more like a series of self-contained compartments where partially completed products arrived in front of them, they carried out whatever functions their jobs required, and the slightly augmented product disappeared from their ambit never to be seen or heard of again unless some fault could be attributed to their personal input.

The actions required from each worker were very clearly prescribed, which is not to say that some of them didn't require considerable skill. People were thoroughly trained for their roles. In fact, no one was allowed to handle an Olsen product unless they were fully competent for their particular task. If someone got fed up with what they were doing, retraining for a more complex job, or simply a different one, was encouraged. Everyone was good at what they did, but nobody could say with honesty that they actually made anything. And nobody had more than minimal control over what they did or how they did it.

After exhaustive research Paul spent the weekend deep in thought. On Monday he crafted a carefully worded report and arranged to present his findings to the Olsen directors. His proposals were radical.

Instead of the existing system of production line assembly he proposed a system of autonomous work groups, each of which would be responsible for the assembly of a complete product. Following training, each group would be led by one of the existing supervisors, who mostly had a wider though still only partial view of the production process. In this way established hierarchies and pay differentials would be preserved initially. Inspectors would become technical advisers but product quality would be the responsibility of the work groups. The groups would agree objectives with their managers and work out for themselves how to plan and carry out their work, within clear guidelines.

As Paul expected, his ideas were hotly debated. He was closely and rather aggressively questioned. Directors wanted to know how Olsen's exceptionally high quality could be assured in such an 'unstructured' environment, how groups of production workers could 'decide for themselves' what they were going to do, and whether he was serious about letting products leave the factory without inspection. He explained that far from the chaos the Directors feared the work groups he proposed would work as highly cohesive teams, each playing a part in a collective task which was clearly understood by all.

As for inspection, instead of being someone else's job it would be every group member's responsibility to make sure that everything that they sent forward met Olsen's exacting criteria in every way. Paul left the meeting fairly convinced that his ideas would be rejected. A week later he received a call from Olsen's Managing Director to say that the board had agreed to implement his proposal.

Over the next three months Paul and a small team of senior managers set about converting one of the production lines, making digital radios, to the new format. They held discussions with staff and met with union representatives, explaining the proposals and setting up training. When the first completed radios were ready for packing they held a party to which everyone who had participated in any way was invited. The Olsen Directors had wanted to examine and test the radios but Paul had insisted that this would send all the wrong signals; the work group had to be trusted to do its own quality assurance.

The Directors compromised by sending the first shipment to selected customers to whom they had explained what was going on. The outcomes of this pilot scheme were promising. The first radios had taken a little longer to produce than under the old system, but this was to be expected. Once everyone got used to the new way of working efficiency should improve. Feedback on quality was excellent. No faults were found in any of the radios and one of the customers remarked that the presentation seemed to be smarter than before.

The real value of the change became clearer as the digital radio team settled down to business as usual. Production speeded up, quality was maintained at the highest level ever, and requests began to filter up to the Directors for small changes in design and components which would improve the products even further at little or no additional cost. In fact, after 'three months' operation the unit cost of the products had fallen by almost 5 per cent whilst average delivery times had come down by several days. No order was late, by any margin, over the whole period. The most notable change, however, was in the workforce itself. The digital radio team assumed an identity, putting a large picture of their product on the wall and praising the new system to colleagues on other lines. There was a new sense of pride in making an Olsen product.

With the experience of the digital radio team behind them Olsen went on to implement group working across its product range. By the end of 2004 they were fully committed to the new system and were confidently predicting increased profits on all but one product. Contrary to fears, faults and returns were well below former levels, despite the absence of inspection. Pay has been increased and the training budget more than doubled, which has contributed to increased interest in working for Olsen and an improvement in the quality of applicants. Olsen still faces stiffer competition than at any time in its history but now feels a new confidence that it can take on its rivals with every chance of staying at the top.

Analysis

The Venerable Bede tells the story of how King Edwin of Northumbria was converted to Christianity in around 625 CE. The king and his nobles were discussing religion when a sparrow flew in from the dark stormy night outside the hall, flew across the warm, lighted room and then disappeared through the window at the other side, out into the darkness once more. One of the nobles said that life was like that; no one knew what had gone before, or what would come after, people only knew what transpired during their brief time in the light and warmth. For the people working on Olsen's production lines this would have been a fair allegory for their work. Partially completed assemblies arrived in front of them from the dark regions of someone else's workspace. They worked on them for a little while, and then the still incomplete assemblies moved off out of their brief responsibility into the unknown once more. For many people this is what work looks like.

The production line, or more correctly assembly line, has been around since the eighteenth century and has been used for all kinds of processes including agriculture, firearms and, of course, vehicle manufacture. It can be very efficient, but it's seldom much fun.

The production line at Olsen was really quite a classic example of Frederick Taylor's 'scientific management' (1911) at work. Taylor, who was probably the first practitioner of time and motion studies, advocated specialization in its ultimate form, with everyone performing a strictly defined and limited task at which he (sic) could become highly skilled. Every task would be timed and measured in great detail. For a while Taylorism gripped American management, who saw it as a way to increase efficiency and control. (Henry Ford was a big fan.) They saw the usefulness of analysis and mistakenly thought, with Taylor, that the conceptual breakdown of work into its component parts should be carried through into actual practice.

One reason why Taylorism fell out of fashion is that it takes no account of human nature. Crainer (1997) says: 'The most obvious consequence of scientific management is a dehumanizing reliance on measurement. Taylor envisaged no room for individual initiative or imagination. People were labor, mechanically accomplishing a particular task'.

People need to have some control over their working lives, and some reason to be interested in whatever it is that they are spending their time to produce. Hackman and Oldham (1980) gave us a better picture of how to get work done when they described the characteristics of a worthwhile job. They say that there should be:

1. 'Skill variety', so that the job utilizes several different skills or abilities, or involves a number of different tasks.
2. 'Task identity' so that the worker sees a task through from beginning to end, and can see an identifiable product or outcome.
3. 'Task significance'; other people are affected by how well the task is done.
4. 'Autonomy'; allowing the worker to plan his or her own work and choose how to do it.
5. 'Feedback', so that the worker receives clear, direct information about how well he or she is doing.

Autonomous work groups often have many of these characteristics, so it isn't surprising that when they replace a system that offered few or none of them improvements are often seen. Not all processes or all situations lend themselves to the kind of change that Paul Morris proposed for Olsen.

Both Volvo and SAAB experimented with the system during the 1980s, and achieved excellent results, although 'these improvements could not be directly or entirely related to the semi-autonomous group form of organisation as other changes occurred simultaneously' (Petzall et al., 2003), but reverted to more traditional forms in the mid 1990s (although in both cases there are suspicions that the autonomous work group principles were undermined by management in some factories).

Specialization obviously isn't a bad thing in itself; the problems start to arise when the scope of jobs is narrowed so much that the principles of good job design advocated by Hackman and Oldham (1980) no longer apply. People need *jobs*, not just repetitive tasks, and that involves being able to see the outcome and purpose of what you do.

Of course, for Olsen it's early days and enthusiasm can wane as people get used to new ways of working. Even so, the changes that have taken place at Olsen Electrical give real grounds to hope that the improvements will be permanent.

THE ESSENTIALS OF THIS CHAPTER:

- Efficiency is not an end in itself, but rather it's just one element in achieving *effectiveness*.
- Rigid control over staff seldom does anything to improve overall effectiveness.
- People need to maintain some level of control over what they do. If they are denied this basic human need they may try to fill the gap in ways that are detrimental to the organization.
- Good job design allows people to see how their work fits in to a wider pattern, and allows some discretion over how things are done.

10

On intrinsic satisfactions from the work itself

He is well paid that is well satisfied.
William Shakespeare; Portia, in *The Merchant of Venice*

Narrative No 9: Inchbourne City Architect's Department

Background

Inchbourne is an English city with a history going back to pre-Roman times. Now it sprawls over almost $20\,km^2$ with modern housing estates and light industrial areas coexisting fairly successfully, if not always comfortably. There is no heavy industry; the nearest major manufacturing centres are 30 or 40 km away, but there are several large office-based employers within the local authority's boundaries.

The city centre has had to keep up with the times and it contains all the usual household name shops and businesses as well as a sprinkling of smaller independent businesses which have managed to survive the corporate offensive. There are many modern buildings in and near the centre but Inchbourne's true character comes from its historic architecture. It has a Norman church, now the cathedral, and both a corn exchange and a wool exchange, dating from the thirteenth and fourteenth centuries respectively, as well as several other smaller medieval, Tudor and Jacobean buildings and an imposing Victorian town hall, all within a few minutes' walk of each other.

The town was granted its Royal Charter in 1490 and its church became the seat of the Bishop a decade later. Unusually, ownership of part of the central area was held from the earliest times by the mayor on behalf of the city, rather than by individuals. The city had always had a turbulent relationship with the nearby Abbey of Saint Cedric of Inchbourne and possibly for this reason as much as from any theological considerations the city fathers enthusiastically supported King Henry VIII's reform of the English church.

When this was followed by the dissolution of the monasteries they looked covetously at the Abbey's vast land holdings and were rewarded for their loyalty by being permitted to purchase part of the Abbey's property at a very advantageous rate. They acquired as much as their funds would allow, which included all the Abbey land within the city walls and several fields just outside. (In fact, hardly anything remained of the actual walls themselves at the time, and nothing is left now, but the traditional city limits still follow the ancient boundaries.)

For these historical reasons the city of Inchbourne is a major landlord, owning properties of all ages from the medieval right up to twentieth century office buildings. To maintain and manage this property portfolio, the majority of which is let to commercial users, Inchbourne has a City Architect's Department, referred to within the local authority as the ICAD, which is responsible for ensuring the structural integrity and capital value of all the city's property, and for maximizing its financial contribution to the local authority's budget. This is increasingly difficult to achieve.

The historic buildings are, of course, legally protected and carefully watched by a whole range of heritage organizations and private individuals. Despite a considerable income from the tourist trade they still represent a financial burden on the city. The modern buildings are ageing and many of them are poorly suited to present day requirements. In 2004 several had been vacant for months and in one case for almost two years. Just mitigating the natural deterioration was an uphill struggle. On the other hand, the ICAD had been successful in redeveloping two large properties in partnership with private developers and were hopeful of doing similar deals over some of the other properties that were near – or past – the end of their useful lives.

The situation

Roy Stoner is in his mid fifties and works in Inchbourne's CAD as a buildings manager. I met him through a mutual friend who asked me if I would 'have a chat' with him with a view to possibly working with him as a coach. (We didn't, in fact, take this idea forward; if we had done so this narrative wouldn't be appearing here, even in disguised form.)

We arranged to meet and he told me all about Inchbourne and quite a lot about himself. He had graduated with a degree in architecture in 1972 and begun work as junior employee with an architect's practice in London. He had gone into the study of architecture with some clear ideas about building design, which leant strongly towards traditional forms, and had been disappointed by the relentlessly modernist orientations of his tutors. He felt that he was out of step with the trends in the profession and even before he left university he had been having misgivings about his vocation, but he had invested too much of himself towards achieving his degree by then for him to change direction. So he went through with it and on towards the completion of his training as what would now probably be called 'an intern' at the practice.

He had found his work at the architect's practice frustrating and sterile. Not only was the pay terrible, the work he was asked to do was trivial and the designs his employers produced seemed to him to be repetitive and bleakly functional. His interest in old buildings hadn't waned and he longed to be allowed to design buildings that had the elegance and aesthetic appeal of the past, married with the practical improvements that had been developed over time. He was certain that this was perfectly feasible but was in no position to promote his ideas.

When his long 'apprenticeship' came to an end he moved to another employer which was a little more to his liking, and at last he began earning just about enough to live on but his heart still wasn't in it. He changed jobs several times over those early years before eventually concluding, sadly, that no one was going to pay him to design the 'modern traditional' buildings that he favoured. By this time he had a family to support, so earning a living took precedence over professional fulfilment.

Just when Stoner had resigned himself to the situation he saw a position with Inchbourne City Architect's Department advertised. It wasn't asking for anyone to design new buildings but it did emphasize the care, refurbishment and restoration of old buildings, along with the management of more modern ones. It was a change of direction for him but he seemed to be more or less qualified for the job, so he applied and was appointed. He moved with his family to Inchbourne and began his career with the ICAD.

Despite being very different from 'pure' architecture, Stoner found his new work fascinating. He adored the old buildings he worked with and found the challenge of restoring decaying stonework and massive beams intellectually rewarding. His early ideas about blending modern facilities with traditional architecture found new outlets as he worked out ways of making Inchbourne's ancient heritage usable and practical for the late twentieth century, and he received several commendations for his sensitive adaptations.

Even the heritage lobby seemed to approve of him. He also found that the more mundane aspects of his work, involving maintenance and refurbishment of the modern building stock, were less disagreeable than he had feared. Since the buildings, however objectionable, were already there he didn't feel that by working with them he was adding to the urban blight in quite the same way as he had when his employers were putting up new monstrosities. On the contrary, he was able, in a small way, to ameliorate their impact on the environment through minor cosmetic changes done alongside the more substantive structural work.

Most of the actual work was carried out by local tradesmen, with bigger firms being called in for the major projects. Stoner found that he could work comfortably with these contractors. He was knowledgeable and it wasn't easy to take advantage of him, but he was also fair and understanding when genuine difficulties came up and often suggested imaginative solutions. He looked on each new project as a challenge. Most were routine, some downright boring, but every now and then one came along which really caught his imagination. For the first time in years Stoner could honestly say that he enjoyed his job. He was respected, even if he was possibly seen as something of an idealist. The local authority pay wasn't spectacular, but he earned enough to look after his family, the holidays were good and the pension plan was generous.

For a while it looked to Stoner as though he was settled in a career that was worthwhile, fulfilling and rewarding in every sense that mattered. There was plenty of variety in his work but no serious change loomed on the horizon. But he was mistaken.

Like all local authorities Inchbourne came under increasing financial pressure during the 1990s and needed to cut back in all aspects of its operations. The ICAD was no exception to this but it was difficult to see how cuts could be made. It had legal obligations to maintain its heritage buildings, although this didn't stop the city administrators and their political masters from questioning every item of expenditure and turning down many proposals which the ICAD considered essential. This both frustrated and saddened Stoner, who found himself struggling to prevent irreversible deterioration in some of the more vulnerable buildings.

The worst effects of the new more stringent financial environment bore most heavily, unexpectedly for Stoner, on the modern building stock. He still believed this to be a source of valuable revenue for the city and had plenty of ideas for refurbishment and alteration, which could have greatly increased its potential. To do this would require some investment, but he was certain that he and his ICAD colleagues could manage the projects efficiently using the usual contractors, which would also have the benefit of keeping a proportion of the money circulating in Inchbourne.

The authority had some difficulty in seeing things that way. As far as the Councillors were concerned the solution to their difficulties lay in cutting costs rather than in increasing revenue. They refused point blank to reconsider cuts in ICAD's budget, which meant that staff were fully stretched and unable to take on much in the way of new projects. Stoner's bosses sympathized and agreed with his ideas. Their response to the situation took inspiration from the successful partnership deals they had done with private developers. If private firms could redevelop Inchbourne-owned property with modest levels of direct involvement of ICAD staff, why not bring in private contractors to handle the less drastic refurbishments? Before long tenders were routinely being sought from consulting firms who would manage the projects on ICAD's behalf, often in return for a share of the revenues to be generated from the upgraded buildings.

Stoner had two problems with this. One was that useful revenue was being diverted away from the local authority's funds, and away from Inchbourne itself, and into private hands. The other was more personal. Instead of being deeply involved in the management of the projects and in the design of the changes that were being implemented, his role was increasingly becoming one of 'client's representative'. He was the consultants' inside contact; ostensibly in charge but in practice just there to handle issues and chair meetings. The consultants decided what was to be done and the city authorities gave their approval. From that point on all he had to do was report progress and make excuses for any failures. Over a period of two or three years what had been an exciting (for him, anyway), challenging and fulfilling career changed to being just a job. He had been in that situation before and had hoped never to be there again.

When I spoke to him Roy Stoner was eight years away from the official retirement age for City of Inchbourne employees. There had been talk of an early retirement scheme, which might allow him to leave perhaps a couple of years before that, but nothing definite had been announced. There were still days when the job brought him some satisfaction but they occurred less and less often. On the whole the job had become a burden to him and he would be glad to leave.

I asked him if his professional qualifications would allow him to change direction once again, perhaps become self-employed or move to a private firm. He told me that he had thought of that but held out little hope. If he undertook any private work the insurance he would need would be prohibitively expensive and in his field claims could arise many years after the work was done, so the premiums would have to be paid for life. This wasn't an option. As for changing employer, his local authority pension would be his major financial asset in the future and he needed to ensure that he achieved the maximum years' contributions. Besides, he didn't believe that his skills, which had become quite specialized, would be valued very highly in the commercial world.

He seemed resigned to the situation. He clearly wasn't desperately unhappy but he had lost the enthusiasm which had characterized his early years at Inchbourne. He told me that several of his colleagues felt the same and he fully expected there to be competition for the early retirement offer, if and when it came. For him, the main benefit of his job would come when he eventually left it to claim his pension. Meanwhile, he intended to serve out his remaining years with the ICAD and make the most of his leisure time.

Analysis

If you search the internet for 'the best job in the world' you get something like 200 000 returns. Clearly, there are plenty of people who get satisfaction from their work. If you look a little more closely at the kinds of jobs that figure as candidates for this accolade they fall into two broad categories. There are those that are fun and exciting for the incumbent, with jobs involving travel as leading contenders, along with getting paid for activities which other people regard as hobbies. I disqualify chocolate tasting and similar jobs on the grounds that they are only good on a temporary basis. The other group of 'best jobs' are those which bring benefits to others. Teachers at all levels from nursery nurses through to university professors seem to be in the majority here, although all the public services, medicine, firefighting, police, social work, and so on are well represented, as well as aid work of various kinds. Many jobs, of course, hit both buttons and so may have a better claim to the title.

There's another side to this: those occupations traditionally designated 'professions' actually get rather a mixed press. For example, despite the readiness of teachers to extol their work the exit rate from teaching in the UK is very high; perhaps as many as 20 000 staff a year (Smithers and Robinson, 2003). Things get worse in other professions: 'Nurses are four times more likely to commit suicide compared with people working outside medicine, ... and doctors are twice as likely to kill themselves compared with people working in other professions' (BBC, 2000). The figures are apparently even worse for vets (BBC, 2005).

The reasons for this are no doubt very complex, as reasons usually are. However, Roy Stoner's experience gives a clue to one possible contributing factor. Professionals, whatever their discipline, spend a long time learning about their subject, usually while they are young and idealistic. They develop ideas of their own and eagerly anticipate being able to put these ideas into practice. For a lucky few the world of work meets all their expectations. The glittering prizes they saw waiting for them as they began their careers do actually fall into their hands. For many, though, these expectations are only very partially fulfilled.

For Stoner the disillusionment set in very early; early enough for him to recognize the need to make a change whilst it was still practical to do so. For a while this turned out better than he could have anticipated and he experienced the all too rare satisfaction of earning his living by doing something which, if not quite 'the best job in the world' was still pretty good. His experience of the climate of his workplace could hardly have been bettered.

The changes which took place around him made his job so much less satisfying and were beyond his control, and this in itself made it harder for him to accept and adjust to them. It would be easy to say that the City of Inchbourne made a mistake in outsourcing the management of its building projects; there is certainly an argument that the long-term diversion of revenues away from the City's exchequer will turn out to be a heavy cost to pay for the easing of the current financial pressures. Probably no one will ever make that assessment.

The harsh fact is that this kind of decision is very far removed from the management issues around the quality of working life of a handful of employees. The organizational climate of the ICAD is very unlikely to have had any influence at all on those making the decisions.

For Roy Stoner the effect of the decision is that he no longer regards his work as anything more than a way of earning his living. It had become for him, in Douglas McGregor's words, 'a form of punishment which is the price to be paid for various kinds of satisfaction away from the job' and so 'we would hardly expect (him) to undergo more of this punishment than is necessary' (McGregor, 1960). From everyone's perspective (except that of the contractors who picked up the profits), it's been a tragic waste.

Narrative No 10: The Sylvia Castleton Trust

Background

Brian Tenby was a successful commodity trader in the City of London. His job meant that he spent long hours in front of a computer screen in a noisy open-plan office, continually on the telephone – often having to shout – against extreme time pressures, surrounded by other people doing much the same work. Vast amounts of money could hang on how quickly Brian could respond to take a client's order or pass the details to a colleague to buy on the trading floor. The work was frantic and stressful but at first Brian enjoyed it. He got a real kick out of a successful deal and could shrug philosophically when things didn't turn out right. Fortunately he won more often than he lost.

He had a useful and growing client list, some of whom trusted him to make judgement calls on their behalf in certain circumstances. Since Brian kept his finger on the pulse of world events that might affect his clients' interests his decisions were usually sound. His clients were pleased with him and so were his employers and the rewards were high. He wasn't yet by any means at the top of the profession, where salaries can reach millions of pounds per year and individual bonuses can look like the GNPs of some of the members of the UN, but he did earn a six-figure salary which he fully expected, based on past experience, to be more than matched by his annual bonus.

At twenty-seven Brian was already beginning to recognize that his present job was a young man's game. The thrill he had once got out of clinching a lucrative deal had slowly transformed over the relatively short course of his career into simple relief that, once again, he had avoided disaster. The 12- to 14-hour days left him weary and despondent and he worried that he was no longer as sharp as he had once been. Almost from the beginning, Brian had nurtured a hazy kind of life-plan in which he saw himself carrying on in his job until he no longer enjoyed the challenge and he had made enough money not to need to work for a living any more. He hoped and expected the latter condition to be achieved before the former, which he thought was the ideal position to be in.

Without detracting in any way from his lifestyle he had invested his considerable surplus income carefully and he tentatively calculated that he would have enough put by to finance his long-term future by the time he was thirty-five. When that point was reached he intended to find an interesting occupation – he didn't yet know what that might be – and work solely for his own pleasure and satisfaction.

Unlike some of his colleagues he had always looked after himself. He drank only in moderation. He knew what constituted a healthy diet, even if he didn't always strictly follow one. He didn't take drugs and he went to the gym two or three times a week. Now he sometimes found that he had to drag himself to the gym. He often missed meals and more than once had realized with a start that he needed a drink to help him unwind. He recognized danger signals but he wasn't ready to give up the high income, and the high-earner status, that came with the job.

Then in 2002 two things happened which were to change Brian's outlook, and his life. The first was that a friend and colleague, who worked in the same office, crashed his Porsche at over 150 km per hour. Not only was Brian's friend killed outright, but two members of a family in another car were also killed, and a third badly injured. The inquest showed that the Porsche driver had been high on cocaine. Brian knew that his friend had regularly used cocaine to wind down from the stress of the trading room and that he had been a fast driver, but somehow had never seen either of these things as potentially lethal. The combination of grief and shock left Brian deeply depressed and, for the first time since he started work, he was forced to report sick. When he returned to work after a few days he was quiet and withdrawn, but he recovered quickly and for a while life and work returned to normal.

Brian's next life-changing experience was that he fell in love. He met Alex whilst on holiday in Greece. He was with a group of male friends and was finding them irritatingly laddish. She was on holiday with her parents and her disabled younger brother. Brian had been returning to the hotel when he saw Alex struggling to get her brother's wheelchair up the steps to the entrance and had stopped to help. They got chatting and before long they both knew that they wanted to see more of each other. As both of them lived in London, not too far apart, this wasn't difficult to arrange when the holiday ended. Both were mature and both had had previous relationships which hadn't worked out.

Alex worked in Human Resources (through which connection I got to hear about their story) and also did voluntary work with a charity called the Sylvia Castleton Trust. Her brother Oliver had been born with cerebral palsy, a condition that can affect movement and speech. In Oliver's case it meant that he had almost no use of his legs or left arm and his speech was very difficult to understand for anyone who wasn't used to it. He also suffered from some lack of control over his facial expressions, which also had the effect of making communication with strangers more difficult. The condition had not, though, impaired Oliver's mental capacity in any way. He had a degree in sociology and had a full-time job in social services. Although he could manage fairly well on his own if necessary, he found it hard work and it was easier for him to live with his parents at their home in Surrey.

As the relationship developed Brian learned more about Alex's charitable work, in which she had first got involved after realizing that many disabled people could not, like her brother, manage a mainstream job and needed employment which was geared to their needs and capabilities. The Sylvia Castleton Trust, named after its founder and major benefactor, was set up to provide an environment in which such people could perform useful work. Its main business – and it was very deliberately operated as a business, despite its charitable status – was the repair and refurbishment of donated furniture, which was restored to a standard which would make it suitable for sale to the general public.

Brian, whose furniture needs were usually supplied by smart chain stores, was surprised to learn that there was quite a thriving market for refurbished second-hand goods and the Trust would very nearly be able to break even on the proceeds if it could obtain enough 'raw materials' to meet the demand. This was, in fact, a real problem. The shortfall in the annual budget was made up by donations and grants, but these were unpredictable, and local authority grants, which had in the past been the Trust's lifeline, were being cut year on year. Fortunately, thanks to the prescience of the late Mrs Castleton, the Trust owned the freehold of its warehouse cum workshop in south London, so it wasn't burdened with rents or mortgage payments.

The Trust employed a full-time manager, who reported to the board of trustees, but this post fell vacant at Christmas 2002 when the manager who had held the job for 15 years retired. Despite her stated intention to go when she reached 60, she had been persuaded to stay on for a further three years, but her husband had recently suffered a mild stroke and it had rather brought home to her the attractions of making the most of their time together. The manager was supported by two full-time assistants, who were sharing the responsibilities of the vacant post on a temporary basis. In addition there were around 20 tutors and supervisors working part-time, some of whom were paid and some volunteers.

At any given time the Trust might have up to 50 disabled people on its payroll, who were paid at least the minimum wage, depending on their skills. Some of these people were physically disabled and others had learning difficulties, but all received whatever training was appropriate so that they could make a full contribution to the business. Items of furniture were sometimes delivered to the workshop, but mostly people rang the Trust and a van was sent out to collect the donation. It was a well-run, viable operation with committed staff and looked set to continue in business for a long time.

The situation

In January of 2003 Alex gave up her small rented flat and moved in with Brian. This change in his life away from work gave Brian a much needed refuge from the stress and pressure. In the office, though, things were just as bad if not worse. The commercial world in which Brian operated was cut-throat and the weak went to the wall. In the past Brian had always been one of the strong and had thrived in this environment, but now it seemed threatening and at times almost overwhelming. He began to see his work as fundamentally useless. It created nothing. It improved nothing. It was essentially parasitic. And it left him exhausted and drained.

On a grey, cold and wet February morning as Brian commuted to his now soulless but still highly lucrative job, he made a life-changing decision. Instead of going straight to the office he sat down with a coffee and telephoned Alex. That evening he wrote to the Chair of trustees at the Sylvia Castleton Trust asking to be considered for the job of manager.

Despite his high-powered job he actually had no experience of management, knew very little about working with disabled people and absolutely nothing about restoring furniture. On paper he was woefully unqualified for the job. He was also currently earning four times the salary on offer, without considering his massive annual bonus. On the other hand, he owned his own home, free of mortgage, he had investments that most young men of his age could only dream about, and he had no commitments. Alex's own job was well paid, by normal standards, and after getting over the initial shock she gave him her full backing. She knew how his work was affecting him and feared for his health, and their future, if things carried on as they were.

When the Chair of the Trust rang him to invite him to an interview Brian found to his own considerable surprise that he was both excited and nervous. These feelings increased when he realized that he wasn't the only candidate. In fact, the trustees had shortlisted three people for the job. Brian felt his own lack of suitability for the role very keenly, and he knew that he couldn't expect any preferential treatment as Alex's partner.

He frankly acknowledged his shortcomings and emphasized his own need to do something more worthwhile with his life, without appearing to want to use the Trust as a form of therapy. He left the interview room feeling very far from confident but determined that if the Sylvia Castleton Trust didn't want him he would find some other socially useful role. Whatever happened he wouldn't stay in his current job.

Of course, Brian was appointed manager at the Trust; otherwise there wouldn't be a story here. He quit his City job and threw himself wholeheartedly into his new role. He learned fast, listening to what the more experienced staff had to tell him and to the disabled employees. His acquaintance with Alex's brother, Oliver, had taught him not to jump to conclusions about disabled people; Oliver's speech impediments and physical difficulties often led people to think he was slow witted, but Brian knew that in fact he was extremely sharp as well as being well educated.

Brian applied this experience in his dealings with the employees at the Trust. Some did have quite severe learning difficulties whilst others' disabilities were purely physical. Brian tried to get to know each one individually and respond to their different needs as best he could. He undertook the same training as a new employee, so he got to know the practicalities of the work. He went out in the vans to collect donated furniture and often came back with more items than had been promised. The staff, some of whom had been sceptical at first, came to respect and like him. His sincerity was clear to everyone and when he made mistakes, as he did, his willingness to take responsibility and do what he could to put things right more than made up for any irritations.

And Brian was a superlative salesman, used to talking clients round and getting people to do him favours cheerfully. He put this talent – the only qualification he had brought with him from his old life – to excellent use, visiting local businesses and private benefactors, contacting the various official and private bodies that made charitable grants, and putting on public relations events of various kinds. The Trust's financial position improved considerably and its profile was considerably enhanced.

For the first time in several years Brian felt totally committed to his work. The days sped by and he was often taken by surprise when one of the staff looked in to his tiny office to ask if he would mind locking up as everyone else had gone home. Two years into the job, he had no regrets at all about giving up his highly paid City job to work for the Trust. He enjoyed his work more than he had ever thought possible and he knew, at the end of each day, that other people's lives had been made better by what he had done.

His personal life, too, could hardly have been better (and it would be rash to assume that this is just coincidence). At the end of 2005 Alex began six months' maternity leave and an old friend of mine was appointed as interim HR manager to cover for her, which is how the details of this narrative reached me.

Analysis

Many people's jobs make them ill. According to McLean (1985) stress causes problems when three factors come together: a person may be *vulnerable* to stress for some reason at a particular time; the *context* in which that person finds himself or herself at that time may have the potential to induce stress; and/or something may happen which places a *demand* on the person which they feel unable or unprepared to deal with. If just one or two of these factors are present there may be no ill effects at all, but when all three come together at the same time the person may suffer damaging consequences.

In Brian's case the context was his highly-pressured, competitive job characterized by continual urgency. He himself was vulnerable because the lifestyle was no longer right for him. He was tired and jaded and needed a change. The demand, or stressor, which completed the three-factor conjunction was the tragic death of his friend in circumstances which were clearly lifestyle related. All this became too much for Brian to take and he began to suffer from the stress-based condition known as burnout, which Sonnentag et al. (1994) define as 'an individual's negative emotional experience leading to a chronic process … experienced as exhaustion on a physical, emotional and cognitive level. Most definitions include withdrawal and decreasing involvement in the job, especially by persons who have been highly involved in their work'.

When people suffer from severe and/or chronic stress at work the adverse consequences may be mitigated, or at least deferred, if they have a 'safe haven' or refuge away from the source of the stress and where they feel secure and valued. Brian was fortunate in meeting Alex at a crucial time and their home life provided him with such a safe haven. All the same, when someone's feelings about their job have become negative, and remained so for a period of time, it is often impossible to go back to previously-held feelings and attitudes. When that happens the only real way forward is for the context to change, which allows the person to regard the negative attitudes as associated with the old context and therefore not applicable to the new one (even if the change is relatively minor). For Brian, a complete change of context seemed like the only way out of the bad place in which he found himself and circumstances provided him with an opportunity to make that change.

Not everyone has the freedom to ignore economic factors in the way that Brian was able to. And not everyone can or would want to work in the kind of care-based organization that the Sylvia Castleton Trust exemplifies. However, the feeling that what we do at work is actually useful or beneficial, in whatever form is meaningful for the individual concerned, is a vital factor in self-esteem. In fact, we are equipped with psychological defence mechanisms which can actually change our perceptions of reality to protect us against the potentially harmful effects that may ensue if we were to perceive that we, as rational, decent human beings were engaged in an activity that was pointless or harmful.

This phenomenon has been identified by Festinger as cognitive dissonance (Festinger, 1957; Festinger and Carlsmith, 1959). Brian is not alone in choosing to resolve this 'dissonance' by changing to a less demanding or, as in Brian's case, more satisfying job. According to an analysis by the British Trades Union Congress of the UK government's *Labour Force Survey*, which interviews 60 000 households, '45 percent of people want to work fewer hours, and more than two million people – 1 in 10 employees – would downshift by giving up pay for a better work–life balance' (TUC, 2006).

This has serious implications for organizations; unless management pays real attention to issues of employees' satisfaction – with the work they do, as well as with their conditions of employment – and healthy balance between work and non-work activities, they will find valuable staff leaving for more amenable work elsewhere. And it will be the most valuable staff – the ones organizations can least afford to lose – who have the widest range of options open to them.

THE ESSENTIALS OF THIS CHAPTER:

- Working day after day at an occupation which is devoid of intrinsic satisfaction is a form of slavery, regardless of the rewards which can only be enjoyed away from the workplace.
- Our self-esteem can be damaged if we don't feel that what we do at work is useful or beneficial.
- If work itself is satisfying, i.e. it meets some of the whole-life needs that everyone has, then money becomes less significant; we don't need to be bribed to do the things we enjoy doing.

11

On innovation – the freedom to try new concepts and approaches

Innovation is the specific instrument of entrepreneurship – the act that endows resources with a new capacity to create wealth.

Peter F Drucker, *Innovation and Entrepreneurship*, 1985

Narrative No 11: Antoneta

Background

Antoneta is a high street fashion retailer with more than 20 shops across the south of England. It sells both men's and women's clothes which are usually quite distinctive, often ahead of trends, and certainly not cheap. It rarely deals in the well-known designer labels but its lines are nevertheless mostly exclusive designs, often commissioned by the company from talented new designers. Several famous names began their careers with a successful Antoneta design.

All Antoneta shops look alike from the outside but shop managers are told that they have 'considerable freedom' to arrange the interior of their shop, subject to head office approval. In practice, most of the interiors look quite similar too, since the head office people have a proprietorial view about what constitutes good shop design and don't usually approve anything very radical. Still, the company recognizes that the place where it takes possession of other people's money is on the nation's high streets, so its shop managers have considerable status, at least in theory.

The shop managers also have an unusual, if not unique, role in ensuring that Antoneta gets the pick of emerging design talent. In its early days the company's founders realized that they could encourage aspiring designers with an easy access route to the company via a shop in their own locality, so it was made part of every shop manager's job to cultivate local talent. Designers can approach local managers with drawings and *toiles* (prototypes or mock-ups of garments). Those designs that the manager considers to show promise are sent on for evaluation to the buying team at head office, who may then order small production runs or give the designer advice on how to make his or her concepts more viable. Designs which prove successful in their 'home' area are then ordered in larger quantities and distributed to all Antoneta outlets.

Antoneta's shop managers can therefore sometimes find their role uncomfortably ambiguous. On the one hand they are expected to be hard-headed administrators, managing staff, dealing with shift rosters, stock handling and processing customer payments and, inevitably, fielding the occasional customer complaint. On the other hand, they have an important part to play in the process of ensuring a continual flow of new designs, which calls for a rather peculiar blend of artistic flair and commercial acumen.

Some have found this very difficult, especially those who have been recruited from other fashion retailers where managers have little or no discretion over what they sell and certainly no significant part to play in the design process. They often either fail to attract new designs at all, or they indiscriminately swamp the head office team with designs that have no chance of going anywhere. These people usually feel, rightly, that they are in the wrong job and move on fairly quickly. Others have taken to the artistic side of the job with enthusiasm, but have fallen short in the practical skills – not to mention the sheer stamina – needed to run a successful high street shop of any kind. These also tend to find more suitable employment, usually of their own accord, although Antoneta have occasionally found it necessary to dismiss a manager whose performance consistently fell below their high standards.

There is considerable competition between the managers on both aspects of their job. As well as the fairly traditional rivalry between outlets over sales figures and successful promotions there is also competition over who can introduce the most successful new designs, and new designers, to the company. Antoneta used to award an annual prize to the 'top' managers in each arena.

Like many retail outlets Antoneta has always regarded its sub-management staff with a degree of ambivalence. Every shop has at least two deputy managers but these are not necessarily regarded as managers-in-waiting. They are free to apply for vacant manager jobs and enjoy the advantage of being guaranteed an interview provided their appraisals are satisfactory, but their success rate is not high; the majority of new managers are appointed from outside the company. There are some quite long-serving shop assistants, too, but most don't stay more than a year or two and many leave even sooner.

This is partly because Antoneta tends to favour young, bright applicants, who are attracted to the company by its reputation as a fashion leader (and the staff discounts). Once there, they find that shop work is quite arduous and often tedious, and customers aren't always as agreeable as one might wish. The pay is no better, although no worse, than most other retailers and staff depend on sales-based bonuses to achieve reasonable income levels. This is only partly within the individual assistant's control so actual pay can be unpredictable. After a while many assistants start to look for some more amenable occupation and being young and bright they often find one quite quickly.

The situation

For several years Antoneta's idiosyncratic approach served them well. Their clothes were distinctive and enjoyed a market sector almost of their own; too big to be termed 'niche', but definitely not mass market. Towards the end of the 1990s, though, the company was struggling to maintain its profits in the face of ferocious competition from other high street chains and the big supermarkets. To add to their difficulties, the turnover of shop managers was approaching epidemic proportions and the supply of really talented new designers seemed to be dwindling. They decided to seek advice about what might be going wrong from Christine Galman, a colleague of mine, who asked me to get involved.

Antoneta's initial view of the situation was that there was something wrong with their recruitment process that was leading to the appointment of unsuitable candidates as shop managers, so that was where we began. It soon became clear that this was certainly true. We followed the recruitment process (just on paper, using the Personnel records) through from advertising of vacancies to appointments, and then beyond to look at the performance records of the new appointees. It was evident to us that some elementary errors were being made.

The jobs were not being accurately described, so people who were well qualified and experienced for a traditional retail management role were applying and getting through to interview even though they had little or no understanding of the creative aspects of the job. This meant that the candidates the interviewers saw were mostly suitable for only half the job. The selectors chose the best of the people that were available to them, but this wasn't meeting the company's requirements. Once appointed, the new managers often found themselves out of their depth and unable to cope with the unusual demands placed on them and either put in unsatisfactory performances or became angry at having been misled and moved on.

It was relatively easy to improve this process. We suggested that Antoneta should make a feature in their advertising of the unusual blend of skills they required, bringing in professionals to design their advertisements and write the copy, and then getting it checked over by an occupational psychologist. This would narrow the appeal, hopefully, to encourage applications from people who were suited to the role and discourage those who weren't. We then suggested that the interviewers used a profiling technique (Gray, 2001a) to try to ensure a better match between the attributes required for the job and those possessed by the candidates. This was done and a few months later four new managers had been appointed using the new approach.

So far so good, but we needed to track the progress of the new appointees to see whether the recruitment problem had been fixed. Market conditions remained difficult and we couldn't help much with that, but we were hoping that Antoneta's competitive edge would possibly be sharpened if the flow of distinctive and exciting new designs picked up once more.

Everyone hoped that the new managers would play a part in this but Chris and I weren't sure that this was the only cause of Antoneta's problems. We asked to be allowed to keep in touch with two of the new appointees for a while, to get an in-depth understanding of how it felt to be one of Antoneta's shop managers. We agreed that we would each focus on one manager, naturally with their full consent, and then compare notes to see if any pattern seemed to be emerging. Olivia Marlowe had been appointed to manage a shop in a town not too far from my home, so she became my main 'informant' in this study.

Over a period of about six months Chris and I talked regularly with our contacts, mainly by phone but also making occasional visits to the shops, and we got to know them quite well. Olivia had impressed the interviewers. She had studied an AVCE (Advanced Vocational Certificate of Education, equivalent to A-levels) in fashion marketing at college and had achieved two single awards in business and art and design. This was an excellent foundation for the work she was now doing and it would have qualified her to go on to study for a Higher National Diploma or a degree, but instead she had decided to get a job and had gone to work for a national chain retailer of clothing, food and household goods. She had advanced to a junior supervisory role but had become bored. Now, at twenty-four, she was excited but also nervous about her first management job.

It was impossible to spend more than a few minutes in Olivia's company without being aware that she was absolutely full of ideas. She set about reorganizing the shop floor layout in ways that she had already worked out in her head, but not been allowed to implement, in her previous job. She thought the existing shift patterns left the shop vulnerable to shoplifting at peak times so she persuaded the staff to change the duty rosters voluntarily. She also designated certain staff members to target particular kinds of customer on the principle that people will buy more if they feel empathy with the assistant.

She didn't seek approval for any of these changes and it wasn't long before the Area Manager took her to task. Olivia didn't back down. She argued with the AM and in the end he let her keep most of her changes, only insisting that the shop layout partially returned to something nearer to the company style. Olivia didn't like this but knew when to make a tactical retreat.

She also set about proactively seeking out fledgling designers in her area. The town itself didn't have a Further Education college like the one she had attended, but there were two such institutions in neighbouring towns and she made contact with the Heads of Department covering fashion and design in both of them. She also used some of her very meagre discretionary budget to put advertisements in the local free newspapers inviting designers to contact her. This again brought her into conflict with the AM, who said frankly that he applauded her use of initiative but all public relations activity had to go through head office. If individual managers started putting advertisements or other material in the press the company could lose control over its image. Olivia told him she thought this was crazy, but didn't repeat the offence.

I learned from Olivia that she didn't really resent the AM's censure, because she understood his position, but all the same she fully intended to stretch the boundaries at every opportunity. What she found more frustrating was that none of the other shop managers would talk to her about anything important. It wasn't that there was hostility between them, most of them got on quite well and the occasional Area meetings were usually good-humoured. She hadn't been at Antoneta long enough to attend one of the annual 'National' meetings (in fact, Antoneta has no presence north of Oxford) but it seemed that these were much the same.

The issue was that there was intense competition between the managers for the best sales figures and the best new designs. If anyone had an idea that might improve either, they kept it to themselves until it was implemented. After that, of course, everyone hurried to try it out for themselves, if they could. Olivia was keen to learn from the others and didn't want to have to wait until word got round that something new seemed to be working out well. Also, she had plenty of ideas of her own and thought that if other shop managers shared her enthusiasm for them head office might be more inclined to adopt them.

Meanwhile she was finding it hard to take the necessary time out from managing the shop to nurture the designer contacts she was making but she had recognized from the start that the company regarded this as a vital part of the job and it was certainly more interesting than the largely routine business of keeping things running smoothly back at base. She put in many hours of unpaid overtime to keep on top of things. She was rewarded with some early successes. Three college students had submitted potentially useful *toiles* already, and one youngster's talent had really impressed the head office team. In addition, sales figures in the shop had improved and 'shrinkage' had reduced. She was doing well.

When I compared notes with Chris I found that her experience had been rather different. Her contact had also understood the importance of the creative side of the job but unlike Olivia he had no previous experience of this. His previous job had also been as a junior supervisor in a big chain, where his responsibilities had been to keep turnover up and losses down without any input into what was sold or how it was displayed.

He had met the selection profile because he was an imaginative amateur designer himself and produced a number of ideas, some of which the company was now evaluating. Unfortunately he seemed unable either to locate or to recognize talent in others. He was approaching his new role at Antoneta in just the same way he had operated in his previous job. His shop was always properly staffed, clean and tidy, and his turnover was as good as or better than Olivia's. He hadn't made any changes on the shop floor and he hadn't forwarded any designs or introduced any new talent. Like Olivia, he was also uncomfortable with the secretive style of his peers, mainly because he wanted to know how to make improvements and no one would tell him.

When I next spoke to Olivia she had just had a blazing row with her Area Manager. She had found an ex-student who was making a precarious living importing artisan jewellery and had cleared a small section in her shop for the young woman to sell her products on a commission basis. She was sure it would pay for itself in terms of the turnover per square metre of floor space, and also bring mainstream business into the shop. The AM had told her that this was completely unacceptable and ordered her to remove the 'alien' business immediately. This was the latest in a series of disagreements and this time she was on the point of resigning, so my call was timely. I persuaded her to persevere, at least for a little longer. I arranged to meet with Chris to prepare our feedback to the company.

We identified several themes from our extended study of our two 'informants', which we thought Antoneta's management might find helpful. First, the company was asking a lot of its managers by specifying a dual role: administrator and talent scout. Neither of us had seen anything quite analogous before and to begin with we were very sceptical about the continued viability of the policy. However, Olivia had changed my mind. I was convinced that Antoneta could still make the policy work for them, provided they could attract and retain the right people, who were rare but valuable.

Second, the culture at Antoneta was working against them. The creativity of the talented people they had in post was, to some extent, being stifled by policy decisions. Chris and I decided to recommend some changes. We thought that the competition between shop managers had almost nothing to recommend it and we would urge the company to stop it. Instead, we wanted the company to encourage the sharing of ideas and experiment. We wanted shop managers to have more freedom to do things their own way, restrained only by 'boundary' rules and, of course, budget limitations. We would also tell the company that it should celebrate 'noble failures' so that everyone would know that it was alright to take risks, quoting the founder of IBM Thomas Watson's aphorism 'The fastest way to succeed is to double your failure rate' (Watson, 1963).

We didn't know how these suggestions would be received and prepared ourselves for a rough ride when we met with the senior management team. Instead, it seemed that there had already been some discussion along these lines and what we had to say fitted with the general mood. This is always a bit deflating for a consultant; we usually like to be at least half a step ahead of our clients. On the other hand it was reassuring to both sides that we had independently arrived at similar conclusions.

Antoneta has now implemented these changes and their shops no longer all look the same. Profits are holding up, although it will probably always be a struggle to fight off the giant corporations. Olivia is still managing her shop and still arguing with her Area Manager who, being no fool, recognizes her occasional outbursts as a sign of the passion and energy she puts into her ideas. Perhaps the most positive development is that colleges all over the south of England, and further afield, now advise their fashion students to visit an Antoneta shop with their designs, which should help to keep Antoneta at the leading edge of fashion in the future.

Analysis

It's important to recognize that creativity and innovation aren't the same thing. "Creativity' is about the generation and sharing of ideas, and 'innovation' is the process whereby creative ideas are implemented' (Drewery, 2003). This means that innovation can be fostered by people who aren't themselves particularly creative, provided they can recognize creativity in others and provide the organizational settings in which it can thrive. Professor Teresa Amabile collected over 12 000 diary entries from people working in creative occupations and identified some key facts about the kind of organizational environment where creativity flourished (Breen, 2004).

One important insight was that 'creativity takes a hit when people in a work group compete instead of collaborate'. This wasn't what Antoneta had thought, but they were willing to revise their opinions. Another of Amabile's findings was that 'people often thought they were most creative when they were working under severe deadline pressure. But the 12 000 aggregate days that we studied showed just the opposite. People were the least creative when they were fighting the clock'. This had implications for Antoneta because a shop manager is always 'fighting the clock'. If creativity and innovation were to be promoted they needed to give their managers more time to think, and this doesn't come free of charge. 'Employers like the idea of innovation ... but people are not given the time and resources to think things through' (McKie, 2002).

An organizational climate in which innovation is blocked or stifled will cause frustration for certain of its members and will reduce overall effectiveness. Some useful people will leave whilst others, like Olivia Marlowe, will be difficult to manage. Paul Sloane, who writes and lectures about lateral thinking, says 'If you want innovators in your team look for people with some particularly bad attitudes – the ones with rebellious, contrary and divergent views. These are the people who some might label as troublemakers. But they are not negative or cynical. On the contrary, they are passionate about their views' (Charlton, 2005). There is always a balance to be struck between anarchy and stimulating levels of freedom, but this is part of management's role and can't be evaded without adverse consequences.

Antoneta's management were wise enough to see the need to step back and take a look at their organization, which can sometimes be easier to do through an outsider's eyes. By making relatively small but important changes they have put their company back on course to remain competitive and successful in a very challenging market.

Narrative No 12: Latcho Security Systems

Background

Latcho Security was formed in 1995 by the amalgamation of two old-established companies. One, P D Jefferson, was a family firm run for the past 15 years by the founder's grandson, Jim Jefferson. The firm specialized in electrical engineering and had an enviable reputation for quality and service. Jim is a first-rate electrical engineer himself, well known in the profession and a frequent lecturer and author of technical papers. He values people who, like himself, are highly qualified and able to make their own mark on the electrical engineering world.

The company had always invested heavily in research and development and held a number of patents, several of which were the result of Jim Jefferson's own work.

Salaries at Jefferson were roughly average, but formal qualifications were an automatic route to higher pay and sponsored study was available to virtually everyone. This policy continued after the merger. Jim was an adequate business manager, but would be the first to admit that he finds administration tedious and would rather get back to the technological problems which are his real passion in life.

The other firm involved in the merger, AMT (which used to stand for Anglian Machine Tools) was originally in the mechanical engineering business, and also had a good reputation. Its CEO, Paul Allen, is a self-made man of little formal education, although highly intelligent and quick to recognize the value of theoretical knowledge, provided it can be applied to real-world problems. Paul believes in on-the-job training and always encouraged supervisors to take an interest in developing their staff, although sponsored external training was unusual in AMT.

The company had some very skilled people, who tended to stay with AMT, possibly to some extent because AMT recognized their skills whilst other potential employers questioned their lack of formal qualifications. AMT paid very well, and erratically paid out big bonuses when major contracts were won or when individuals did something noteworthy. Paul enjoyed running AMT and just got involved enough on the engineering side to keep his hand in.

Despite their very different backgrounds Jim and Paul had been good friends for years. Their businesses were mainly complementary, although there was a small area of overlap where they competed fiercely and with great enjoyment, in much the same way as they competed at golf. But by the early 1990s both companies had been feeling the cold wind of competition and had reluctantly begun to face up to the harsh truth that neither business had much future; there was almost nothing they could make or sell that couldn't now be obtained from multinational corporations at prices they couldn't hope to match. For a while Jim and Paul discussed the gloomy outlook from the perspective of two individuals with separate problems simply commiserating with each other, but gradually the idea began to take shape that perhaps there could be something they could do jointly which would make the prospects look brighter.

For several years a fairly minor part of AMT's business had been assembling burglar alarm units which were mainly purchased by very small installation companies. There was a reasonable profit margin on these units and the company often got requests for adaptations or non-standard facilities. When Paul mentioned this Jim Jefferson became thoughtful. Over the next few months the two friends knocked ideas back and forth between them, did some research and gradually developed a business plan. By the spring of 1994 they were ready go into the industrial and domestic security business and a year later, with the approval of their shareholders, the two companies merged, with Paul as CEO and Jim as Technical Director.

Savings were made by selling off the former AMT premises, and some staff savings were made through a voluntary redundancy/early retirement offer. A few employees who were already over the normal retirement age were also allowed to take the 'package', which made an excellent impression on those who remained. Both companies had always had good staff relations and this seemed to survive the merger intact, although some employees were naturally apprehensive about the proposed change of direction. Latcho now employs approximately 230 people.

The new company thrived. In practice, the change was relatively smooth as existing business ran down slowly and the security business developed steadily until eventually it was the new company's only activity, although in fact quite a wide range of products and services were involved. Staff were retrained to manufacture, assemble and install the security systems, and the R&D people were kept fully occupied expanding the product portfolio and designing custom adaptations to suit specialized requirements.

Jim Jefferson and Paul Allen worked well together. They did have disagreements, but recognized each other's strengths and managed to resolve their differences without impairing their friendship. Morale in the company was good, once things had settled down after the merger. Initially the different approaches to pay and qualifications had caused some friction, but the two principals had both managed to compromise a little and by 1998 they had a prosperous company, punching above its weight in terms of market share and optimistic about the outlook.

The situation

Problems began for Latcho in a very small, almost unnoticed kind of way. In the first couple of years the R&D team, almost all of whom were ex-Jefferson people with one or two later additions, had been fully occupied in developing the new product range. In this they had been led by customer demand, relayed to them via the customer contact people. As Latcho's staff became familiar with the market they were able to define requirements, for which R&D then devised solutions.

The basic needs were, in fact, quite simple, consisting mainly of surveillance and recording equipment and various kinds of alarms. The differentiators were mostly in the detailed design: cosmetic factors, reliability, size and cost. To address these needs Latcho concentrated on producing their own distinctive versions of products which were already well understood in the market. Jeffersons had been ahead of the game in applying innovative and, usually, cost-effective technology to product design and the radical change in the customer base actually made surprisingly little difference to the daily work in R&D.

The time came, however, when Latcho's product range covered just about every need reported by the field staff. Reliability was excellent and Latcho were able to undercut the competition with their charges for routine maintenance whilst still showing a very healthy profit on this activity. Product upgrades were continuous, but tended to be undemanding as far as R&D were concerned; new components became available which were smaller and/or more powerful than before, and these were incorporated into existing designs, but there really wasn't any pressing need for the kind of cutting-edge development work they had been used to at Jeffersons. Being highly motivated technicians this didn't deter some of them.

New product ideas continued to come out of R&D and its staff would lobby the field people and management for support. Jim Jefferson certainly didn't discourage this. He completely understood, and shared, the passion for 'pushing the technological envelope' and he took the view that for every half-dozen ideas that would go nowhere there was one potential winner.

Paul Allen saw it very differently. He thought of R&D in much the same way as he thought of component suppliers; if a need was identified he wanted something to meet that need, quickly and cheaply. If there was no specific need he didn't want to spend money on keeping R&D people amused. As he put it: 'if I'm not going anywhere I don't buy petrol'. Jim Jefferson argued that the R&D unit had to be kept operational, or it wouldn't be there when it really was needed, and Paul understood that perfectly well.

He also understood, although he wouldn't concede the point to Jim, that the staff had to be kept occupied otherwise they would soon find other jobs. In the end an unsatisfactory compromise was reached whereby Paul wouldn't concern himself over much with what went on in R&D, so long as they responded rapidly when called on, but he wouldn't provide a budget for what he considered to be little more than hobby activities. The department complement was to be cut by not filling two vacant posts. Jim reluctantly agreed to this, thinking himself quite lucky that he was able to keep the department more or less intact and understanding at an intellectual level, if not at an emotional one, the need for rigorous budget control.

Back in R&D the ruling caused frustration. They were pleased to have permission to pursue their own schemes and projects, which removed some uncertainty and apprehension, but in most cases it wasn't actually possible to do so without funding. Some of the undoubted intellectual talent in the department turned towards the existing product range and a stream of suggested enhancements began to make its way to the field staff and management. Most of these had little or no commercial application and would simply have added cost and maintenance overheads without bringing in any additional revenues, but one or two provided genuine customer benefits and were adopted.

For Paul Allen this was what R&D was for, and Jim Jefferson didn't disagree with this. All the same, he was concerned that his talented team would soon begin to drift away and he still harboured dreams that his people might come up with a new 'killer product' that would make Latcho's reputation. The chances of this happening seemed to dwindle as time went by and the morale in R&D slowly but steadily declined.

A possible way round the problem presented itself to Jim Jefferson out of the blue. He was having dinner with a friend, a fellow engineer who worked for a major manufacturer of construction machinery, who enthused to Jim about a project he was working on. It seemed to Jim, who didn't know much about the construction business, to have very little to do with the company's mainstream products and he questioned his friend about it. 'Oh yes' he was told 'it's my personal project. It's skunkwork'.

Jim had heard the term before and thought it sounded devious and not quite respectable. 'What happens if the company finds out?' he asked. But apparently it was accepted practice in his friend's company for engineers to have semi-private projects going on. No time or budget were allowed for this unofficial activity, but a certain amount of 'padding' was built in to the approved projects under the heading of contingency requirements which, if not required, could be utilized by project staff with no questions asked.

Jim was amazed. Having run his own company for many years he had often allowed people to work on their own ideas; it was part of his philosophy of management, but he couldn't imagine letting people divert funds, and time, to private initiatives without formal authorization. He was also fairly sure that Paul wouldn't like it at all. Back in his office at Latcho he started to review the time and budget allocations of all the official work in R&D. As he had thought, it was all fairly tight, but past experience had made him insist on realistic estimates so there was a certain amount of contingency allowance on most jobs.

He pondered the idea for several days and when a senior member of the R&D team came to argue the case for a pet design he wanted to work on Jim said, almost on the spur of the moment; 'OK, work on it alongside your work on the Newbury job and book the time and costs to that budget head'. When his subordinate had gone away, delighted if a little stunned, Jim wondered whether he had just done something he would regret. However, time went by, the Newbury project was still brought to a successful completion and the atmosphere in R&D had perked up a little. So the next time someone came with a similar request Jim didn't hesitate very long in giving his approval.

After a while people stopped asking. It became accepted that 'skunkwork' was allowed so long as official work didn't suffer and approved budgets weren't exceeded. In fact, several quite useful developments came about as a result of this hands-off attitude and neither Paul nor any of the other directors seemed to notice. If they did, they raised no objection. The atmosphere in R&D had never been more positive. Everyone seemed absorbed in their work. Budgets, which Jim had often had a struggle to get people to take seriously, were now regarded with a kind of reverence and bringing work in on time and on or even under budget had become a matter of considerable pride. Even Paul Allen was impressed and began to take a supportive interest in the work in R&D, which previously he had regarded as Jim's domain.

Paul's awakened interest led to his asking R&D people questions about their work. He was always well informed about the development projects which were in progress because he knew why they were needed. His questions were intelligent and he was liberal with his encouragement. He respected superior knowledge, wherever he encountered it, and his interest was genuine. People liked talking to him because he always listened to them.

Women are badly under-represented in engineering disciplines in the UK and it was partly because of this that Jim had taken a particular (but entirely professional) interest in the career of one of his staff, Anna Rossini, who was studying part-time for a PhD. Paul regarded academic qualifications as purely instrumental but knew that Jim regarded them as very important so he accepted the cost of supporting people like Anna as a necessary overhead.

When he met Anna in the staff canteen he asked her how her studies were going. During the conversation he learned that she was working on a design for efficient electricity generation from streams and rivers, which he thought was fairly interesting in a casual kind of way until he heard that she had nearly completed a prototype device in the company's laboratory. He asked a few more questions and said he would look in later in the week and see for himself. Anna was pleased and flattered, but Paul had realized from her answers that her prototype must have cost a fair amount and he thought the company was probably paying for it. He couldn't see much connection between Anna's project and Latcho's business so he wanted to know where the funds were coming from. When he next saw Jim Jefferson he asked him outright how Anna's project was being funded.

Jim and Paul liked and respected each other and had always discussed everything to do with the business before making any important decisions. Jim had never really felt comfortable keeping Paul in the dark about the skunkworks and now that Paul had asked a direct question he explained just how private projects like Anna's were being funded. Paul was furious. The two friends had argued before, frequently, but Jim had never seen Paul so angry. They both went home to cool off but the next day relations were very strained. Jim felt terrible.

He knew he should have kept Paul in the picture but even worse he realized that the reason he hadn't done so was because he knew, or guessed, that Paul wouldn't approve. He was all too aware that Paul knew this too. He apologized unreservedly for his 'economy with the truth' and offered to stop the skunkworks immediately. Paul, who was not a volatile man and knew the dangers of making decisions whilst emotions were running high, said he would take a couple of days to think about it.

At this point Latcho's Finance Director (a friend of a friend of mine, to whom I'm indebted for this narrative) took a hand. He has all the characteristics of a stereotypical accountant and might have been expected to favour tight control of every penny. However, he had his finger on the pulse of many aspects of Latcho's organizational life besides its financial affairs and he now pointed out to Paul that the R&D department was actually functioning extremely well. The unofficial work was in effect costing the company nothing because its costs were at least balanced by the benefits in kind of a committed and increasingly financially responsible workforce. He recommended that Paul should approve the unorthodox status quo.

Paul regretted his row with Jim, although he didn't for one moment think it had been his fault. He still believed that Jim had been wrong to conceal the use of company resources in the way he had and, to be fair, Jim now thought so too. After considerable hard thinking, Paul decided to go along with the skunkworks. He and Jim settled their differences and Jim was delighted that he wasn't going to have to pull the plug on the various projects that were going on in the background.

Both men were aware that they had come close to losing the trust there had always been between them and saw the episode as both a lucky escape and a valuable learning experience. Latcho is still in business and expanding at a slow but healthy rate.

Analysis

There are two important themes in the Latcho story. The first is the need for creative people to be allowed to create. The term 'skunkwork' seems to have been first used by Lockheed during the Second World War, although the name derives from an American comic strip called L'il Abner, drawn by Al Capp. It didn't originally mean unofficial or private work, but rather something secret and out of the mainstream. The more common meaning of the term now, as I've used it here, is for something that hasn't been approved, but which management vaguely know about and tolerate unofficially.

Augsdörfer (2004) says there are 'other names for it and some are firm specific: Friday afternoon work; work behind the fume cupboard; freelance work; under the counter work; under the table work; pet-project; discretionary research; intrapreneurship; free wheeling; illicit research; scrounging; renegades work; work in the shadow- or underworld. Also very imaginative are the French, which call it "research under the wick" or the Germans, which call it U-Boot, where a new product suddenly emerges on the commercial surface like submarines suddenly breaking the sea surface'. The message of all this is that skunkwork is quite widespread, which wouldn't be the case if it didn't have benefits for the organizations that tolerate it.

In the case of Latcho Security, the benefit was that it allowed the creative people in R&D to pursue their own agendas, which made them happy. However, this freedom wasn't unconditional. Project budgets and deadlines still had to be met and the staff in effect were utilizing the slack in the schedules and budgets which they had created for themselves. The firm gained because staff developed a new respect for budgets and schedules, which they had previously regarded more as guidelines than fixed parameters. Also, the freedom the staff enjoyed led to enhanced commitment and engagement, which led in turn to more effective work by the people concerned.

Stenmark (2000) studied the effects of allowing people to pursue their own projects in a Swedish motor company. He concluded that 'self-initiated activities are powerful because they are driven primarily by intrinsic motivation'. He goes on 'It is recognized that creativity often requires extra-ordinary dedication and commitment, and that most employees would willingly do far more than the company could possibly ask of them if only they were allowed to work with things in which they were really interested'. He suggests that permission to work on a personal project can be a far more effective motivational mechanism than financial rewards, which seems to be borne out by events at Latcho.

The second theme here is that 'trust is a fragile commodity. Like glass, once shattered, it is never the same again' (Handy, 1985). By concealing his actions from his colleague Jim Jefferson ran a severe risk of destroying their relationship. Whilst the friendship seems to have survived, it is predictable that it will take some time for trust to be fully restored, if it ever is.

The essentials of this chapter:

- Without innovation organizations rapidly fall behind their competitors.
- Innovation and creativity are not the same thing. Innovation is the process of implementing creative ideas. Innovators don't have to be creative themselves, but they do have to recognize and respect creativity in others.
- If creative people never get the chance to see their ideas implemented they will either stop producing ideas or go somewhere else where their talents are valued.
- Innovation doesn't always work. The freedom to innovate implies freedom to make mistakes.
- Innovation isn't free; it uses time and money, but it can be highly cost-effective. It takes a highly competent management team to understand and make use of this.

12

On purposive threat

In time we hate that which we often fear.

William Shakespeare; Cleopatra, in *Antony and Cleopatra*

Narrative No 13: Smith Jospin Construction

Background

Smith Jospin is a major construction and civil engineering company. It dates back to the mid-nineteenth century, when one Elias Smith built a row of six terraced houses in Bristol and made a substantial profit from their sale, which he reinvested in further construction projects. Over the years the company's fortunes have been extremely mixed. There have been two bankruptcies and several mergers, both voluntary and forced, culminating in an agreed merger with Fred Jospin and Sons in the late 1970s.

Today's company is one of the UK's larger plc's and has won some very big public and private contracts including commercial premises, civic buildings, housing developments, hospitals, schools, roads and bridges. Its success in these fiercely competitive bidding contests has been attributed to ruthless cost-cutting and it has been alleged by disgruntled rivals that some of its bids have been unrealistically low, depending for eventual profitability on overpricing subsequent change requests. On the rare occasions when Smith Jospin has bothered to answer such charges it has dismissed them as no more than sour grapes, pointing out the many projects which have been brought in on time and budget.

However, it has been forced more than once to defend itself in the courts against accusations of not meeting its contractual obligations. It was recently sued over the late delivery of a major government building in the north of England but was able to show, or at least to convince the court, that its contract terms didn't oblige it to complete the work by any particular date – to the client's considerable surprise. On the whole, though, it has a solid reputation, and its bridges don't fall down.

The company directly employs several thousand people as 'staff', and tens of thousands more either as casual labour or through sub-contractors. Most of the permanent staff are based at Smith Jospin's headquarters in west London, although many spend much of their time on location. For staff members pay and conditions are fairly good, although this doesn't apply to the 'casuals', who get strictly the market rate for their skills, and the company doesn't ask its sub-contractors about their employees. There are no frills, though. The company was one of the first in

175

the UK to drop its (far from generous) final salary pension scheme and it has never offered other forms of reward.

Emma Litchford qualified as a civil engineer in 1990 and began work as a junior planner with one of Smith Jospin's competitors, where she achieved successive promotions and eventually ran out of 'head room'. She moved to Smith Jospin in 2000 as a Project Manager, although this title was used rather freely in Smith Jospin and in fact she had never been given overall responsibility for an entire project, even a small one. In the summer of 2001 the company won a contract to build a major shopping complex in the west of England, involving a large central mall, outlying shops and leisure facilities, car parks and access roads. Emma was assigned to the project team and in due course put in charge of access.

Work on the project was supposed to begin in January 2002 but continuous heavy rain delayed site clearance. When this was eventually begun it was discovered that large areas of the site were waterlogged just below the surface. Since part of the shopping complex and associated service areas were to be below ground level this represented a serious concern and extensive additional drainage systems had to be incorporated into the plans.

No financial or schedule allowance had been made for this in the contract and the client pointed out that a comprehensive topographical survey had been made available to Smith Jospin when they were invited to tender for the work; they should have known that there would be drainage issues and couldn't now offload the consequential costs or change the agreed completion date. The project was therefore in some difficulty from the start; it would be hard to show a profit on the job unless there were substantial chargeable change requests, and if the job wasn't finished on time there would be penalty charges to pay for every day it over-ran.

The situation

To begin with Emma found the project interesting and her own work on it moderately challenging; it was certainly the biggest job she had been involved in so far. From the start, though, she was aware of a rather odd atmosphere among her colleagues. At the first weekly project team meeting she attended she thought everyone seemed defensive.

From experience she knew that there was always a lot of uncertainty at this very early stage in a project, with things to clarify and issues to sort out, but although people asked plenty of questions, as far as she could tell none of the queries were about people's own work. She came away with the distinct impression that it 'wasn't done' to acknowledge any uncertainty about one's own area of responsibility. She also learned that the leader of the bid team and three of her people had left the company. It wasn't explicitly admitted that they had been sacked because of the groundwater problems but it seemed highly likely. Emma took note of all this and resolved to make sure that nothing went wrong with her part of the project.

It was clear to everyone that bringing the project in on time was going to be a close call. The Project Director was a quietly spoken but forceful character who listened to everyone's contribution to discussions and then gave clear instructions. He seemed to be aware of everything that was going on. Emma felt that she could work with him successfully and learn from him.

Her first task was to provide an access road which would be used for site access during the construction and subsequently as the main service road into the shopping complex. It would therefore be subject to some very heavy use initially by construction machinery and thereafter by delivery lorries as well as lighter vehicles. It was clear that the unexpectedly soft terrain required more substantial foundations than had originally been planned but Emma was sure she could handle this without major problems.

The design work, of course, wasn't her responsibility, but she knew and worked alongside the surveyors and other professionals, and she understood her own role very well. Whilst the access road was under construction Emma felt that the eyes of everyone on the project were on her because until the road was ready for use the site was only accessible to the very heaviest machinery and all-terrain vehicles. No one could get fully up to speed and the Project Director, who carried overall responsibility for the contract, was constantly calling her mobile phone for up-to-the-minute progress reports. As far as Emma was concerned the work was progressing more or less to schedule, but she was in no doubt that the Director was far from satisfied. She got the idea that colleagues were trying to avoid her but dismissed this as pure imagination.

With at least a week's work remaining on the task the Director called Emma to say that the plans had been revised yet again and he needed the access road ready for use by construction traffic two days earlier than scheduled. Emma knew exactly what remained to be done and explained the position to him; she was confident that the previously agreed date could be met but she doubted whether it could be improved. The Director was calm but insistent. It was Emma's responsibility, he told her, to deliver her own tasks according to the current plan. In Smith Jospin people were judged by results. Emma was already worried and this did nothing to reassure her, but she took the message to heart and spent every hour of the next few days urging her people to greater efforts. She took her paperwork home with her and got very little sleep.

The access road was eventually ready for use a full day ahead of the previous schedule. The last day was traumatic because the Director insisted that the job was 'late' and called her repeatedly to ask when the road would be open. Emma believed she had done well to shave a day off the original date and felt disappointed that instead of acknowledging her achievement the Director took her aside and reminded her that the project schedule was everyone's responsibility. The rest of the tasks assigned to her 'needed to be delivered on time'. Still, with this highly visible task completed she was able to turn her attention to the many other elements of the project for which she was responsible, none of which would have much impact on the rest of the work until shortly before completion.

The Project Director hardly bothered her at all apart from routine interactions at weekly project meetings when she spoke briefly to report progress on her 'work packages', which fortunately were mainly on schedule. Other members of the team had more significant problems which made them the centre of attention. By the half-way stage of the project two of Emma's colleagues had been replaced and at least one other, to Emma's own knowledge, had been warned that he had to push his tasks forward if he wanted to stay on the project.

Emma's next problem concerned a section of car park which should have been surfaced in time for a site inspection by the client's senior management team. The idea was that they would be able to drive up to the main entrance to the shopping mall, park where the shoppers would eventually park their cars, and go in to the still roofless building to view the work in progress. However, it hadn't been possible to complete the surfacing work because sub-contractors were running late installing cables and other services under the proposed car park area. If Emma had proceeded with the surfacing it would have had to be dug up again and subsequently reinstated.

The Director told her that it was each project manager's responsibility to overcome obstacles in their own area of the project, implying that if the car park wasn't surfaced in time for the visit he would hold her responsible. Emma protested that she had no control over the sub-contractors, there were deep trenches across the area and it simply wasn't possible to do as she was being instructed. Since this was, in fact, perfectly obvious the Director had to accept the situation but Emma had no doubt that she would be blamed if events didn't proceed according to plan. She made the best of the situation by arranging for a strip of surfacing to be laid to a point as close as possible to the entrance and a temporary walkway installed from there. It didn't look good, took almost a day to implement and had to be stripped out afterwards; all wasted time and expense to Emma's mind, but she felt she had got away with it this time.

A second incident was potentially more serious. Part of the site of the new mall required a section of hillside to be cut away, leaving level ground with a steep bank behind. Emma wasn't responsible for this task but was peripherally involved because one of her access roads would eventually run behind the new buildings on the fringe of the level ground. Whilst the ground was being levelled a minor landslip occurred and a heavy digging machine slid down the embankment. The driver was hurt and the machine damaged, and several days' additional work was incurred in shoring up the embankment.

Emma's colleague who was responsible for that particular groundwork was dismissed. Emma thought this was unfair, because surveyors had inspected the hillside and given the go-ahead before work began; there was no possible way that Emma's colleague could have anticipated the accident. She had her own problems with the incident, however, because for a while it seemed that she would share the blame. Once again she was told that Project Managers were responsible for all aspects of the tasks assigned to them, but was 'let off' with a warning.

Emma, relatively new to the job and fairly sure in her own mind that she was performing competently, now began to feel seriously worried about the effects this project, and this Project Director, might be having on her career prospects. She was sleeping badly, and found herself checking and rechecking every aspect of her work. Even though her own deadlines were now 'off the critical path' of the project she felt that she couldn't let anything over-run, but her obsessive attention to detail was making everything take longer than it should. She became short-tempered and the easy familiarity of her relationships with her own team began to cool and become more formal.

By late summer the project was nearing completion and there seemed a real possibility that it would still be possible to perform the handover to the client on the contractually agreed date. Emma had successfully completed most of the road systems and car parking for which she was responsible. Her one remaining task was the installation of an escalator and footbridge from the local station. Emma had worked on railway projects before and felt confident that she could handle this one.

The escalator had been ordered from a specialist supplier and would be installed by their engineers. Emma had to coordinate this work and manage the construction of the footbridge by Smith Jospin people. As work began on this task the Project Director came to see it for himself. Emma was sure she had thought of everything and was eager to show her boss that she was in control. He seemed satisfied but as he left he warned her: 'you do realize that this is a high-visibility installation?'. She assured him that she did. He went on: 'some very important people use this station and time's running out. We don't want any more mistakes'. His meaning was clear. Emma's performance wasn't considered satisfactory and this was her last chance. If she got this wrong her future looked very uncertain.

For a while everything went according to plan. The escalator was installed ready for testing and the pylons which were to support the bridge were constructed. Each day, and sometimes two or three times in a day, the Project Director called Emma to check progress. Each call left her more concerned and she began to worry whether she might have missed something vital. The day before the task was due for completion there was a hold-up in delivery of the prefabricated walkway for the bridge, which had to be in place for testing the escalator. After many increasingly frantic calls to the suppliers it finally arrived late in the afternoon. With no possibility of getting it installed in normal hours Emma authorized overtime for the workers and had some floodlights rigged so that work could go on through the night. This would certainly exceed the budget allocated for the task but Emma felt she had no choice; better that than over-run.

The job was completed ready for final testing around two in the morning and the whole team, including Emma, was exhausted. She told everyone to go home and return early the next day. When she arrived on site she found to her alarm that the Project Director was already waiting for her but she put a brave face on and assured him that subject to final testing the job was complete. They went up onto the bridge and Emma gave the signal to test the escalator. As soon as it started rolling it jammed and Emma felt the onset of panic. The engineers made some adjustments to the alignment between the escalator and the bridge and tried again. This time it began to roll smoothly. Emma felt sick with relief. Her last task on the project was successfully completed.

The handover of the project was eventually made two weeks later than contractually agreed. This resulted in liquidated damages amounting to many thousands of pounds but Smith Jospin regarded it as a partial success. They had still made a profit, just not as much as they had hoped. However, over the next six months problems began to develop. Emma's bridge had to be closed when signs of crumbling were noticed in the supporting pylons. The linkage to the escalator shifted on its mountings and extra supporting strips had to be installed. The cost ran into thousands. Within the complex, numerous instances of rushed work and cost-cutting were identified and Smith Jospin were presented with lengthy 'snagging' lists which they were legally obliged to put right. The profits melted away and by the time the complex was finally compliant with its specification the losses were considerable. The Project Director lost his job, as did three more of Emma's colleagues.

Despite the bridge problems, Emma remained with Smith Jospin. Whilst in many ways she would have been glad to get out she was fairly sure that her association with the project would make it difficult to find another job, at least for a while, so she bided her time. It wasn't until early in 2005 that she finally moved to another company. By then she had worked on two other, smaller, projects which had been more successful and she felt that her CV was once again fairly respectable.

Her new employer sponsored her to attend a training course which is where I heard her account. I asked what she thought was the most significant part of her experience with Smith Jospin and why she thought there had been so many subsequent problems. She said: 'People were scared. The company let you know that you'd be out if you didn't perform and that went all the way through. The Project Director was under that pressure, he put us under the same pressure and we were supposed to pass it down to our people. I can't work like that. I did my best to shield my people from it but I couldn't always do it. I got to the point where I felt that I was just waiting for it to happen, really. I saw other people lose their jobs. I still suffer from it now. It really sort of finished me off, to be perfectly honest, because I got so worn down by it. All my projects had gone well, this was the first one that had gone badly. What happened was that people cut corners. Everyone had to cover their own backs so they did whatever they had to so that no one could point the finger. It was only later that all that started to come to light'.

Analysis

Robert Heller (1994) says 'The theory of management by fear doesn't appear in any textbooks or feature in any seminars; nor is it taught in any business schools. Yet MBF may be more pervasive than any other influence on individual performance and corporate results'. Smith Jospin is a company which believes that the way to get people to perform is to make them understand that there will be painful consequences if they don't come up to scratch. As Heller says, this is still a widespread opinion amongst organizational management and, as I found when I researched the subject, among people who are actually on the receiving end of its consequences:

> There were mixed opinions on whether a level of purposive threat was likely to be conducive to enhanced performance. Several informants were fairly clear that it was unhelpful, whilst others suggested, with varying emphasis, that some beneficial effect on performance might result from the application of coercive pressure, on themselves or others.
>
> Gray, 2001b

In a general sense, when people feel threatened their response depends on how much control they perceive themselves to have over the situation (Schachter and Singer, 1962). If they think they can handle the threat they are likely to feel anger, if they don't they are likely to feel fear. Anger makes us want to fight, and in the workplace this can take the form of 'militancy or support for extremist viewpoints. Or it may go further, including denigrating the organisation or senior personalities, or even direct sabotage of procedures, systems, or property' (Gray, 2004).

Fear leads, at least superficially, to compliance, but it's likely that this will be without enthusiasm and the heightened stress levels are likely to lead to lower quality work, poor decision-making, disengagement and resentment. A more satisfactory resolution may be to remove oneself from the threatening situation. The people who are most likely to be able to do this are those who have the highest 'market value' to alternative employers; just the kind of people most companies would want to retain.

Emma Litchford found herself threatened, if not initially with the loss of her job, at least with damage to her career. The intention of these threats was undoubtedly to focus her mind on the task in hand and force her to take care of every detail. She responded by trying to do just that, which is a natural response and helps to explain why so many people still believe in this management style. However, a more significant effect was that she and others in the same position became more concerned with the negative goal of avoiding penalties than with the positive one of doing the best possible job. As Heller says: 'People running scared are likely to go the wrong way – away from the action'.

Emma found her confidence drained so that she had to check and recheck everything she – and others – did. This is undesirable for two reasons: first, if people know that the boss will check everything they do the responsibility is transferred from them to the boss. They are likely to do what the boss tells them and no more. The second effect is the obvious one that all that checking of detail takes valuable time and distracts from the broad view. The result is likely to be less effective work. My own research confirms this tendency: 'Analysis of purposive threat levels and project success, however, shows a clear negative correlation, calculated as -0.4, between purposive threat and successful project outcomes' (Gray, 2001b). The message here is: threats don't belong in the manager's toolbox – their effects are likely to be counter-productive.

Narrative No 14: Branton, Boardman, Stephens

Background

Branton, Boardman, Stephens is a legal firm based in the English Midlands. It has 12 partners, none of whom is named Branton, Boardman or Stephens, and about 20 other qualified solicitors who are employees of the partnership. There are also a few part-qualified solicitors and almost 30 support staff. The firm's history is not unusual in the profession in that it is the product of a long process of mergers and takeovers so that it can (and does) plausibly claim to have been founded in 1862. However, like the old broom that has had five replacement heads and three new handles, there really isn't much connection between today's BBS and the one-man practice founded by J S Stephens, Esq., nearly 150 years ago.

When Jyoti Rasmani joined the firm from university in 1993, BBS had a varied practice covering all the routine legal requirements of a provincial town: commercial, personal and criminal. Her continued training at BBS took up a further four years, first in part-time study of the Legal Practice Course, followed by two more years as an 'official' trainee solicitor. Over this period she was able to get an introduction to most of these areas and by the time she was fully qualified she had decided that the variety and interest of general practice would provide most of what she wanted from her career in the profession.

Jyoti's emergence as a fully qualified solicitor coincided with changes in the legal aid (public funding) system in England and the beginning of the *conditional fee agreement* arrangement, better known as 'no win no fee', by which solicitors would take on the risk of a civil action, often moderated by insurance cover, in the knowledge that a successful action would result in their fees being paid by the respondent.

Several of the BBS partners were eager to seize this opportunity for additional business whilst others, either because they were more traditionally-minded or because their main interests were in commercial or criminal work, thought it was both undignified and risky. The discussion went on for some time but in the end the observation that whilst BBS dithered other legal firms seemed to be making money from the new system gave the 'modernizers' the upper hand and the firm began taking on no win no fee business.

The situation

Almost from the start Jyoti found herself uncomfortable with the work she was asked to do. She had no problem with the actual work of pursuing claims on behalf of clients who had suffered losses or injuries; that had been a standard part of her job since she joined BBS, even before she qualified. Now, though, she was doing very little else and she felt that her career was being funnelled into an increasingly narrow range against her will.

This was compounded by concerns about the methods being used by BBS to exploit the commercial opportunities the new system offered. Publicly funded work, previously known as legal aid cases, had never been very profitable but had provided a basic level of business on which junior lawyers could cut their teeth. The conditional fee arrangements, if carefully selected (or cherry-picked, as Jyoti perceived it) could be much more lucrative. After a slow start BBS was now doing well out of this work and more of the firm's efforts were being diverted into it. With this change of focus came what Jyoti felt were changes in the character of the firm she had joined as an idealistic young graduate.

Initially, in the time-honoured fashion of the English legal system, BBS had waited for clients to come to them. Now they were energetically, even aggressively, marketing their services to the public. Agents were employed on commission to bring in business and more than once Jyoti had learned from clients that the tactics used by these agents had been very persuasive. In some cases accident victims had been approached in hospital and invited to make claims through BBS. Conversely, the firm sometimes refused to take on perfectly valid smaller claims which, as Jyoti knew, could often be very important to the client in both personal and financial terms. She felt that this was unethical and it was certainly not the way BBS had handled things in the past, but her objections were dismissed as 'unrealistic' when she raised her concerns with her boss.

At the beginning BBS had required clients to take out insurance policies, financed in some cases by loans arranged by the firm itself, to cover costs if their case was lost. Even where the case was successful, repaying these loans could eat into the compensation awarded and if expert witness fees were involved it some-times happened that even successful litigants could end up with little or nothing at the end of the process.

This situation eased a little when BBS found itself losing business to firms which offered guarantees that clients would never have to pay the insurance premiums; if it proved impossible to recover the costs from the respondent they would be written off. The BBS partners didn't like this idea much but they realized that it was a marketing ploy they would have to adopt if they were to stay competitive. Jyoti felt that this was, at least, a small concession to what she regarded as good practice, but she soon discovered that it made BBS even more reluctant to take on the lower value, or lower profile, cases so on balance it didn't represent much of an improvement.

Along with what she saw as the distortion of her workload, the new commercial orientation of BBS brought economic changes for Jyoti. As a student and even as a trainee solicitor her pay had been, frankly, derisory. After qualification she had been put on a slightly more reasonable salary but it was still not enough to allow her the kind of lifestyle she associated with members of 'the professions'. However, she knew that this was quite normal and that the compensation for the slow start, in terms of remuneration, would come as she moved up the seniority levels within the firm. This was something which all new solicitors at BBS could reasonably expect if they were competent and conscientious, and Jyoti was both.

As BBS transformed itself from an old-fashioned firm of professional advisers into a dynamic business enterprise, the partners began looking to the commercial world for ideas about how to maximize profits and improve performance. They had already, in a sense, adopted the principle of payment by results when they accepted the new no win no fee approach. This led naturally on to the payment of commissions to agents for introducing clients and from there it was a relatively short step to the concept of performance-related pay for their own employees.

Jyoti, though, hadn't seen this coming and was taken by surprise when her boss told her, enthusiastically, that in future she would be able to boost her income considerably. He explained that she would be offered a new contract which guaranteed that she would receive basic pay of about two-thirds her current salary, supplemented by a percentage of the profits from every case she handled. Jyoti asked for time to think about it. The revised basic pay would certainly not be enough for her to live on, but the cases she had handled recently had mainly been successful and, based on the explanation her boss had given her, she calculated that the proposed new arrangements would have given her a substantially higher overall income.

After careful thought she decided that she really didn't have very much choice if she wanted to continue her career with BBS. Although it had been made clear to her that she was free to continue on the old basis and she didn't regard either her boss personally or the firm in general as intimidating or unfair, she still felt sure that not accepting the new deal would effectively mean that she wouldn't progress much further. She told her boss the next day that she would accept the new contract and he had seemed genuinely pleased.

For a while the new system worked generally to Jyoti's advantage. Each successful case she worked on brought her additional payments, ranging from token amounts where she was a minor contributor, through to quite substantial figures where she took the lead. When a case was unsuccessful she got nothing, but overall her monthly income was never less than it had been before and frequently much higher. The only down side to all this was that she found herself actively participating in the new BBS culture of cherry-picking cases. She felt bad the first time she turned a case down because, despite its good prospects of a successful conclusion, there was very little profit in it. The next time it was a little easier and after a while she got used to it. Her next moral dilemma was when she found herself tempted to advise a prospective client to drop a case because the workload it entailed made it unattractive. She pulled herself up short, realizing that knowingly to give unsound advice was a professional Rubicon she wasn't willing to cross, but she found herself thinking very hard about her situation.

After talking things over with friends and family, and with one of her former university tutors (who subsequently asked her to tell me about her experiences), she decided that for the sake of her own self-esteem she would have to take control of her case load. Over the next few months she put questions of profitability ruthlessly aside and accepted cases purely on their own merits. This had two consequences. First that her income dropped significantly, although she was still earning more than she had under the old contract. Second, she began to get increasingly anxious enquiries from her boss about her 'performance', meaning the contribution she was making to profits. Cases with which Jyoti had begun dealing were taken from her and given to more 'reliable' employees and her boss began sending her case briefs with increasing insistence that she take on cases he had selected for her. Rather than provoke a confrontation she did as she was asked and her income began to rise once more. However, employees of Jyoti's status were expected to bring in their own business rather than simply handle work found for them by the partners, so her performance in this respect still didn't exactly delight her boss.

She found herself trapped in a situation she had neither wanted nor willingly accepted. To earn enough to meet her needs she had to be selective about the cases she took on and this meant turning away cases she thought were deserving. Often the prospects of success in the courts for these cases were problematic, but there was a much better prospect of settling out of court, at a reduced level of damages. This didn't fit the profile of an 'attractive' case for BBS.

The work she did take on almost always had a high probability of success in the courts, and therefore an even higher prospect of a more substantial out of court settlement. Jyoti didn't always feel the cases were very deserving. In fact, she thought some of them came close to being fraudulent. She wished she could go back to the kind of general practice – honest and fairly rewarded – for which she had entered the profession, but by now she was dependent on the 'performance-related pay' which brought her basic salary up to a viable level.

In 2004 Branton, Boardman, Stephens figured in a highly critical report by a consumer group in which they, among other law firms, were accused of 'ambulance chasing' – misleading clients about fees and giving bad advice about the admissibility of claims. There had already been two complaints to the Law Society about BBS's conduct of cases, both of which had eventually been rejected but which had tarnished the firm's reputation and brought it to the group's attention. As a direct consequence the firm had been the subject of an intensive investigation including a 'sting' operation in which bogus clients approached BBS for advice. BBS maintained that their advice had been sound and made veiled threats of legal action but the consumer group stood its ground and after a little more sabre rattling BBS backed down. One of the bogus cases was one of those that had been taken from Jyoti and she realized that she could easily have been named in the scandal, although she was sure that the advice that she would have given would have been legally correct and above board.

Jyoti began making enquiries about alternative employment. It wasn't easy as other firms weren't eager to employ people from BBS, but eventually she was able to find a job with a small firm in another town, where she was able at last to develop her general practice skills. Her pay was less than it had been at BBS, but it wasn't linked to 'performance', except in the sense that as she proved herself to be capable and conscientious her pay was increased. Her ambition is eventually to become a partner in this or another similar firm, but above all to be free of the need to subjugate her better judgement to the need to maintain the performance-related element of her income.

Analysis

The job of a legal adviser involves many ethical choices and over the years systems have developed to provide guidance and protection for all the parties involved. Changes in the basis on which a profession's traditions and procedures are founded are bound to throw up new uncertainties and, realistically, temptations, before things settle into new patterns. Almost all paid work is, in a fundamental sense, market driven in that someone must want or need the services provided and someone must be willing to pay for it. These two 'someones' are not always the same. In the case of legal aid or publicly funded legal work it was private citizens who required the service but the state which paid the bills.

There are other similar three-party relationships in medicine, education and other social and charitable contexts. The UK is in a phase of transition where direct payments are encroaching on state funding in many areas and Jyoti found herself at the start of her career in this situation of transitional turbulence in her own profession. For a while she allowed herself to be carried along with the prevailing mood.

In the case of conditional fee arrangements an early free-for-all quickly attracted severe criticisms. The Citizens Advice Bureau (CAB, 2004) compiled evidence from 385 reports over a two-year period and concluded that: 'There is no effective joined-up system for regulating conditional fee arrangements to ensure consumers are protected on both quality of advice and costs'. The CAB was particularly concerned that 'The system does not deliver anything effective to consumers on rehabilitation. … The arduous legal processes and money only results of our current system of compensation often mean that victims are not being sufficiently helped to resume a normal life in both society and the workplace'. Jyoti was unhappy with her own role in this process but felt unable to escape from it.

Her dependence on the 'performance-related' element in her remuneration locked her into a situation which made her unhappy and damaged her self-esteem. This is not unusual in such systems. My own research showed that supplementary payments of this kind may come to be regarded as part of people's anticipated remuneration, which could be withheld as a kind of penalty if they failed to achieve targets. 'In short, reward mechanisms which were intended to be an incentive came to be regarded effectively as a form of threat' (Gray, 2000b). This is, in fact, a very common kind of purposive threat even though in many (most?) cases it isn't initially intended that way. People who are locked in to a problematic situation by 'golden handcuffs' like this typically have to resolve the psychological conflicts it creates by subconsciously changing their perceptions in some way (Festinger and Carlsmith, 1959) or else risk suffering from varying degrees of stress and depression.

The operation of performance-related pay and other kinds of financial incentives is a highly complex and often counter-intuitive area of psychology and the simplistic assumptions that are often made about it have the potential to be very damaging in a variety of ways. Jyoti was able to resolve her personal 'dissonance' by changing her job. Not everyone finds such a satisfactory way out.

THE ESSENTIALS OF THIS CHAPTER:

- Purposive threats are threats which are consciously directed at individuals to coerce their behaviour or sometimes from malice.
- The perception of threat is in the mind of the recipient. Even if words or actions are not intended to be threatening, if they are perceived as such the consequences will be the same.
- Threats may be positive – that something unpleasant will be done as a penalty for non-compliance, or negative – that some anticipated reward will be withheld. The effects of either form are similar.
- People typically feel either fear or anger as a response to being threatened. If they feel powerless to 'fight back' or get away the probable response is fear. In the workplace this may take the form of worry, concern or stress.

- People may feel that they have no choice but to comply with the wishes of those who threaten them. They are very unlikely to do this with enthusiasm and will suffer stress levels that are likely to result in lower quality work, poor decision-making, disengagement and resentment.
- The most valuable employees may not have to put up with feeling threatened. They are likely to move on at the earliest opportunity.

13

On environmental threat

No one can put in his best performance unless he feels secure.

W Edwards Deming, *Out of the Crisis,* **1986**

Narrative No 15: Broma Stores

Background

Walkers Foodmarkets was a chain of supermarkets with retail outlets in more than 20 towns across north-east England. It began in a small way with one greengrocer's shop in a small town near Newcastle, opened by brother and sister George and Harriet Walker in 1948. The shop flourished, partly because both siblings were astute business people and partly because Harriet insisted from the start on stocking a wider selection of food products than would normally have been found in a greengrocer's shop at that time. Within a few years the couple had three other shops, all within a radius of a few miles.

By this time George and Harriet were both married with children. In the 1950s it was still usual for women to give up work when they married, and certainly when they had children. Harriet continued working after her marriage but she did withdraw from day to day work in the business when her first child was born, whilst retaining her partnership and continuing to be a very active contributor of ideas. She often helped out on the shop floor when necessary and she was a useful troubleshooter when problems arose with suppliers, staff or customers.

As part-owner of a provisions company Harriet managed to avoid much of the routine shopping which burdened many 1950s housewives. Trekking from one shop to another, queuing to be served and, frequently, queuing again to pay was considered quite normal at the time but Harriet had most of her requirements sent from her own shops. When an item she required wasn't stocked Harriet asked why not, and under pressure from her the product range steadily expanded. She soon became convinced that there was no reason why a greengrocer shouldn't supply most kinds of food requirement. In fact, she began to feel that the whole concept of 'greengrocer' was hopelessly old-fashioned. She had visited department stores in the cities and reasoned that a local food shop could operate on the same kind of lines, except on a smaller scale.

George Walker was clever and meticulous, which made him a good business manager. He knew that he didn't have Harriet's imagination but he respected her judgement and gave her vision his full backing. They began by refitting the largest of their shops and taking on experienced staff to handle the new lines of business, such as butchery, which required specialist skills. All this left them quite financially exposed but the change proved to be a masterstroke. Business boomed and the Walkers quickly converted their other shops to the new system. More and bigger shops followed, the partnership became a limited company and innovations such as customer self-selection and checkouts put Walkers Foodmarkets Ltd at the forefront of food retailing in their region.

The company's fortunes suffered the usual vicissitudes over the ensuing decades but the general trend until the early 1980s was expansion and improved profitability. Then profits began to level off and later, to decline gently. All the same, when George decided to retire in 1989 his shares in Walkers were still worth many millions of pounds. Harriet's daughter, Liza Harrington, took over from George as Managing Director whilst Harriet herself continued to take an active, but arms length, interest in the firm.

Meanwhile, the food retailing business in England had changed beyond recognition. The ideas that had put Walkers at the cutting edge in the 1950s were now basic expectations. A handful of giant corporations now controlled the sector and smaller players were increasingly forced to specialize or offer enhanced services to remain competitive. Many didn't survive in the harsh new competitive environment. Harriet had lost none of her business acumen and Liza, who had been to business school, had to agree with her that the future for second division players like Walkers didn't look too rosy. They had already been forced to close three of their shops after one or other of the big chains opened stores nearby, and there was nothing to stop the same thing happening to their entire enterprise.

At a board meeting in 1998 the idea was first discussed, in absolute secrecy, of selling the Walkers enterprise to one of their competitors. Over a period of many months Liza and one or two trusted senior managers let it be known, discreetly, in the right places that Walkers might be prepared to consider sensible offers for their company. As all the shares were held by nine family members, and they were already on side, it took some time for these enquiries to become public knowledge and by the time they did Walkers were already in serious negotiations with Broma Stores.

Broma weren't up with the big four supermarket chains but they did have a substantial market share in north-west England and saw the Walkers shops as a route for expansion into the North East, where they had only a handful of outlets. Walkers was a well-run organization, probably rather better managed than Broma itself, and its shops were almost all in very good locations. With Broma's superior resources behind it there was considerable potential for it to do well. Broma saw it as an attractive acquisition, at the right price.

Walkers' negotiating position was less strong. The leading supermarkets weren't interested in buying-up a smaller competitor, preferring to choose new sites for themselves and build their own outlets from scratch. There was some interest from other operators but they turned out to be mostly hoping to acquire selected Walkers outlets, rather than the whole company. The Walkers negotiators settled down for some hard bargaining whilst Liza and the rest of her senior team concentrated on keeping the company running as though nothing unusual was going on. They even opened another shop during this period.

The situation

Shortly before Christmas of 1999 contracts were signed which transferred ownership of Walkers Foodmarkets Ltd to Broma Stores. The sale price had been less than Walkers had hoped for, but still several of the shareholders began the new millennium as multi-millionaires. Liza had negotiated her own contract with Broma which put her on the board for five years, after which she planned to retire.

Up to this point only a few senior managers had been aware of the takeover plans but now the details of the deal were announced to the rest of the staff. It came as a severe shock and it would hardly be an exaggeration to say that there was something close to panic among some of them. Shop managers had been given no more warning than their staff about the change and the assurance by the senior managers and directors, whom they had never had any reason to distrust in the past, that they would have better security and prospects with Broma only partially eased their concerns. They already knew that competition was fierce and they had heard rumours that Broma were tough people to work for. Their pay and conditions were protected under employment legislation, but their future prospects certainly weren't and they didn't know how they would fit in to the new regime.

Broma had announced that they didn't intend closing any Walkers shops, although in the handful of locations that were served by both Walkers and Broma outlets it was intended that the smaller of the two shops would eventually close and the business transfer to the larger site. Walkers shops would begin selling Broma brands and they would be supplied from Broma's central distribution warehouses. As Broma didn't have sufficient distribution capacity in the area the Walkers central warehouse would be retained. Over time it was intended that one by one all the Walkers shops would have a 'makeover' and would emerge rebadged as Broma outlets. The staff had nothing to worry about as they would all be needed for the new operation.

For a while it looked as though the takeover would go smoothly. As promised, shop floor staff at the Walkers outlets noticed hardly any changes, except that unfamiliar brands began to appear and old ones vanished. For middle and junior managers, too, change came slowly. In some ways, the effect of this was to make matters worse. Senior Broma people visited the Walkers shops regularly and made supportive remarks, congratulating shop managers and junior staff on aspects of their work. Almost every visit included 'suggestions' for small changes which would improve efficiency. These changes, whilst never very radical individually, always took established Walkers practice a step towards the Broma way of doing things.

As had been promised, there were no redundancies, even when two Walkers shops were closed and the trade transferred to nearby Broma premises. In just one instance the move went in the other direction and a smallish Broma outlet was closed, but in all three cases it was the Broma manager who ended up in charge of the merged business, with the Walkers people as deputies. But although no one actually lost their jobs recruitment at Walkers shops was virtually frozen. Broma managers dropped none too subtle hints that they thought Walkers had been over-staffed and this situation needed to be resolved over a fairly short timescale. Where recruitment was essential for operational reasons the vacancies were filled by transferring staff between branches.

It wasn't long before rumours began to spread that Broma were thinking of rationalizing the newly acquired business and this would mean compulsory trans-fers for management-level people as less profitable shops were closed, and extra pressure on everyone as vacancies were left unfilled. There was also talk that the promise of no redundancies might last only for a limited time, after which Walkers people would find themselves being weeded out.

The general atmosphere took a turn for the worse when the time for Walkers' annual pay review came and went without any announcement from the Broma management. At this point officials of the union which represented a small minor-ity of Walkers people tried to contact Broma to make representations on behalf of their members, but Broma said that they didn't recognize any unions and wouldn't discuss employees' pay or conditions with third parties. In fact, Walkers hadn't recognized any unions either; recognition is a formal agreement between an employer and the union and since not many people belonged to a union there had been no pressure for such an agreement.

However, Walkers management hadn't been hostile to unions and had frequently spoken to union officials informally about individual employees' concerns when requested to do so. On at least two occasions union experts had contacted Walkers with specific requests for changes over health and safety issues and Walkers had readily agreed to comply, seeing the requests as quite helpful in terms of protecting employees' welfare (and, of course, avoiding legal complications if there had been any accidents).

Broma took a different view, regarding unions as essentially there to cause trouble. Not enough of their staff were union members for them to be obliged to accept union recognition and they intended to keep it that way for as long as possible. The union backed off at this point but a few more Walkers people made enquiries about membership. Others felt that if the union couldn't do anything for them there wasn't much point in paying the membership dues.

Eventually the pay problem was resolved, in a way, because three months after the missed review at Walkers the time came round when Broma staff pay was reviewed, and the ex-Walkers people were included in this exercise. There was disappointment, though, when the review awarded them only a token increase. It was pointed out that comparable jobs had been more highly paid at Walkers than at Broma, not by much, admittedly, but there was a differential, and so some jobs would have to 'mark time' until pay equalized. A small increase was awarded as a 'gesture of goodwill'. The gestures made by ex-Walkers staff on hearing this were quite unrelated to goodwill.

Few of the ex-Walkers people felt like protesting too loudly, though, because by now they were concerned for their futures. Although the Broma–Walkers agreement had been represented to them as a merger it wasn't long before the reality began to become apparent; that Walkers was effectively consigned to history and ex-Walkers people, at all levels, were now Broma employees and had to do things the Broma way if they wanted their careers to progress. For shop floor employees this didn't really matter too much. They found themselves working, perhaps, a little harder than before because there weren't quite so many of them, and their bosses were just a little less accommodating over shift arrangements and requests for time off, but it was all fairly marginal.

Managers were more directly affected. There were new, more detailed and prescriptive record systems to operate. Targets were made a little tougher and senior management scrutiny became more intrusive. At the same time they began to notice that, contrary to their previous impressions, the market sectors addressed by the two companies had not been quite the same. Most of the customers served by Broma and by Walkers had been very similar, but Walkers' appeal, and product range, had extended to some more discriminating and higher-spending customers. Broma's range had extended in the other direction, serving customers whose budgets were severely restricted. As 'low end' Broma products came into the shops and Walkers higher-range goods disappeared from the shelves there was a corresponding subtle but discernable change in the clientele.

Managers of former Walkers shops felt themselves to be under increasing pressure. Just as targets for sales and turnover figures were being raised, and demands to reduce costs were becoming more insistent, the customer base was shifting, very slightly but unmistakably, towards a lower-spending profile. Walkers shops had always been fairly uniform in their appearance and atmosphere, and the core product range had been much the same throughout the company. However, Walkers management had always been sensitive to local variations and shop managers had been encouraged to make suggestions aimed at serving local needs. Now managers felt increasingly that their views were not being heard, or perhaps not being respected, and they were simply being told which products to stock.

A year after the takeover morale was very low, not only in the former Walkers outlets but, to a slightly lesser extent, across the whole Broma enterprise. Takings had fallen by a few percentage points in the former Walkers areas and customer complaints of poor service, and even rudeness, had increased. Wastage levels had risen as products were still on the shelves as they went out of date, and senior managers were alarmed to find when they visited shops that stock rooms were sometimes untidy and even dirty. Even more disconcerting, the teams working on refurbishing and 'Broma-izing' the Walkers shops reported that they were getting poor cooperation from local staff, which was delaying the project and adding to costs.

Broma's management were concerned and baffled by all this. From their own perspective they had done everything they could to make the merger a success. They had kept their promise of no redundancies, even though Walkers had employed more people than were really justified, and they had been willing to allow staffing levels to fall slowly through natural wastage. They had awarded pay increases, admittedly small ones, to ex-Walkers staff despite the fact that they were paid more than Broma people for the same jobs, to cushion the impact of equalization. They had every intention of treating everyone the same as far as career prospects were concerned and actually thought that the high calibre of many of the Walkers people made them very suitable for promotion through the Broma organization. They also couldn't understand why shop managers weren't happy to have local product range decisions decided by Broma's professional market research people, instead of having to sort it out themselves, often, it seemed, relying on guesswork.

Liza Harrington, who perceived herself to be the focus of some dissatisfaction among her new boardroom colleagues, felt that she had to do something to improve the situation. She privately sought advice from one of her former business school tutors, now semi-retired, with whom she had kept in touch over the years (and who later introduced her to me).

He suggested that she should go and talk, in confidence, with as many of the middle and junior managers as she could to find out at first hand what the problem was. He warned Liza that it could be an uncomfortable experience because she was likely to be seen as having 'betrayed' the Walkers people, so there would be a lot of fence-mending to do before much progress was made. He also told Liza that her fellow Broma directors must be kept fully informed, and agree to the scheme, or they might suspect Liza of underhand behaviour.

Liza was tough but not devoid of emotional intelligence. She put the idea to her colleagues and was pleased to get a mainly positive response. She then began the long and at times painful task of one to one discussions with managers at all levels across the former Walkers enterprise. At first it was very difficult. There was suspicion and resentment and she even received a couple of resignations pointedly handed to her personally when she visited sites.

However, word began to spread that she appeared genuinely to want to put things right and the tenor of her meetings steadily improved. Oddly, she thought, the performance of shops began to improve even before she came to call and at the end of four months' hard work the whole of the former Walkers part of Broma had increased its turnover and profits. Resignations had more or less stopped and a handful of ex-Walkers people had applied for vacancies at more senior levels in the Broma organization. The tensions in the top management team relaxed and Liza's own standing improved considerably.

The extended Broma network is still facing an uphill struggle to maintain its profitability in the face of the market domination of the big four supermarkets, but its customer base has remained fairly loyal and it has managed, so far, to stay viable. One effect of Liza Harrington's valiant efforts has been to make the Broma top team more aware of the need to listen, rather than make assumptions. This has had some very useful spin-offs, not least the return of some of Walkers' 'high end' customers as Broma extended its product range towards the quality side of the spectrum in response to requests from local managers. There is still some unease about the future among ex-Walkers staff, but this is now a minority view and diminishing as relationships, and trust, develop. On the whole there is good reason to be cautiously optimistic about Broma's future.

Analysis

The most significant kind of environmental threats that can impact on organizational climate, mentioned by 39 per cent of informants in my own research (Gray, 2001b) and by other writers (Kanter, 1983; Burke, 1988; Winkfield, 1995; Belassi and Tukel, 1996), is that of change which is beyond the control of the people affected by it. This was the kind of threat that affected the staff at Walkers. Mergers and takeovers don't have a very good track record of success.

Cartwright and Cooper (1993) say that 'merger is rarely seen as being a marriage of equals by the members of at least one of the partnering organizations' and in the case of an acknowledged takeover, like the acquisition of Walkers by Broma, there is clearly no question of equality. This inevitably means that staff of the acquired partner will at the very least find themselves having to adopt the processes and practices of the acquirer. In broad terms, this means that they will have to learn to live in a new and possibly alien culture.

When individuals leave one organization and join another they also find themselves having to adapt to a new culture, but in that situation nature is on their side; we are 'programmed' to notice and take on the behaviours of those around us. When the people around us are the same as before but we are all required to change the way we do things we often find it very difficult. The outcome can be stress, demotivation, resentment, suspicion, hostility and anxiety. Sometimes the easiest, perhaps the only way for individuals to handle this is to remove themselves from the situation; either by absenteeism, which often increases markedly after mergers, or by resignation (Cartwright and Cooper, 1993).

As these problems have been well researched organizations considering mergers or acquisitions really ought to be aware of and plan for them. Mitchell Marks and Philip Mirvis (Sales and Mirvis, 1984; Marks and Mirvis, 1986, 2001) have been studying mergers and acquisitions, and their effects on employees, for over 20 years. They have identified a 'merger syndrome' involving 'defensiveness, fear-the-worst, rumours of job loss, loss of benefits, pay freezes, etc. ... intensified by increased centralisation and lack of communication'. This leads to lowered productivity and increased staff turnover.

Linda Holbeche of Roffey Park Management Institute has researched more than 40 mergers and acquisitions in the UK and Europe and believes that the people issues are absolutely crucial for long-term success. She found that 'companies that were strongly HR-led predicted and resolved many of the people issues during their mergers, leading to real integration and synergy' (Holbeche, 2001).

Not many companies are 'strongly HR-led'. In a survey of 4000 'senior HR practitioners', carried out in summer of 2003 (Emmott, 2003), only 21 per cent of respondents said that they were board members. Even if they were on the board, HR directors 'were often not expected to play a proactive and strategic role'. Even worse, from the perspective of the HR profession, 'small but not insignificant minorities say their CEO has negative views about the influence of HR on board decisions'. Input to decision-making about people issues doesn't, of course, have to come solely from HR professionals (although it might be expected that they would be a prime source of specialist advice), but if such input is entirely absent there is bound to be trouble.

As Marks and Mirvis found, many of the pitfalls arise from lack of effective communication: 'You can never over-communicate during mergers' (Holbeche, 2001). In Broma's case communication was seriously defective. The Walkers management wanted to keep their negotiations secret until a deal was done, and there can be sound commercial reasons for this, but it won't be cost-free and the consequences have to be considered as part of the cost side of the equation.

Once their acquisition of Walkers had been agreed Broma failed to communicate with their new workforce in a way which was meaningful to them, leaving them feeling anxious and threatened. This had an immediate, and I would argue inevitable, detrimental impact on almost all aspects of performance. Crucially, Broma hadn't realized that communication is a two-way process; telling is never enough, they needed to listen too. When, through Liza Harrington's efforts, they began to do that things immediately began to improve and from there it was possible to begin to repair the damaged trust and confidence.

Narrative No 16: The Suffolk Buss

Background

The Suffolk Buss is an old coaching inn on England's North Sea coast. There had been an inn on the same site since the seventeenth century but the present buildings – the inn itself and an adjacent separate stable block – date from the 1820s. By the early 1900s the place was virtually derelict. There had been a collection of fishermen's cottages clinging to the coast a mile or so to the east (from which the pub's name derives – a buss was a type of fishing and cargo boat used along the east coast), but these had long since disappeared into the sea and passing trade had rerouted itself along safer and more populated highways.

It's likely that nothing would now remain of The Suffolk Buss if its adjacent stretch of bleak, stony coastline and cold grey sea hadn't been brought to the attention of well-heeled middlebrow English society in the years following the Second World War by Benjamin Britten and his Aldeburgh Festival. Within a few years Aldeburgh and other nearby small towns like Southwold and Woodbridge had become fashionable and consequently prosperous.

The Suffolk Buss was restored and opened as a country pub in 1975 by Ronald and Audrey Bolton, a retired couple from Ipswich who used their savings to pay for the refurbishment work. It was moderately successful and provided an adequate income for its owners, although if they had properly costed-in their capital outlay it's doubtful if they could have convinced an impartial observer that it was a worthwhile investment. With no nearby community it relied on visitors so its trade was extremely seasonal. On fine weekends in summer it would often be packed, with people waiting to be served forming long queues through the bars and up the steps outside the door. Midweek even in summer there would be no more than a handful of customers, and in winter the place was empty more often than not. Out of season the Boltons sometimes wouldn't bother to open up and they almost always locked up well before the official closing time.

The pub was unremarkable in every way, except that it was a 'free house', i.e. not owned or tied in to any of the major drinks companies. It sold local draught beers and a selection of bottled drinks, much like other similar establishments of the time. Food was very much an afterthought. Crisps, nuts and other packaged snacks were available, and Audrey would make sandwiches if the pub wasn't too busy. Ron discouraged this because he thought it a waste of time, but Audrey had read somewhere that coaching inns were obliged by law to serve food to travellers if requested, and she set great store on doing the right thing.

Ron Bolton died in 1995 and Audrey, who was almost 80 by then, retired finally to a sheltered housing complex in Felixstowe. The Suffolk Buss remained empty and for sale for more than a year. In January 1997 William Noakes and Frances Yates came to view the empty pub. Bill and Frankie were a couple with a two-year-old daughter and a solid but rather volatile relationship. They had decided that running a pub together would give them and their daughter a better lifestyle than their boring office jobs and they had spent more than a year looking for somewhere suitable that they could afford.

They had no experience of the licensed trade, but were neither foolish nor naïve. They had researched the business thoroughly and felt that they had a good theoretical knowledge of how it worked. They also had a very clear idea of the pros and cons of the locality. Their visit in the depths of winter was part of that research; they had already visited many pubs during the season, so they knew how much business there was to be done at peak times, and they had spent time in the area in winter so they understood how deserted (and, frankly, how dreary) it could be then.

They now felt ready to buy, if they could find the right place at the right price. Audrey Bolton's solicitor had provided them with the last few years' accounts for the pub, which didn't make good reading. Now they were on the premises Bill and Frankie could see that it had been hopelessly old-fashioned, and that it needed considerable decorative work and upgrading. However, it was a large building, structurally sound, and with more accommodation than they would need for themselves so they would be able to open two or possibly three rooms for the bed and breakfast trade. The pub kitchen was rudimentary, but there was room for it to be extended so it would be possible to provide meals, which would draw in additional trade. As a result of their visit they put in an offer for the pub, which was accepted, and they took up occupation in early March.

If Bill and Frankie were to make a success of their venture it was essential for the pub to be open for business by late spring; they had to make enough profit during their first season to carry them through the winter. After that they hoped to be able to build up the trade a little so that there was at least some minimal income all year round. They set about the refurbishment work, doing much of it themselves and hiring in trades people as and when necessary. They kept the Suffolk country pub style, but gave the place a clean, more modern look and spent their money wisely on furnishings and accessories.

By the middle of May they had completely redecorated the bars, setting part of one bar aside for use as a dining area. They had knocked down the repellent original outside customer toilets and in their place built a small extension along the whole of the back of the building to house new toilets and a bigger kitchen. Their own living accommodation was still to be upgraded, but they had refurbished two of the bedrooms for use by guests. They had spent over their budget and there was still much work to do but they were ready to open as the summer season began to build up.

The first two years were a struggle, but The Suffolk Buss managed to attract enough trade to cover its costs and slowly began to build a reputation. Local residents would drive over for a weekend drink or pub lunch and in time visitors got to hear about it and would make a point of calling in on their way to and from the region's tourist attractions. Frankie did deals with local farmers to place signs in fields visible from the main roads, which brought in an unexpected amount of extra trade.

The real breakthrough came when Frankie approached several coach companies and suggested that the pub would be the ideal place for coach trips to stop for lunch or coffee. This put a strain on the kitchen at first, but fortunately there were people in the nearby villages who were glad of the chance of some part-time work, so Bill and Frankie were able to hire staff to handle the extra load.

By 2002 The Suffolk Buss was a prosperous and thriving business, employing two full-time and 12 part-time staff, as well as the two proprietors. Bill and Frankie refurbished the old stable block as their own home and converted their old accommodation in the main building into additional guest rooms, making a total of six ensuite double rooms for bed and breakfast customers. The business was still highly seasonal, but there was enough 'background' trade through the autumn and even in winter to cover the overheads. Bill and Frankie began to talk about where the business could go from there.

The situation

At the end of the 2002 summer season it had become clear that The Suffolk Buss was serving enough meals both at lunchtimes and in the evenings to justify a full-time chef. In fact, the skills required were not of a very high level; very little of the food provided was prepared on site but the quality of the bought-in catering packs had improved steadily, in step with customer demands. The chef's role was to reheat the dishes according to instructions and present the food attractively. Salads, garnishes and other fresh components needed to be handled sensitively, though, and someone with the correct food hygiene certificates needed to be on the premises whenever food was being handled. The kitchen operation needed to be reorganized and the first step was to hire someone to take charge.

Early in the spring of 2003 Bill and Frankie took on Danute Martynas, who had been working in a London hotel kitchen for a couple of years and had completed a National Vocational Qualification in food preparation and cooking, which gave her all the background knowledge she would need to handle the pub's catering requirements. Danute proved to be everything Bill and Frankie could have hoped for, and more. She was bright, eager to please and resourceful. When she gave instructions to the other staff, who were now technically her subordinates, she made them sound more like sensible suggestions. If there was any resentment amongst the others at having a young, foreign woman imposed as their boss it quickly evaporated under the influence of her sunny personality.

Danute was also invaluable in a crisis. When a delivery didn't turn up and supplies in the freezers were running low she toured local shops buying fresh produce at trade prices and produced a short, bistro-style menu which attracted many compliments. This made Frankie think hard. Over the next few weeks she contacted local producers to find out what fresh produce was available, at what prices and in what quantities. At the end of this exercise she was convinced that it would be feasible to move The Suffolk Buss restaurant considerably up market.

Up to this point she hadn't been ready to share her ideas with Bill, who was aware only that she was checking out alternative suppliers. He was very dubious. The current system required only basic skills from the kitchen staff, was fairly cheap, and satisfied most of the customers. The delivery failure which had prompted Frankie's new vision had been a rare occurrence and it would be easy to guard against the risk of its happening again simply by holding bigger reserves in the freezers. Turning this comfortable operation into a 'gastro-pub', as he called it, would involve higher restaurant prices, food which might well not appeal to the coach party trade which formed the backbone of their business, and greater risks of being let down by small independent suppliers. Fresh food would also be highly seasonal, which could make the already marginal winter operation even more problematic.

These were sound arguments but Frankie wasn't deterred. She talked it over with Danute, who would be vital to the success of the project, and found her to be highly enthusiastic. In fact, for Danute it represented an opportunity to become what she had wanted to be since arriving in England – a real chef. Fired by Danute's infectious enthusiasm, the other kitchen staff were also keen to take part. Frankie tackled Bill again, suggesting that they begin in a small way, with a daily 'specials' board in addition to their regular menu. Bill still wasn't convinced but couldn't think of a strong reason to veto this fairly modest proposal so he reluctantly agreed.

Danute's specials proved very popular with a section of the customers. As Bill had predicted, the coach party trade were reluctant to order the higher priced and sometimes exotic dishes from the board, preferring the more traditional and cheaper fare, but a minority of customers ordered and praised the specials, and it was undeniable that repeat business increased as individuals returned to see what would be on offer next.

The impact on the bed and breakfast trade was mixed. Most of these customers seemed to want the same kind of reasonable quality mass catering that the pub had always provided, but a minority seemed very willing to pay higher prices for the specials. Bill, who took care of ordering the bar stocks, also noticed that the more expensive beers and wines were turning over quicker than before as customers ordered something more suitable to complement Danute's cooking.

There were mistakes, though. Demand was unpredictable and if the fresh produce wasn't used quickly it couldn't be kept. Running out was less expensive but caused annoyance to the customers. When Bill assessed the impact on profits of the experiment he was inclined to think it was costing more than it was worth.

Frankie disagreed. She thought that the high motivation of Danute and her kitchen team was a great asset that should be exploited. She also thought that the reason profits weren't rising was the half-hearted way they had approached the change. Her plan was to give up on the pre-prepared food delivered by the contractors ready to reheat and serve, which she thought prevented The Suffolk Buss from being taken seriously by the discerning public. They would only really start to be successful if they grasped the nettle and moved over 100 per cent to 'real cooking'.

Bill thought this was far too risky and their disagreements often turned into private rows. The couple, who had never been reluctant to express strong opinions to each other, now found themselves rowing more frequently, and not only about work. Frankie saw the danger signs and decided that their relationship must take priority, for their own sakes, and for their little girl's. In the end she knew that she wouldn't take the chance of a really serious rift with Bill over a business decision.

Meanwhile Danute's enthusiasm was undiminished. She continued to think up new recipe ideas and discreetly added items to the daily specials board until Bill told her to keep to two or three items each day. Wastage continued to be fairly high and sometimes a menu item was unsuccessful. When this happened Bill got quite angry and made critical remarks about Frankie's 'hobby' costing the business money. Danute was upset and apologized but Frankie told her there were bound to be occasional failures and she shouldn't let it bother her.

Danute heard the couple arguing and couldn't fail to be aware that her bosses didn't agree about the restaurant's future. She became anxious and whereas before she had shared half-formed ideas with Frankie, bouncing them back and forth, refining them and discarding those that didn't really work, now she kept things to herself until she had thought them through. She became more cautious about ordering and as a consequence her dishes became a little more conservative. She still wanted to take the project forward and was impatient with the uncertainty about how far it would go. Frankie reassured her and gave her every encouragement, but couldn't make any promises whilst Bill was so sceptical.

Some of Danute's sparkle seemed to fade and this had an effect on the other kitchen staff. They had been caught up in the enthusiasm for making the pub something really different and in a way they perceived their own status to be enhanced by working in a place which seemed to be really going somewhere, but this effect was beginning to wear off. They were all aware by now that no decisions had been made about the restaurant's future and Danute's subdued demeanour did nothing to raise the mood. Danute knew what she wanted but by now was feeling quite despondent and let down. It hardly seemed worth putting her heart and soul into the task if there was a good chance that it would all come to nothing. The other staff picked up on this feeling and began to slacken off. Frankie had to point out cleaning tasks that had been neglected, something she hadn't had to do since the early days of running the pub.

Also for the first time it became necessary to speak to one or two employees about their timekeeping, and there were examples of sloppy service in the restaurant. Two part-time staff complained about their wages and left when Bill turned down their requests for a rise. It took a long time to replace them, which put an extra burden on everyone. Frankie and Danute found themselves having to intervene in petty squabbles among the staff and generally the cheerful, energetic atmosphere which had built up at The Suffolk Buss now seemed to be in danger of ebbing away.

By the end of the season the experiment had been inconclusive. It appeared that additional raw materials costs had been covered, and profits on the specials seemed to be marginally higher than on the regular menu. There was also additional turnover on alcohol sales, which might be attributable to the special menus. This left Bill and Frankie still facing the crucial decision of whether to continue as they were or to begin the next season as a fully committed gastro-pub. Bill still thought the change was very risky, whilst Frankie thought it an opportunity to make a real name for the business. Both partners assumed that Danute would be part of the future, whichever way they decided to go. They decided to continue the experiment through the winter, when the coach trip and bed and breakfast trades were much reduced but there would be local residents who might drive out to the pub for meals. By the spring they thought they would be able to make up their minds.

Things picked up a little at Christmas, when The Suffolk Buss offered a traditional Christmas lunch using only organic produce. It was a great success but in the dog days of a cold, wet Suffolk January morale dropped again. Whilst Bill and Frankie deferred making up their minds about the pub's future, Danute came to a decision about hers. In early February she told Frankie that she was leaving.

I heard this story from Bill, who I met through the Chamber of Commerce. By that time, although he still thought the gastro-pub project carried very real risks, he had come to regret not giving it his support, partly because he had seen other establishments make a name for themselves by taking that route. The nature of his pub's existing trade made direct comparisons tricky, but all the same he now thought it could have worked. Frankie had forgiven him, but they were both sorry to lose Danute, who had been in many ways an ideal employee, as well as a very likeable colleague.

I asked him if he knew what Danute was doing now and was rather pleased to hear that Frankie had managed to keep in touch with her. She had left The Suffolk Buss for another posting with nautical connections, as chef on a traditional Thames sailing barge which catered for dinner parties and receptions whilst cruising off the Essex coast or in the Thames Estuary, or quite often whilst remaining moored up at the dockside in Essex, Kent or London. There she was able to cook the kinds of menus she had wanted to serve at The Suffolk Buss, and apparently she was becoming quite celebrated. Bill and Frankie are still thinking of making the change and if they ever make up their minds they have a useful learning experience to guide them.

Analysis

For Bill and Frankie there was a genuine difference of opinion about the viability of their project, but no personal animosity. The kind of dispute described here can be exponentially worse and more damaging when personal enmity, rivalries and power struggles are involved. In this case it's clear that Bill and Frankie had different comfort levels when it came to accepting risk; Bill was more risk-averse than Frankie, although he was certainly not excessively cautious – they had, after all, both given up their paid employment and used all their capital to buy the business in the first place.

In fact, Bill's caution about the restaurant was quite reasonable, because the risk he identified of alienating their existing customer base in the process of attracting a new, possibly more lucrative but certainly unquantified clientele, was genuine.

This said, their different personality attributes could have been a real strength in this and similar situations. Frankie's willingness to embrace new ideas complemented Bill's level-headed wish to preserve the gains they had already made. He had not yet completed the process of internally consolidating the (successful) outcomes of the risks they had already taken, and wasn't yet ready to take new ones. Frankie was a few steps ahead of him in this natural process and probably needed to wait for him to catch up.

This wouldn't have mattered too much if Danute hadn't received the impression from Frankie, who represented senior management as far as she was concerned, that the project was 'officially' approved. Danute invested a great deal of herself in making things work and when uncertainty was introduced, and continued over an extended period, she felt herself to be undermined. By allowing their own disagreements to impact directly on the staff Bill and Frankie seriously reduced the chances of success.

A more sensible approach would have been to conduct a careful risk assessment, letting Danute and the other staff know what was being considered but making it very clear that no decision had been made or was imminent. That way, the contribution the employees could make would be towards the decision-making process, rather than towards the implementation of the new policy. If everyone understands this the terms of the psychological contract are much clearer, and the outcome towards which people are working is the eventual decision. This may bring disappointment, but that possibility is understood all along, so trust is maintained, closure is achieved, and people can pick themselves up and get on with the next task. Of course, repeated disappointments of this kind will eventually take their toll, but one or two can be accepted without too much damage to morale.

Disagreements or disputes among senior managers, about policy or support for specific initiatives or even on a personal basis, are often perceived by subordinate staff as a kind of threat – the seriousness, and the impact, of which depends on how much the dispute matters to the individuals affected by it. When the disagreement casts doubt on the value of the work people are doing, and whether they will be required or allowed to continue doing it, the damage to self-esteem and commitment can be considerable: 'there's little point in putting your heart and soul into a task or project if there's a real possibility that someone "up there" will pull the plug on it before it's finished' (Gray, 2004).

- Environmental threats are threats which arise from natural events, from pressures in society which are not being directed by intelligence, or causes or policies determined remotely from the affected individuals so that for practical purpose they may be regarded as being undirected. This kind of perceived threat produces feelings of personal insecurity and uncertainty.
- Organizational change often feels threatening, especially when people don't know what's going on and/or feel that they have no influence over events.
- Mergers and acquisitions can be quite extreme forms of organizational change, and almost always make people feel threatened. Decisions which affect their future in an immediate and potentially harmful way are made without reference to them or their needs. These events are often characterized by secrecy, which increases their threatening nature.
- Because people usually feel less threatened if they are kept informed, and much less threatened if they feel they have some input into decisions, communication and consultation can have a powerful mitigating effect in organizational change situations.
- Disputes and disagreements between senior people often feel threatening to more junior staff, mainly because of the uncertainty which such disputes provoke. As well as introducing tension and generalized hostility, they may give rise to doubts about the 'continuance of context', i.e. whether a current situation will continue: enthusiasm for a current task or project is undermined if there seems a real possibility that it will be stopped before completion by management decision or external forces.

14

The way ahead

γνωθι σεαυτόν – *'Know yourself'*
Inscribed over the entrance to the temple of Apollo at Delphi

In Chapter 4, I presented research evidence from a variety of sources which shows that a benign organizational climate can be linked to high performance. I would argue that, because people matter and life isn't a rehearsal, we all have a moral obligation to do whatever we can to foster a benign organizational climate anyway, regardless of any economically-based performance issues. If the two desired outcomes – employees' individual well-being and organizational performance – had turned out to be mutually antagonistic then the ethical dilemma which I outlined in Chapter 1 would have to be faced, summed up by Bottery (1992): 'Should not ethical questions come before those of effectiveness? Would one want to countenance management methods . . . which were effective but ethically unacceptable?'.

Fortunately (and not only because I'm cynical enough to think that the answers to Bottery's questions in some boardrooms would be 'no' and 'yes' respectively) the research shows that it's in the economic interests of organizations, and of managers at all levels within them, to work towards the kind of climate which will be perceived as benign by most of the people who work there. Not only will people feel better about their work, their organizations, their colleagues and their managers, they will also, usually and over a sensible timescale, become more valuable employees in purely economic terms as well.

If this principle is taken as established, it seems reasonable to suppose that managers will want to do what they can to improve the climate of their own organizations, or at least those parts of the organization for which they have some responsibility and control. Because an employee's perception of climate is influenced very strongly by the behaviour of managers, and especially by the behaviour of his or her immediate supervisor (McGregor, 1960; Reichers and Schneider, 1990), it is possible for individual managers to bring about improvements 'simply' by making changes in their own behaviour.

Of course, changing our behaviour isn't really simple at all. There is a long and arduous process involved which means that, like losing weight or giving up smoking, changing our workplace behaviour needs willpower, determination and constant self-observation to avoid slipping back into the old habits. How difficult this will be depends, fairly obviously, on how big a change is needed (and issues of credibility and trust may arise if someone's habitual behaviour appears to undergo a sudden, major change). But change certainly is possible and, as several of the narratives illustrate, the change that is needed may be fairly minor, especially if warning signs are noticed and acted upon at an early stage.

The process of improvement begins with self-knowledge. When people consulted the oracle at Delphi, seeking guidance about big decisions, the advice they received was famously opaque and ambiguous. In the end they had to make their own interpretations of the oracle's pronouncements and make their own decisions. The real wisdom of Delphi, often overlooked, was the advice to 'know yourself', carved into the lintel of the temple doorway.

To know where we are now, where we want to be, and what our strengths and weaknesses are provides us with the base from which rational decisions can be made. In an organizational context the emphasis is often on the 'where we want to be' element of this, which leads to the development of vision and mission statements, strategic plans, and other very worthy and valuable corporate artefacts. None of these is of much use, however, without a realistic assessment of current status. It's only when we know both our intended destination and our current location that we can realistically plan how to get from here to there.

The wider issues of strategy, departmental purpose analysis or forward planning are questions to be considered elsewhere. Our concern here, as a precursor to improvement, is limited to making a realistic assessment of the current state of organizational climate and this is hard for an insider to achieve. If we are members of the organizational system we want to assess, it's almost impossible to arrive at meaningful conclusions based solely on our own observations or feelings. As T E Hulme says: 'it is almost insuperably difficult to become critically conscious of our own habitual assumptions' (in Arnold, 1995).

A prerequisite for, I suppose, almost any improvement process is the realization that something could be better than it currently is. All too often, this realization comes rather late, when a problem has become serious enough to thrust itself into the consciousness of the people concerned. Because we are intimately involved in the system's functioning we get used to its characteristics and don't notice the subtle changes which are taking place all the time. Of course, if there's a big or sudden change we will probably be aware of it, but it's the cumulative effects of small, incremental changes that build up to produce negative alterations in the climate which adversely affect the people involved without their necessarily being aware that anything is happening.

Charles Handy (1990) gives the vivid, if gruesome, parable of the boiling frog to illustrate this tendency. If one tries to put a frog into a pan of hot water the frog will immediately jump out (apparently – I can't vouch for this and have no intention of trying it), but if the frog is placed in a pan of cool water which is then slowly heated to boiling point the frog doesn't notice the incremental change in the temperature and stays put, allowing itself to be boiled to death.

There are two main ways to avoid this trap. One is to ask someone else, who isn't a member of our own organizational system, to observe the climate and provide feedback. An experienced observer can often detect a prevailing mood or 'atmosphere' in an organizational setting which may not be apparent or definable to the people who live with it every day. Despite the fact that this kind of observation is inevitably likely to be superficial, the insight it provides can still be very useful.

It may, of course, be difficult to define a mood or an atmosphere in terms which are specific or focused enough to suggest a course of action for improvement, but where there is a discernable (to a stranger) anomaly or dysfunction it may well be sufficient to point the manager's attention to particular issues which can be directly addressed.

Where simple observation isn't enough, some more formal research will be needed. For the reasons explored in some depth in Chapter 5, the most cost-effective way of doing this is usually by means of some kind of survey in which people are asked to express their feelings about a range of climate factors. There are several ready-made survey questionnaires available for this purpose; which one to use is largely a matter of choice and confidence. The OCA (Organizational Climate Assessment) instrument that I and my colleagues currently use is based on our own research (Gray 2001b, 2002) so we feel comfortable in analysing the results, but it would be arrogant to suggest that it's necessarily any better than other instruments in use elsewhere and, of course, it's perfectly possible for someone who has some experience of research methods to design their own.

A word of caution is appropriate here for anyone thinking of doing any kind of research in their own (or anyone else's) organization.

> Clearly, there is little point in collecting information unless you intend to act on the messages it conveys. In fact, the process of collecting information . . . is never neutral. People always make assumptions about why you are doing it and it often raises expectations that something is going to change, which is likely to be unsettling and can lead to disappointment and suspicion of bad faith if the anticipated action doesn't happen.
>
> Gray, 2004

When I carry out a survey of this kind I like to prepare the ground by explaining, either verbally or in a covering letter, why the research is being done and the use the organization intends to make of the information the survey provides. This has the dual benefit of reassuring the people whose cooperation is required that there's no sinister motive behind it, and also of providing context, which seems to cut down on queries and, I think, improve response rates.

The answers to the OCA questionnaire can be analysed in two ways. One is to give a simple overall numerical climate index with a maximum value of 72. This is moderately useful in itself because it gives a broad indication of how the people who work in the organization or group perceive the climate there. The higher the index, the more benign the climate. In very general terms, a score in the upper quartile, i.e. 55 or above, suggests a climate which is conducive to successful and productive work. If the score is much below this it suggests that there may be aspects of the organization's climate that would repay some attention, and a very low score is an indication that something is going badly wrong and needs immediate corrective action.

The other kind of analysis that the OCA permits is a breakdown of results for each individual factor. In normal circumstances one would expect all eight factors to return roughly similar scores because they are all members of the same system (see Chapter 5 for an explanation of this concept) and are constantly exercising influence on each other, as illustrated in Figure 14.1.

It's important to restate here that all these factors deal with people's perceptions. A remark by a manager to a subordinate may, quite genuinely, not have been intended as any kind of threat, but if it was perceived as such the effect is the same. Managers may believe themselves ready and willing to listen to people's concerns, but if people don't perceive this to be the case then free expression of concerns is effectively suppressed.

As an example of this I once asked a senior manager: 'Can middle and junior-ranking people get their ideas and concerns heard by senior managers?'. His answer was: 'They can but they don't'. Two more junior people told me: 'There is a . . . kind of blame culture. It would be denied, but there is. . . . Hence there is this thing "if I stick my head above the parapet it's bound to get knocked off at some stage"' and: 'Staff do feel inhibited in saying something because they think "I'm going to be victimized for saying this". That's still an issue'.

This discrepancy between the perceptions of manager and subordinates would probably continue indefinitely because neither side would ever understand that the other side saw things differently. It's the perceptions, regardless of whether or not they are objectively justified, which affect the organizational climate.

Each factor in the organizational climate system interacts with every other factor and also with factors in the external environment which may be undefined

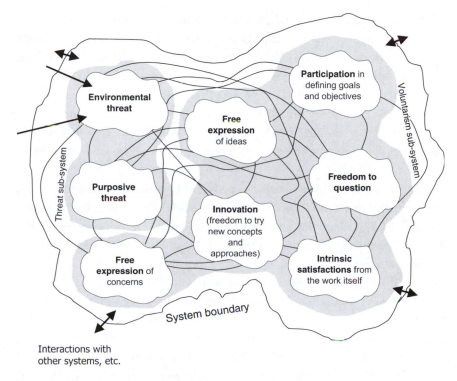

Figure 14.1 A system map of eight organizational climate factors.

and/or unrecognized, 'providing information about current and anticipated status which promotes self-adjustment' (Checkland, 1984). These interactions may act to strengthen or weaken the impact of each factor to an extent which can't be assessed or predicted (Stacey, 1992).

Because of this, the amount of influence on the overall climate which each individual factor can exert tends to be self-compensating, meaning that over time they even out so that an increase or decrease in one is followed sooner or later (usually sooner) by similar changes in all the others. In fact, isolated changes in individual factors within the six positive factors, which I have collectively labelled 'voluntarism', seldom last very long, because these factors interact very rapidly.

Of the two negative factors, purposive threat has strong intra-systemic interactions with the other factors, meaning that it's an intrinsic characteristic of particular attitudes and ways of behaving associated with managers or others who are in constant interaction with the people who are affected by it, and therefore its influence on other factors within the system is direct and immediate.

Environmental threat, on the other hand, almost always originates outside the system, so it's quite likely to take people by surprise. All the same, the perception of environmental threat isn't immune from the influence of the other factors. How much influence they can exert depends to a large extent on the nature of the environmental threat, but where a benign organizational climate exists there is more likely to be trust in communications from management and confidence that the welfare of employees is likely to be taken into account in decision-making. This can soften the impact of environmental threats if this is feasible in the specific circumstances.

Conversely, where the climate is not perceived to be benign, the perception of environmental threat can seem more menacing and people may feel more helpless and isolated. This means that organizations with relatively benign climates are often more resilient to the effects of environmental threats: they have 'healthier immune systems' which can help them to withstand externally sourced problems. What this means is that if any factor seems to be out of step with the overall pattern it may be an indication of something potentially significant happening within the organizational system under scrutiny. The most likely explanation, from experience, is that it may indicate a new or developing situation which requires attention.

In the narratives, I illustrated each of the eight factors in the organizational climate system with two examples. These scenarios are not, of course, the only situations in which individual climate factors may become apparent, either as indicators of a poor overall climate or as drivers, beginning as independent changes but very soon starting to drag the overall perception of climate down. These accounts are intended to facilitate learning by observation of other people's mistakes, or their successes. This kind of vicarious learning is a highly developed skill in human beings; we do it all the time, either by direct observation or indirectly by reading or other media of communication, and of course we do it in the workplace too. For some reason, though, there seem to be certain workplace situations which make people reluctant to make use of other people's experiences.

Many years ago I was working as an internal consultant in a very large corporation, and I frequently came across managers struggling to handle a difficult situation. Quite often I would be aware of another manager who had recently faced and dealt with a similar problem elsewhere in the company, and I would pass on contact details so that my new client could benefit from our colleague's experience. Rarely was this kind of suggestion followed up.

I could speculate about the nature of the barrier which obstructed this fairly simple short-cut to learning: perhaps asking for help was seen as an admission of weakness, perhaps colleagues were seen also as competitors, or perhaps the challenge of reinventing the wheel was too tempting to pass up, but the truth is that I don't really understand it. I'm not alone in observing it, though.

In a different context, Douglas Adams (1990) says 'Human beings, who are almost unique in having the ability to learn from the experience of others, are also remarkable for their apparent disinclination to do so' and even Voltaire was supposed to have asked, rhetorically, 'Is there anyone so wise as to learn by the experience of others?'. I suspect that the narrative, as a didactic device, was first developed as a means of overcoming this barrier.

I hope that the accounts which I have set out will have had enough similarity with real-life situations to stimulate ideas about useful action plans for improvement. To support this process, the following guidance relates to each of the eight climate factors individually.

The freedom to express ideas. Action to improve this factor usually focuses on the removal of obstacles; if they have any interest at all in what they do for a living, people can't help having ideas about it. If those ideas aren't reaching places where they can be developed and put to productive use, it's almost always because something is getting in the way.

In EAEP, the freedom to express ideas was suppressed by an outdated 'them and us' management view that the role of junior people was to implement the instructions and ideas of their bosses. People were valued for their skills, but not for their ideas. Because people felt frustrated and under-valued, in time this had a negative impact on the overall climate. In Gonville Data Services ideas were effectively suppressed because they were hi-jacked, and people started keeping their ideas – their intellectual property – to themselves. Other ways in which the free expression of ideas can be stifled include repeated rejection of suggestions, denigration, fault finding, apathy, and a lack of effective communication channels by which ideas can be shared.

If people are encouraged to put ideas forward, and those ideas are treated with respect as well as realism, then it's very likely that the flow will be healthy and valuable.

Formal suggestion schemes are one way of addressing this need, but they do have to be operated honestly and energetically. Features of successful suggestion schemes are that they have the full backing of senior managers, they provide some kind of incentive, which doesn't have to be financial, everyone knows about them, and they're kept relevant by continual review. As with most processes and policies, suggestion schemes usually work best if the people they are meant to serve have a hand in designing and, perhaps, operating them (Fowler, 1994; Charlton, 2005).

Formal suggestion schemes certainly aren't the only means by which ideas can be expressed in the workplace. In some ways formal mechanisms like this are less than ideal, although they may be the only practical way to implement an organization-wide policy. Ideas can and will be expressed, though, informally, so long as someone is willing to listen and respond positively to them. Managers who show by their everyday behaviour (and it has to be every day – occasional erratic demonstrations of interest are useless) that they welcome and value the contributions of their people will almost certainly find that the flow of ideas never dries up.

The freedom to express concerns. A concern indicates that something is perceived to be wrong. On the whole people don't like to tell their bosses that they think something isn't right because it sounds negative. This gets even worse when the concern is about something which affects the individual, because then it can sound like whingeing.

All the same, if concerns can't be expressed, and addressed, they don't just go away. Instead they can simmer and ferment until they develop into serious issues. Because of this, a competent manager makes a positive effort to let people know that they can raise concerns whenever they feel uncomfortable about anything, and that such expressions of concern will be treated as positive inputs to the proper functioning of the organization.

At Mackenzie's House, the manager rejected expressions of concern because she perceived them as an attack on her authority. This is almost always a big mistake. Concerns aren't personal disputes until one or other of the people involved makes them so. Kept impersonal, they have the character of issues to be resolved, like all the other workplace issues that are part of everyone's working life.

At Toreston Housing the concern was about ethical standards and correct practice. Again, if anyone had been available to listen to Michael Byrne's worries the whole sorry episode could have been resolved at a much earlier stage. Where concerns are about standards, legal issues, safety or a host of other broadly environmental matters, including competitor activity, everyone in the workforce can act as the eyes and ears of the organization, providing early warning of potentially damaging problems. Not to utilize this highly valuable resource is folly bordering on culpable negligence.

The management action required to ensure that this climate factor is positive is to have formal channels by which concerns can be expressed safely and in confidence. These channels must be seen to work at all times, unlike the whistleblowing policy at Toreston Housing, which was described in loving detail in the manuals, but didn't work in practice.

However, for most types of concern formal mechanisms like this aren't relevant. If the main objective is to deal with small concerns before they become serious, then a willingness to listen and respond is by far the most effective approach. Like all management behaviour, this has to be sincere and consistent, or it will fail. I readily acknowledge that a certain amount of patience is needed to implement this policy; some people seem to have more than their fair share of concerns, but this is really the only cost to be set against the considerable benefits.

The freedom to question. In ancient Rome, a victorious general who was awarded a 'triumph' rode in his chariot through the city's streets, escorted by his soldiers, military bands, captives and loot, and surrounded by cheering crowds. Riding at his side would be a slave who continually whispered in his ear: 'remember you are only a man'. I think that the equivalent for senior people in modern organizations would be an executive toy which repeated at intervals: 'you make mistakes like everyone else' and 'everyone you meet knows things you don't know'.

Mark Wodman's boss didn't like to have his policies or instructions questioned. As a consequence, things went badly wrong in his department, with probable repercussions on his own career. At Franklyn Tapes, processes which were developed to ensure that things were done 'right' ended up stifling progress and initiative.

Questioning serves two purposes. The first is to clarify; if people understand clearly what their managers are trying to achieve they can contribute much more effectively to successful outcomes. They can also work much more independently, without constant references back to check that they're doing what's required, and to ask what they should do next. The second value of questioning is to draw attention to risks and errors before they lead to serious consequences.

This is an area where there's considerable room for improvement. There may be cultural forces in the UK which link questioning with negative attributes such as 'disloyalty', 'insubordination' or 'lack of commitment'. In my own research (Gray, 2001b) only just over half of my informants said that they felt able to question or challenge their superiors. All the same, if managers encourage positive questioning then the quality of decisions, and of their implementation, can only improve. Overall perceptions of climate are also likely to improve because people will feel that they have a voice in what is done and how it's done.

Participation in defining goals and objectives. There are plenty of good reasons why people should be encouraged to participate in defining the goals and objectives that they are to be asked to achieve at work. One reason is quite simply that it produces better outcomes. A survey by the consulting firm Deloitte Touche

(1998) showed significant correlations between business growth and human resource management practices that foster involvement and participation. This is consistent with the study of over 650 projects by Baker et al. (1988) which found that participation by the project team in setting schedules and budgets was significantly associated with project success, whilst a lack of such participation was associated with project failure. Some of the reasons for this were discussed in Chapter 5.

Another reason why people should have a say in what they are asked to achieve is that it's good for their health. 'Emotional distress, lowered self-esteem and job dissatisfaction result from non-participation (in decision-making) of workers' (Sauter et al., 1992). French et al. (1982) concluded from a major investigation of job stress that:

> The findings suggest that participation may be an important organizational mechanism for allowing employees to improve their adjustment to the demands of the job by having a say in the decisions which determine those demands.

Robert Karasek has been a leading figure in research on participation since the 1970s. In a series of studies he has established clear links between 'low decision latitude' and increased risk of cardiovascular disease (Karasek and Theorell, 1990). Other studies have reported broadly comparable results.

Harborough Response set out, as a consciously decided policy, to remove the modest level of participation that employees had previously enjoyed. Their intention, apparently, was to improve efficiency and increase the level of control that senior managers were able to exercise. This turned out to be counter-productive; staff turnover, sickness and commitment all deteriorated. At Olsen Electrical, staff had never had much input into what they did and how they did it, so nothing was being taken away from them. The world moves on, though. People's expectations change and organizations have to keep up: 'change is like getting old – there is only one alternative' (Ayling, 1995). When Olsen introduced a new way of working, which put employees in control of what they did, results improved markedly and people felt better.

Where investigation shows that participation in decision-making is low, managers need to address the issue quickly. Of course, not everyone wants the same level of autonomy, and some people may take longer than others to adapt to the freedom and the responsibility that goes with it. So the comfort levels of individuals need to be taken into account. This is possible; one aspect of participation is that it can allow the freedom to ask to be told what to do. This may seem contradictory, but in fact it puts control into the hands of the employee, which is what participation is all about.

The key demand on managers is that they try, continually, to extend the amount of participation by their people, but respect individuals' comfort levels. This requires observation and active listening, and flexibility, which is all quite hard work, but the effort is well worthwhile.

Intrinsic satisfactions from the work itself. Everyone wants to enjoy their work. For most people, enjoyment in this context is actually quite a complex mixture of involvement, challenge, feedback, usefulness, reward, continuity, variety and relationships. Organizations are not primarily designed to provide their employees with enjoyment, or satisfaction, but this doesn't mean that there's any incompatibility between the organization's primary task, whatever that may be, and the satisfaction employees may derive from their work.

On the contrary, although the evidence for a direct link between overall *job* satisfaction and productivity is rather mixed (see Chapter 3) there certainly is incontrovertible evidence that the satisfaction people get from a task or activity increases their motivation to perform that task (Lawler, 1973; Kanfer, 1994), and this in turn has a positive impact on outcomes.

When people can't derive satisfaction from their work they become frustrated, demotivated and, sometimes, resentful. They may also suffer from stress-related health problems.

Roy Stoner, at Inchbourne City Architect's Department, had found his job totally absorbing, and having experienced a very different situation earlier in his career, he was well placed to appreciate the worth of doing a job he loved. Whilst this continued, his contribution to his organization was very valuable, but when the situation changed he was left just marking time until his retirement, which was still a long way off. The value of his contribution would certainly have dropped.

Brian Tenby left a job that made him a great deal of money, but at what he came to see as an unacceptably high cost to his health and happiness. By moving to the Sylvia Castleton Trust he found true satisfaction from his work which was worth more to him than a high salary and bonus. His contribution to the work of the Trust was remarkable; there's no doubt that his employers, and those they set out to serve, benefited considerably from his enjoyment of his work.

Managers, realistically, can't ensure that everyone derives intrinsic satisfaction from their work, but they can follow established best practice to make this more likely. The principles of good job design defined by Hackman and Oldham (1980), which I mentioned in connection with Olsen Electrical, provide guidelines that are still excellent advice for building the potential for satisfaction into jobs:

1. 'Skill variety', so that the job utilizes several different skills or abilities, or involves a number of different tasks.
2. 'Task identity' so that the worker sees a task through from beginning to end, and can see an identifiable product or outcome.
3. 'Task significance'; other people are affected by how well the task is done.
4. 'Autonomy'; allowing the worker to plan his or her own work and choose how to do it.
5. 'Feedback', so that the worker receives clear, direct information about how well he or she is doing.

If these are followed there is a much better prospect of helping people to achieve satisfaction in their work and, conversely, if people are not deriving intrinsic satisfactions from what they do, the design of their jobs is a good place to start looking for causes.

Innovation – the freedom to try new concepts and approaches. One of the defining characteristics of our species is our ingenuity – our ability to solve problems by applying new methods, new technology, new techniques, and new concepts. As soon as we accept that human beings have a certain characteristic, whatever it may be, we tacitly acknowledge that to deny that characteristic expression is likely to have adverse consequences for the individual(s) concerned. People have a need to try new things, and to test out new ways of doing things.

At the organizational level, 'No organisation can survive without innovation. There must be an adaptive process that allows the organisation to take on board new ideas and translate them into practical results' (Cox, 1998). Although it might be tempting to trace a direct link between individual freedom to innovate and the organizational need for innovation there are very important differences. At the organizational level innovation can be a highly controlled process, involving a series of steps from idea generation, through validation and careful planning and on to implementation (Gray and Judge, 2002).

Innovation by individual employees or groups of employees can often be a great deal less formal, and in the specific context of innovation as a climate factor it is this informal freedom to try things out which probably has the strongest influence on perceptions of climate.

In the narratives on this topic (Chapter 11) I cited Drewery's (2003) comment that innovation and creativity are quite different things. You don't have to be creative to innovate, but you do have to recognize creativity when you see it and be ready to put it to use. It's this application of ideas which is true innovation.

At Antoneta creativity was highly valued, but policy and practice tended to get in the way of putting it to use. A similar situation arose at Latcho Security, where a team of highly creative, talented people was being stifled by the organizational constraints imposed upon them. When the constraints were lifted, or at least relaxed, they began once more to produce actual product developments some, but not all, of which the company could use.

Innovation implies risk. When new things are tried they don't always work. Freedom to innovate doesn't imply total licence to take wild, uncontrolled risks and it doesn't imply that management is absolved of responsibility for the consequences when things go wrong. The responsible approach to employees' freedom to innovate is to set boundaries and exercise 'light touch' control. It's a compromise, like most of life. When people are free to do things their own way, which implies trying out new things from time to time, they feel a greater sense of ownership of what they do. Denial of this freedom saps commitment and motivation.

Purposive threat. Purposive threats are directed at individuals to coerce them into doing something, doing more of something, doing something better or, occasionally, to stop doing something. They come in two kinds: those that are intended as threats and are perceived as such, and those that are perceived as threats but weren't actually intended that way. Since the perception of threat is a subjective function of the recipient, the effects of both kinds are much the same.

It's been established that purposive threats are a very ineffective way of improving performance, and they can be extremely damaging to overall perceptions of climate. It follows then that where enquiries – whether by means of observation, surveys or some other method – show that there is a perception by individual employees that they are subject to such threats, it's in the interests of managers to do what they can to change that perception.

The best course of action depends to some extent on which of the two kinds of purposive threat is identified.

Emma Litchford experienced intentional purposive threat at Smith Joplin. The general form of such threats is: 'meet the deadline or you're off the project', 'our incentive scheme is that people who achieve their sales targets get to keep their jobs', or 'you won't be considered for promotion if you only work your contracted hours'. The management action required to change people's perception of such purposive threats is fairly straightforward: stop doing it. There are much more effective approaches to performance management which contribute to, rather than detract from, a benign organizational climate (Gray, 2004).

Sometimes purposive threats originate more remotely, for example from more senior managers. This requires the exercise of diplomacy on the part of the 'change agent' who is trying to improve the climate of his or her organization or department. The objective is still the same, though, to remove the threat and replace it with something more positive.

Threats are often associated with bullying, although this isn't always the case – even people who are subjected to purposive threats sometimes regard them as a legitimate management technique (Gray, 2000b, 2002) and don't perceive themselves to be bullied, as such. Climate investigations do sometimes bring bullying behaviour to light; sometimes the actions of one bullying colleague (and it isn't always a manager or supervisor) are the single main cause of deteriorating organizational climate. Bullying should never be tolerated. Effective action to deal with it requires organizational processes to be in place, and to be invoked. All organizations should have such processes; if they haven't, this needs to be addressed as a matter of urgency.

There is quite a comprehensive literature on bullying at work (e.g. Compton-Edwards, 1995, 1996; Spiers, 1996; Vartia, 1996; Bies and Tripp, 1998; Lewis, 1999; Hammond, 2001; Caulkin, 2005; Tehrani, 2005; Woodman and Cook, 2005; CIPD, 2006; Richardson, 2006; Stephen and Hallas, 2006), which would repay the attention of all managers, but two key facts are particularly relevant here. One is that bullying is widespread. The other is that bullies don't stop bullying of their own accord; they have to be stopped and this requires senior management to step in.

Where purposive threats are not intentional managers are unlikely to be aware that policies or actions are perceived as threatening until this is revealed by enquiries, such as climate investigations. Typically, unintentional threats are the obverse effect of something intended to be positive: 'achieve these targets and you'll get a bonus' ('fail to achieve these targets and your bonus will be withheld') or 'make a success of this project and you'll be in line for promotion' ('if you drop off on this one you can forget your promotion prospects'). This is the kind of situation which affected Jyoti Rasmani at Brandon, Boardman, Stephens.

All kinds of incentive schemes, formal or informal, are subject to this kind of dual interpretation. It would be going too far to suggest that it's always a mistake to offer incentives, but it does always carry risk. Perceptions can change over time, so that something that started out as a genuine incentive comes to be regarded as a basic expectation. The possibility of the incentive being withheld is then almost sure to be seen as a form of threat. On the whole, I would advise that reward should be based on overall contribution and special incentives should be rare.

Environmental threat. Of all the climate factors this is the one which managers are least likely to be able to control. Environmental threats are threats which are not explicitly directed at, and are not explicitly intended to coerce, the individual or individuals who experience them, or to procure any specific behaviours.

They may arise from natural events, from pressures in society which are not being directed by intelligence, or from causes or policies determined remotely from the affected individuals so that for practical purpose they might just as well be undirected. All of which means that individual managers close to the people who are affected by the perception of such threats are, almost by definition, remote from the source of the threat. This may mean that they are powerless to influence the source of the threat, although this isn't always the case. Sometimes it may be possible for the 'change agent' to intercede with senior managers to point out the effects on individuals of a policy or decision and request some modification.

The most prominent source of environmental threat, based on my own research (Gray, 2000b), is organizational change – actual or anticipated – especially where people expect it to impact on them or their work but feel that they have no influence over events. This is what happened at Broma Stores.

Disputes between senior people, where these had the potential directly to affect more junior people or the work they are doing, are also likely to give rise to uncertainty and insecurity. The effects of this are illustrated by what happened at The Suffolk Buss. Disagreements between senior managers, whether it's about policy or commitment to specific actions or even if it's personal, can also have a negative impact on organizational climate. As far as possible, it's usually best if senior people avoid involving subordinates in disagreements like this, although it's still a good idea to consult with all the stakeholders before deciding on a policy.

Other kinds of threat, even physical hazards, don't seem to have anything like the same adverse effects. In fact, the real source of all such threats is people's perceived helplessness in the face of events which may in extreme cases have devastating effects on their lives, and in the face of decisions which will be made without reference to or without consideration of people who will be, perhaps drastically, affected by them.

The most effective way to address this, and mitigate its effect on organizational climate, is to consult people and keep them informed. If people feel that their voice is being heard and, at the most basic level, that people making decisions which may affect their well-being are actually aware of their existence and care what happens to them, the fear which change generates can be much reduced.

Systemic improvement. So far in this chapter I have outlined a process of improvement based on, first, identifying the current state of an organization or department's climate, then focusing on specific climate factors which may need special attention. For each of these I have suggested possible courses of action to address problems and issues.

Because of the systemic nature of organizational climate, every factor is likely to have some impact on all the others, so the aim must always be to take a broad view; attention to detail is simply a means to an end. What we are trying to achieve is an organization which provides its members with security from external threats and doesn't encourage or permit purposive or coercive threats. I have a particular affection for the concept of people as *members* of an organization, with its connotations of belonging. As a manager I once had a conversation with a union official who told me that she had to look after the interests of her members. My response was 'that's fine, I support that; they're my members too'.

The ideal organization I envisage has a senior management team who work out their differences without involving their subordinates, except to consult and profit from people's knowledge and experience. They have, or develop, clear objectives and support, and they take a constructive interest in the work that's going on. A climate of free and open discussion is facilitated, where policy can be questioned, ideas put forward and views expressed in safety. Employees participate fully in the definition of their goals and targets, which are sufficiently demanding to provide challenge and stimulation but are seen by all as realizable and desirable.

Working in this ideal organization is found to be intrinsically satisfying, and financial and other extrinsic rewards are seen to be fair and liberal, within the constraints of sound organizational governance.

This isn't just a utopian dream. Such organizations exist and others aspire to be like them. Organizational climate is very susceptible to aspirations; the will to change things for the better is a powerful source of energy which is contagious. I encourage every manager in every organization to take the first step towards a better, more productive climate. Happiness, which is where this book began, is quite likely to be met along the way.

THE ESSENTIALS OF THIS CHAPTER:

- A benign organizational climate is also a productive one.
- Improvement begins with self-knowledge. The first step towards a better climate is an assessment of how things are now.
- Climate is systemic; all the factors influence each other. If one is noticeably different from the others, it may indicate a new or developing situation.
- The eight climate factors can be addressed individually. There are actions that can be taken to improve each of them.
- In the end, though, it's the overall, systemic, perception of climate which impacts on performance.
- Wanting things to be better is an excellent starting point. The will to improve is contagious.

Bibliography

Adair, J. (1990). *Understanding Motivation*. Guildford: Talbot Adair Press.

Adams, D. (1987). *Dirk Gently's Holistic Detective Agency*. Basingstoke: Pan Macmillan.

Adams, D. (1990). *Last Chance To See*. London: William Heineman.

Adams, J. S. (1963). Toward an understanding of inequity. *Journal of Abnormal and Social Psychology*, **67**, No 5, 422–436.

Adela, J., McMurray, D. R., Scott, R. and Pace, W. (2004). The Relationship Between Organizational Commitment and Organizational Climate in Manufacturing. *Human Resource Development Quarterly*, Vol 15, No 4, 473–488.

Allen, N. J. and Meyer, J. P. (1990). The measurement and antecedents of affective, continuance and normative commitment to the organization. *Journal of Occupational Psychology*, **63**, 1–18.

Al-Shammari, M. M. (1992). Organizational Climate. *Leadership and Organization Development Journal*, **13,** 6, 30–32.

Amabile, T. (2004). See Breen, B. (2004).

Anderson, N. and West, M. (1994). The Personality of Teamworking. *Personnel Management*, November, 81.

Arkin, A. (1997). Hold the production line. *People Management*, 6 February, 22–27.

Arnold, R. (1995). *The Improvement of Schools Through Partnership: School, LEA, and University*. Slough: EMIE/NFER.

Augsdörfer, P. (2004). Path dependency in unplanned R&D. *Working Papers*, Ingolstadt, Germany: University of Applied Sciences.

Ayling, D. (1995). *Enter The Hippo*. Buckingham: Key Publishing Office.

Bagehot, W. (1869). *Physics and Politics.* Various sources.

Baker, B. N., Murphy, D. C. and Fisher, D. (1988). Factors Affecting Project Success. In *Project Management Handbook*, 2nd edn (D. I. Cleland and W. R. King, eds), pp. 902–919, New York: Van Nostrand Reinhold.

Bandura, A. (1977). *Social Learning Theory*. Englewood Cliffs, New Jersey: Prentice Hall.

Baron, A. and Walters, M. (1994). *The Culture Factor*. London: IPD.

BBC (2000). *'Suicide risk' for doctors and nurses*. http://news.bbc.co.uk/1/hi/health/944503.stm

BBC (2005). *Vet suicides outstrip UK average*. http://news.bbc.co.uk/1/hi/health/4310596.stm

Beech, N. and Crane, O. (1999). High performance teams and a climate of community. *Team Performance Management*, Vol 5, No 3, 87–102.

Belassi, W. and Tukel, O. I. (1996). A new framework for determining critical success/failure factors in projects. *International Journal of Project Management*, Vol 14, No 3, 141–151.

Bies, R. J. and Tripp, T. M. (1998). Two Faces of the Powerless: Coping With Tyranny in Organizations. In *Power and Influence in Organizations* (R. M. Kramer and M. A. Neale, eds), pp. 203–219, London: Sage.

Bilmes, L. (2001). Scoring goals for people and company. *Financial Times*, 26 November, p. 8.

Blair, T. (1998). Speech on *The Millennium Bug*. http://www.number10.gov.uk/output/Page1161.asp

Bland, A. (2000). Fight stress, not ill health claims. *People Management*, 7 December, 51.

Bottery, M. (1992). *The Ethics of Education Management*. London: Cassell Educational.

Boulton, P. and Coldron, J. (1991). Happiness as a criterion of parents' choice of school. *Journal of Education Policy*, **6**, 2.

Breen, B. (2004). The 6 Myths of Creativity. *Fast Company*, December, 75.

Briner, R. (2002). Untangling the links in the HRM performance chain. *People Management*, 24 January, 50.

Browning, G. (2006). How to … Measure. *The Guardian Weekend*, 20 May, p. 11.

Buckingham, M. (2001). What a Waste. *People Management*, 11 October, 36–40.

Bunting, M. (2004). *Willing Slaves*. London: Harper Collins.

Burke, E. (1756). *On the Sublime and Beautiful*, part ii, ii. Various sources.

Burke, R. J. (1966). Are Herzberg's Motivators and Hygienes Unidimensional? *Journal of Applied Psychology*, Vol 50, No 4, 317–321.

Burke, R. J. (1988). Sources of Managerial and Professional Stress in Large Organizations. In *Causes, Coping and Consequences of Stress at Work* (C. L. Cooper and R. Payne, eds), pp. 81–105, Chichester: John Wiley and Sons.

Burke, W. W. and Litwin, G. H. (1992). A Causal Model of Organisation Performance and Change. *Journal of Change Management*, Vol 18, No 3, 523–545.

CAB (2004). *No win no fee no chance*. www.citizensadvice.org.uk

Cartwright, S. and Cooper, C. L. (1993). Of Mergers, Marriage and Divorce – The Issues of Staff Retention. *Journal of Managerial Psychology*, Vol 8, No 6, 7–10.

Cartwright, S., Cooper, C. L. and Barron, A. (1993). An Investigation of the Relationship Between Occupational Stress and Accidents Amongst Co Car Drivers. *Journal of General Management*, Vol 19, No 2, Winter, 78–85.

Caulkin, S. (1999). Sweatshops – the wrong call. *The Observer*, 28 November, p. 12.

Caulkin, S. (2005). Sugar and spite vs Jamie's sauce. *The Observer*, 27 March, p. 12.

Caulkin, S. (2006). Well get this! High morale equals high productivity. *The Observer*, 25 June, Business p. 9.

Charlton, J. (2005). Eureka! The benefits of staff suggestion schemes. Personneltoday.com

Checkland, P. (1984). *Systems Thinking, Systems Practice*. Chichester: John Wiley.

Checkland, P. and Scholes, J. (1990). *Soft Systems Methodology In Action*. Chichester: John Wiley.

CIPD (2006). *Harassment at work*. Factsheet. London: CIPD.

CMI (2006). *Team Briefing*. Dictionary entry. Chartered Management Institute. www.managers.org.uk

Coats, D. (2006). *Who's afraid of labour market flexibility?* London: The Work Foundation.

Compton-Edwards, M. (1995). *Is your workmate your worst enemy?* Press release 27-7-95, IPD.

Compton-Edwards, M. (1996). One in eight UK workers are victims of bullying reveals new IPD survey. Press release 28-11-96, IPD.

Congreve, W. (1695). *Love for Love*, III. Viii. Various sources.

Cooper, C. L. (1994). The Costs of Healthy Work Organizations. In *Creating Healthy Work Organizations* (C. L. Cooper and S. Williams, eds), pp. 1–5, Chichester: John Wiley.

Cox, G. (1998). The Creative Organisation. In *The Gower Handbook of Management* (D. Lock, ed), Chapter 3, Aldershot: Gower.

Cox, T. (1993). *Stress Research And Stress Management: Putting Theory To Work*. Sudbury: Health and Safety Executive.

CQMJ (1993). *Center For Quality Management Journal*, Vol 2, No 4, Fall.

Crainer, S. (1997). *The Ultimate Business Library*. Oxford: Capstone Publishing.

Creswell, J. W. (1994). *Research Design: Qualitative and Quantitative Approaches*. London: Sage.

Cromwell, O. (1650). Letter to the General Assembly of the Church of Scotland, 3 August.

Deci, E. L. (1972). Intrinsic Motivation, Extrinsic Reinforcement, and Inequity. *Journal of Personality and Social Psychology*, Vol 22, No 11, 13–120.

Deci, E. L. (1992). The History of Motivation in Psychology and Its Relevance for Management. In *Management and Motivation*, 2nd edn (V. H. Vroom and E. L. Deci, eds), pp. 9–29, London: Penguin.

Deloitte Touche (1998). *Business Success and Human Resources*. London: Deloitte Touche.

Deming, W. E. (1986). *Out of the Crisis*. Cambridge, Mass.: MIT CAES.

Denison, D. R. (1996). What Is The Difference Between Organizational Culture And Organizational Climate? A Native's Point Of View On A Decade Of Paradigm Wars. *Academy of Management Review*, Vol 21, No 3, 619–654.

Despres, C. J-N. (1995). Culture, surveys, culture surveys, and other obfuscations: a reply to Migliore and Martin. *Journal of Strategic Change*, Vol 4, 65–75.

Drewery, K. (2003). *Harnessing creativity and innovation*. London: The Work Foundation.

Drucker, P. F. (1954). *The Practice of Management*. New York: Harper and Row.

Drucker, P. F. (1985). *Innovation and Entrepreneurship*. London: Heinemann.

Drucker, P. F. (1998). *On the Profession of Management*. Boston, Mass.: Harvard Business Review Books.

Drummond, H. (2000). *Introduction to Organizational Behaviour*. Oxford: Oxford University Press.

Easterby-Smith, M., Thorpe, R. and Lowe, A. (1991). *Management Research*. London: Sage.

Economist Intelligence Unit, The (1992). *Making Quality Work – lessons from Europe's leading companies*. London: The Economist Intelligence Unit.

Ekvall, G. (1996). Organizational Climate for Creativity and Innovation. *European Journal of Work and Organizational Psychology*, **5** (1), 105–123.

Emmott, M. (2003). *HR Survey Where we are, where we're heading*. London: CIPD.

Erlandson, D., Harris, E., Skipper, B. and Allen, S. (1993). *Doing Naturalistic Enquiry: A Guide To Methods*. London: Sage.

Festinger, L. (1957). *A Theory of Cognitive Dissonance*. Evanston, USA: Row, Peterson.

Festinger, L. and Carlsmith, L. M. (1959). Cognitive Consequences of Forced Compliance. *Journal of Abnormal and Social Psychology*, **58**, 203–210.

Fowler, A. (1994). How To Manage Suggestion Schemes. *Personnel Management Plus*, July, 28–29.

Freedman, J. L., Cunningham, J. A. and Krismer, K. (1992). Inferred Values and the Reverse-Incentive Effect in Induced Compliance. *Journal of Personality and Social Psychology*, March, 357–368.

French, J. R. P., Caplan, R. D. and van Harrison, R. (1982). *The Mechanisms Of Job Stress And Strain*. Chichester: John Wiley.

Gabriel, Y. and Schwartz, N. S. (1998). *Organizations, from concepts to constructs: Psychoanalytic theories of character and the meaning of organization*. Conference paper, Jerusalem, ISPSO: The International Society for the Psychoanalytic Study of Organizations.

Galbraith, J. K. (1997). *The Good Society: The Humane Agenda*. Boston, Mass.: Houghton Mifflin.

Garnier, J-P. (2006). Speech given at CBI conference, reported by Khalid Aziz in *Management Today*, March, 14.

Gavin, J. H. and Mason, R. O. (2004). The Virtuous Organization: The Value of Happiness in the Workplace. *Organizational Dynamics*, **33** (4), 379–392.

Gordon, G. G. (1985). The Relationship of Corporate Culture to Industry Sector and Corporate Performance. In *Gaining Control Of The Corporate Culture* (R. H. Kilmann, M. Saxton, R. Serpa and Associates, eds), pp. 103–125, Oxford: Jossey-Bass.

Gordon, G. G. and Cummins, W. (1979). *Managing Management Climate*. Lexington, Mass.: Lexington Books.

Gray, R. (1998). *Organisational Culture and the Psychological Contract*. Kumpania Consulting. www.kumpania.co.uk

Gray, R. (2000a). *Motivation: a review of the literature*. Kumpania Consulting. www.kumpania.co.uk

Gray, R. (2000b). Organisational Climate and the Competitive Edge. In *Dimensions of Competitiveness: Issues and Policies* (L. Lloyd-Reason and S. Wall, eds), pp. 3–24, Cheltenham: Edward Elgar Publishing.

Gray, R. (2001a). *Cluster Profiling in Personnel Selection*. Chelmsford: Earlybrave Publications.

Gray, R. (2001b). Organisational Climate and Project Success. *International Journal of Project Management*, Vol 19, No 2, 103–109.

Gray, R. (2002). *The Padua Paradigm*. Chelmsford: Earlybrave Publications.

Gray, R. (2004). *How People Work*. Harlow: FT/Prentice Hall.

Gray, R. and Judge, A. P. (2002). *Product and Service Development and Quality Function Deployment*. Chelmsford: Earlybrave Publications.

Guion, R. M. (1973). A Note on Organizational Climate. *Organizational Behavior and Human Performance*, Vol 9, 120–125.

Guzzo, R. A., Jette, R. D. and Katzell, R. A. (1985). The Effects of Psychologically Based Intervention Programs on Worker Productivity: A Meta-Analysis. *Personnel Psychology*, Summer, 275–291.

Hackman, J. R. and Oldham, G. R. (1980). *Work Redesign*. Reading, Mass.: Addison Wesley.

Hammond, D. (2001). Someone to lean on. *People Management*, 6 December, 30–37.

Handy, C. (1985). *Understanding Organizations*, 3rd edn. Harmondsworth: Penguin.

Handy, C. (1990). *The Age Of Unreason*. London: Arrow Books.

Hatchett, A. (2000). Ringing true. *People Management*, 20 January, 40–42.

Heller, R. (1994). Management By Fear. *Intercity*, March, 13.

Herzberg, F., Mausner, B. and Snyderman, B. B. (1959). *The Motivation to Work*. New York: John Wiley.

Hockey, G. and Hamilton, P. (1983). The Cognitive Patterning of Stress States. In *Stress and Fatigue in Human Performance* (G. R. J. Hockey, ed), pp. 331–362, Chichester: John Wiley.

Hofstede, G. (1991). *Cultures And Organizations.* London: Harper Collins.

Holbeche, L. (2001). How to handle mergers and acquisitions. *People Management,* 8 November, 56–57.

Hollway, W. (1991). *Work Psychology and Organizational Behaviour.* London: Sage.

House, R. J. and Widgor, L. A. (1967). Herzberg's dual-factor theory of job satisfaction and motivation: A review of the evidence and a criticism. *Personnel Psychology,* **20,** 369–389.

Hussey, J. and Hussey, R. (1997). *Business Research.* Basingstoke: Macmillan.

Ilgen, D. R. and Klein, H. J. (1988). Individual Motivation and Performance: Cognitive Influences on Effort and Choice. In *Productivity in Organizations* (J. P. Campbell, R. J. Campbell and Associates, eds), pp. 143–176, London: Jossey-Bass.

Jacobs, R. and Campbell, D. T. (1961). The perpetuation of an arbitrary tradition through several generations of a laboratory microculture. *Journal of Abnormal and Social Psychology,* No 62, 649–658.

James, O. (2005). Toil and trouble. *The Observer OM ,* 7 August, p. 8.

Janis, I. L. (1982). *Groupthink: Psychological Studies of Policy Decisions and Fiascos,* 2nd edn. Boston, Mass.: Houghton-Mifflin.

Jones, A. P. and James, L. R. (1979). Psychological climate: dimensions and relationships of individual and aggregated work environment perceptions. *Organizational Behaviour and Human Performance,* Vol 23, 201–250.

Jung, J. (1978). *Understanding Human Motivation: A Cognitive Approach.* New York: Collier Macmillan.

Kanfer, R. (1990). Motivation Theory and Industrial and Organizational Psychology. In *Handbook of Industrial and Organizational Psychology,* Vol 1, 2nd edn (M. D. Dunnette and L. M. Hough, eds), pp. 75–170, Palo Alto: Consulting Psychologists Press.

Kanfer, R. (1994). Work Motivation: New Directions In Theory And Research. In *Key Reviews In Managerial Psychology* (C. L. Cooper and I. T. Robertson, eds), pp. 1–53, Chichester: John Wiley and Sons.

Kanter, R. M. (1983). *The Change Masters: Corporate Entrepreneurs At Work.* London: George Allen and Unwin.

Karasek, R. and Theorell, T. (1990). *Healthy Work: Stress, Productivity, and the Reconstruction of Working Life.* New York: Basic Books.

Kelman, H. C. (1958). Compliance, identification and internalisation: three processes of attitude change. *Journal of Conflict Resolution,* No 2, 51–60.

Kilmann, R. H., Saxton, M., Serpa, R. and Associates (1985). *Gaining Control Of The Corporate Culture.* Oxford: Jossey-Bass.

Kofman, F. and Senge, P. M. (1993). Communities of Commitment: The Heart of Learning Organizations. *Organizational Dynamics,* Vol 22, No 2, Autumn, 5–22.

Konrad, A. M. (2006). Engaging employees through high-involvement work practices. *Ivey Business Journal online,* March–April, 1–6.

Landsbergis, P. A., Schurman, S., Israel, B., Schnall P. L., Hugentobler, M., Cahill, J. and Baker D. (1993). Job Stress And Heart Disease: Evidence and strategies for prevention. *New Solutions,* **3** (4), 42–58.

Lawler, E. E. (1973). *Motivation In Work Organizations.* Monterey, California: CalBrooks/Cole Publishing Co.

Lawler, E. E. and Suttle, J. L. (1972). A Causal Correlational Test of the Need Hierarchy Concept. *Organizational Behavior And Human Performance*, 7, 265–287.

Lawthom, R., Patterson, M., West, M., Staniforth, D. and Maitlis, S. (1995). *Organizational Climate*. Conference paper – Occupational psychology conference, Coventry, January, British Psychological Society, 19–24.

Lazarus, R. and Folkman, S. (1984). *Stress, Appraisal, And Coping*. New York: Springer.

Leary-Joyce, J. (2004). *Becoming an employer of choice: make your organisation a place where people want to do great work*. London: CIPD.

Lewin, K. (1952). *Field theory in social science: selected theoretical papers* (D. Cartwright, ed). London: Tavistock.

Lewin, K., Lippitt, R. and White, R. (1939). Patterns of aggressive behavior in experimentally created 'social climate'. *Journal of Social Psychology*, 10, 271–299.

Lewin, R. and Regine, B. (1999). *The Soul at Work*. London: Orion Business.

Lewis, J. (1999). Climate of betrayal. *Personnel Today*, 23 September, 36–37.

Likert, R. (1932). *A Technique for the Measurement of Attitudes*. New York: Columbia University Press.

Litwin, G. H. and Stringer, R. A. (1968). *Motivation and Organizational Climate*. Boston: Mass.: Harvard University Press.

Lucas, W. (2006). How to create a learning culture. *People Management*, 14 September, 46–47.

Makin, P., Cooper, C. and Cox, C. (1996). *Organizations and the Psychological Contract*. Leicester: BPS Books.

Manning, T. (1990). Beyond Corporate Culture. *IPM Journal* (South Africa), February, 23–25.

Marks, M. L. and Mirvis, P. H. (1986). The Merger Syndrome. *Psychology Today*, 20, 36–42.

Marks, M. L. and Mirvis, P. H. (2001). Making mergers and acquisitions work: Strategic and psychological preparation. *Academy of Management Executive*, May, Vol 15, Issue 2, 80.

Maslow, A. H. (1943). A Theory of Human Motivation. *Psychological Review*, Vol 50, 370–396.

McGregor, D (1960). *The Human Side Of Enterprise*, 25th Anniversary edn (1985). New York: McGraw-Hill.

McKie, A. (2002). *Virtual Value: Conversations, Ideas and the Creative Economy*. London: The Industrial Society.

McLean, A. A. (1985). *Work Stress*. Reading, Mass.: Addison-Wesley.

McLuhan, R. (1998). Feelgood factors. *Personnel Today*, 12 February, 26–27.

Meek, V. L. (1988). Organizational Culture: Origins and Weaknesses. *Organization Studies*, Vol 9, No 4, 453–473.

Menday, J. (1996). *Call Centre Management: A Practical Guide*. Newdigate: Callcraft.

Miles, M. M. and Huberman, A. M. (1994). *Qualitative Data Analysis*. London: Sage.

Morgan, G. (1986). *Images Of Organization*. London: Sage.

Oppenheim, A. N. (1992). *Questionnaire Design, Interviewing and Attitude Measurement*. London: Pinter.

Pass, S. (2005). On the Line. *People Management*. 15 September, 38–40.

Patterson, M., Lawthom, R., West, M., Maitlis, S. and Staniforth, D. (1996). *What is it Like to Work Here? The Climate of UK Manufacturing*. Sheffield: University of Sheffield.

Patterson, M., West, M., Lawthom, R. and Nickell, S. (1997). *Impact of People Management Practices on Business Performance*. Issues in People Management Series No 22. London: IPD.

Patterson, M., Warr, P. and West, M. (2004). Organizational climate and company productivity: The role of employee affect and employee level. *Journal of Occupational and Organizational Psychology*, No 77, 193–216.

Patterson, M., West, M., Shackleton, V., Dawson, J., Lawthom, R., Maitless, S., Robinson, D. and Wallace, A. (2005). Validating the organizational climate measure: links to managerial practices, productivity and innovation. *Journal of Organizational Behavior*, No 26, 379–408.

Payne, R. L. (2001). A Three Dimensional Framework for Analyzing and Assessing Culture/Climate and its Relevance to Cultural Change. In *International Handbook Of Organizational Culture And Climate* (C. L. Cooper, S. Cartwright and P. C. Early, eds), pp. 107–122, Chichester: John Wiley.

Peters, T. and Waterman, R. H. (1982). *In Search of Excellence*. London: Harper and Row.

Petzall, S., Abbott, K. and Timo, N. (2003). *Australian Industrial Relations In an Asian Context*, 2nd edn. Melbourne, Australia: Eruditions.

Porter, L. W., Lawler, E. E. and Hackman, J. R. (1975). *Behavior in Organizations*. New York: McGraw-Hill.

Purcell, J. (2000). Pay per view. *People Management*, 3 February, 41–43.

Reeves, R. (2002). Reality Bites. *Management Today*, September, p. 35.

Reichers, A. E. and Schneider, B. (1990). Climate and Culture: An Evolution of Constructs. In *Organizational Climate and Culture* (B. Schneider, ed), pp. 5–39, Oxford: Jossey-Bass.

Richardson, M. (2006). *Harassment and Bullying*. London: Incomes Data Services.

Robertson, I. T., Smith, M. and Cooper, D. (1992). *Motivation Strategies, Theory and Practice*. London: IPD.

Robinson, D., Perryman, S. and Hayday, S. (2004). *The Drivers of Employee Engagement*. IES Report 408. London: Institute of Employment Studies.

Rogg, K. L., Schmidt, D. B., Shull, C. and Schmitt, N. (2001). Human resource practices, organizational climate, and customer satisfaction. *Journal of Management*, No 27, 431–449.

Roncoroni, S. (1997). Quoted in A. Arkin 'Hold the production line'. *People Management*, 6 February, 22–27.

Rose, S. (2003). Natural conclusion. *The Guardian Review*, 17 May, p. 21.

Rousseau, D. M. (1995). *Psychological Contracts In Organizations*. London: Sage.

Rubin, H. J. and Rubin, I. S. (1995). *Qualitative Interviewing – The Art of Hearing Data*. London: Sage.

Sales, A. L. and Mirvis, P. H. (1984). Acquisition and collision of cultures. In *Managing Organizational Transitions* (R. Quinn and J. Kimberley, eds), pp. 107–133, New York: Dow Jones.

Sartre, J-P. (1943). *Being And Nothingness*. Translation. H. Barnes (1969), London: Routledge.

Sauter, S. L., Murphy, L. R. and Hurrell, J. J. (1992). Prevention of work-related psychological disorders: a national strategy proposed by NIOSH. In *Work and Well-Being: An Agenda For The 1990s* (G. Keita and S. Sauter, eds), Part II, Washington DC: American Psychological Association.

Scase, R. (2001). Why we're so clock wise. *The Observer*, 26 August, Business, p. 9.

Scase, R. (2002). Bullies who let Britain down. *The Observer*, 2 June, Business, p. 8.

Schachter, S. and Singer, J. E. (1962). Cognitive, social and physiological determinants of emotional states. *Psychological Review*, **69**, 379–399.

Schein, E. H. (1985). *Organizational Culture And Leadership.* Oxford: Jossey-Bass.

Schneider, B., Brief, A. P. and Guzzo, R. A. (1996). Creating a Climate and Culture for Sustainable Organizational Change. *Organizational Dynamics*, Spring, 7–19.

Seddon, J. (1999). Quoted in S. Caulkin *Sweatshops – the wrong call. The Observer*, 28 November, p. 12.

Skillsoft (2006). *IT pros more likely to suffer from stress, says survey.* Press release, www.skillsoft.com/EMEA/news/19-May-06.asp

Sloane, P. (2005). See Charlton, J. (2005).

Smithers, A. and Robinson, P. (2003). *Factors Affecting Teachers' Decision to Leave the Profession.* Liverpool: University of Liverpool.

Sonnentag, S., Brodbeck, F., Heinbokel, T. and Stolte, W. (1994). Stressor-burnout relationship in software development teams. *Journal of Occupational and Organizational Psychology*, **67**, 327–341.

Sparrow, P. R. (2001). Developing Diagnostics for High Performance Organization Cultures. In *International Handbook Of Organizational Culture And Climate* (C. L. Cooper, S. Cartwright and P. C. Early, eds), pp. 81–106, Chichester: John Wiley.

Spiers, C. (1996). Bullying at work: the cost to business. *Training Officer*, October, Vol 32, No 8, 236–238.

Stacey, R. D. (1992). *Managing Chaos.* London: Kogan Page.

Stansfeld, S., Head, J. and Marmot, M. (2000). *Work-related factors and ill health: The Whitehall II study.* London: HSE Books.

Stenmark, D. (2000). *The Role of Intrinsic Motivation When Managing Creative Work.* Conference paper, Singapore, ICMIT: International Conference on the Management of Innovation and Technology.

Stephen, T. and Hallas, J. (2006). *Bullying And Sexual Harassment: A Practical Handbook.* Oxford: Chandos Publishing.

Swan, J. (2005). Inflexibility Drives Out Silent Majority. *People Management*, 19 May, 101.

Tagiuri, R. and Litwin, G. H. (1963). *Organisational Climate: Explorations of a Concept.* Cambridge, Mass.: Harvard University Press.

Taylor, F. W. (1911). *The Principles of Scientific Management.* New York: Harper and Row.

Taylor, R. (2002). *Britain's World of Work – Myths and Realities.* Swindon: ESRC.

Teasdale, E. L. and McKeown, S. (1994). Managing Stress at Work: The ICI-Zeneca Pharmaceuticals Experience 1986–1993. In *Creating Healthy Work Organizations* (C. L. Cooper and S. Williams, eds), Chapter 8, Chichester: John Wiley.

Tehrani, N. (2005). *Bullying At Work: Beyond Policies To A Culture Of Respect.* London: CIPD.

Tennyson, Lord, A. (1854). *The Charge of the Light Brigade* (poem). Various sources.

Thorndike, E. L. (1911). *Animal Intelligence: Experimental Studies.* New York: Macmillan.

Trafford, V. (1997). *An Unravelling of Research Methodology.* Danbury: Anglia Business School.

Trapp, R. (1992). No easy street to Total Quality. *The Independent*, 17 November, p. 26.

Trice, H. M. and Beyer, J. M. (1985). Using Six Organizational Rites to Change Culture. In *Gaining Control of the Corporate Culture* (R. H. Kilmann, M. J. Saxton, R. Serpa and Associates, eds), pp. 370–399, Oxford: Jossey-Bass.

Trompenaars, F. and Woolliams, P. (2003). *Business Across Cultures.* Chichester: Capstone.

TUC (2006). Nearly half the workforce wants fewer hours. *Changing Times News*, No 70, 10 March; www.tuc.org.uk/changingtimes

Vartia, M. (1996). The Sources of Bullying – Psychological Work Environment and Organizational Climate. *European Journal of Work and Organizational Psychology*, **5** (2), 204–213.

Vroom, V. H. (1964). *Work And Motivation*. Chichester: John Wiley.

Waley, A. (c1943). *Censorship* (poem). Various sources.

Wallace, J., Hunt, J. and Richards, C. (1999). The relationship between organisational culture, organisational climate and managerial values. *International Journal of Public Sector Management*, Vol 12, No 7, 548–564.

Watkin, C. (2001). How to improve organisational climate. *People Management*, 28 June, 52–53.

Watkin, C. and Hubbard, B. (2003). Leadership motivation and the drivers of share price: the business case for measuring organisational climate. *Leadership and Organization Development Journal*, **24**/7, 380–386.

Watson, T. Jnr (1963). *A Business And Its Beliefs: The Ideas That Helped Build IBM*. New York: McGraw-Hill.

West, M. (2005). Hope Springs. *People Management*, 13 October, 38–39.

Wiley, J. W. and Brooks, S. M. (2000). The High-Performance Organizational Climate: How Workers Describe Top-Performing Units. In *Handbook of Organizational Culture and Climate* (N. M. Ashkanasy, C. P. Wilderom and M. F. Peterson, eds), pp. 177–191, London: Sage.

Williams, D. G. S. (1998). 'Organizational climate and performance: an empirical investigation'. PhD thesis, University of Surrey, Guildford.

Williams, S. (1994). *Managing Pressure for Peak Performance*. London: Kogan Page.

Wilson, B. (1984). *Systems: Concepts, Methodologies And Applications*. Chichester: John Wiley.

Winkfield, N. (1995). Bad timing: attitudes to the new world of work. *The time squeeze*, Demos Quarterly, 5/1995, 2–11.

Wood, D. A. and LeBold, W. K. (1970). The Multivariate Nature of Professional Job Satisfaction. *Personnel Psychology*, **23**, 173–189.

Woodman, P. and Cook, P. (2005). *Bullying at work: the experience of managers*. London: Chartered Management Institute.

Working Families (2005). Time, Health and the Family: What Working Families Want, quoted in *Inflexibility Drives Out Silent Majority* (J. Swan) *People Management*, 19 May, 101.

Worrall, L. and Cooper, C. (2006). Managers just soldiering on. *Professional Manager*, May, 30–32.

Yeo, K. T. (1993). Systems Thinking And Project Management – Time To Reunite. *International Journal Of Project Management*, Vol 11, No 2, May, 111–117.

Yerkes, R. M. and Dodson, J. D. (1908). The relation of strength of stimulus to rapidity of habit-formation. *Journal of Comparative Neurology and Psychology* **148**, 133–146.

Index

Index